SELMA, 1965

*A question to our colored population which everyone with
ability to think and reason should weigh seriously:*

*On what grounds can you justly claim access to the ballot,
and thus governmental rule, won by the white man's tears and
blood? By this privilege in some states of the South you could and
would gain every office from constable on up to the governorship.*

This eventuality is absolutely unthinkable and impossible.

*But what right can you justly claim to equal social privileges with
a race who through more than four thousand years has risen in the
realms of education, invention, discoveries, and accomplishments,
to heights never dreamed of throughout the past ages?*

*Why should you seek to force your way into the privileges
of a society in which you are not wanted and to which you have
not been invited?*

*. . . [Once] in my native state of Mississippi, I stood in an
audience of thousands and listened to a speech by James K.
Vardeman [sic], who was governor and later U.S. Senator,
designated by aliens as a "red-neck demagogue," from the
backwoods of Mississippi, but who proved himself to be a sage
as well as a prophet.*

*He said: "We'll continue to build higher the old rail fence
of voting privileges, rail by rail, just as the Negro race
tries to climb over it. When we come to the time that no higher
rail can be found to obstruct him, we'll reach back and pull
down the old rifle and make it sing "Good-by Honey I'm Gone."*

When the federal inquisitors marched on the Cradle of the Confederacy, there was telecast perhaps all over the nation a portion of the farcical court which they conducted in that city. I was visiting on the border of the Mason and Dixon Line, at the time and this greeted my eyes. A negro man from Barber [sic] County Alabama was on the witness stand to tell how he had been cheated of his right to register and vote. The episode was something like this: "How long did you wait in the ante-room?" "Several hours." "Did anyone tell you to come in and register?" "No one at all." "Did anyone say anything to you?" "Yes, a man came along and asked me what I was doing there." "What did you say?" "I said I was waiting to register." "What did he say to that?" "He said, 'to hell out of here!' " I, of course do not approve of profanity in any form. But the "red-neck" from the backwoods of Mississippi was indeed a prophet. There was no rifle brandished in this instance, but it does not take very much imagination to hear again that tune, "Goodbye, honey, I'm gone!"

There is no doubt but that those registrars were longing for that last and final rail to raise the voting fence higher. The man who finds it, and makes it effective once for all, will deserve the eternal gratitude of the entire Southland.

> —from *The Pending Tragedy in the South,* by the
> Rev. George W. Cheek, Sr. D.D., former pastor
> of the Alabama Avenue Presbyterian Church,
> Selma, Alabama. Privately Printed, ca. 1959.

BOOKS BY CHARLES E. FAGER

White Reflections on Black Power
Uncertain Resurrection:
    The Poor People's Washington Campaign

SELMA, 1965

by Charles E. Fager

Charles Scribner's Sons
New York

Library of Congress Cataloging in Publication Data

Fager, Charles E.
  Selma 1965

    1. Selma, Ala.—Race question.   2. Civil rights—
Selma, Ala.   3. Selma-Montgomery Rights March, 1965.
4. Selma, Ala.—Politics and government. I. Title.
F334.S4F34   323.4'09761'45   73–1110
ISBN 0–684–13764–X

1 3 5 7 9 11 13 15 17 19 H/C 20 18 16 14 12 10 8 6 4 2

Printed in the United States of America

MAPS ON PAGE x: Copyright © 1968 by William Robert Miller from
the book, *Martin Luther King, Jr.: His Life, Martyrdom, and Meaning
for the World.* Published by Weybright and Talley. Reprinted by
permission of the publisher.

Quotations from the Unitarian Church Archives are used by
permission of the Unitarian Universalist Association.
Quotations from "Crumpled Notes (Found in a Raincoat) on Selma"
are used by permission of Maria Varela.

CREDIT IS GRATEFULLY ACKNOWLEDGED FOR USE OF THE FOLLOWING
PHOTOGRAPHS IN THIS BOOK: Numbers 3, 5, Courtesy of James
Gutman; 23, 26, 27, Matt Herron, Black Star; 24, Ivan Massar, Black
Star; 10, Vernon Merritt, Black Star; 15, Courtesy of Orloff W.
Miller; 12, Charles Moore, Black Star; 1, 2, 6, 7, 11, 13, 16, 17, 18,
19, 20, 21, 22, 25, 29, John Phillips, Baldwin Street Gallery of
Photography, Toronto; 8, 9, Courtesy of the *Selma Times-Journal*; 28,
Courtesy of Reverend Ralph E. Smeltzer.

In Memory of
CAROL SELIGMAN OLIVER
and ADELAIDE LEE
Peaceful American women
who died in exile
from a nation that
gave them no peace,
one within and one
without its borders.

"MY DAUGHTER, SHALL I NOT
SEEK REST FOR THEE, THAT
IT MAY BE WELL WITH THEE?"
—Ruth, 3:1

Dear Mr. Fager:

I read with interest the copy of the galleys of your book *Selma, 1965*.

Your book seems to be a fair account of the Civil Rights Movement in Selma during 1965. It appears to me to be a factual account of events that took place in Selma, Alabama, and the Marches of 1965.

Yours very truly,

Wilson Baker

Sheriff, Dallas County

SELMA

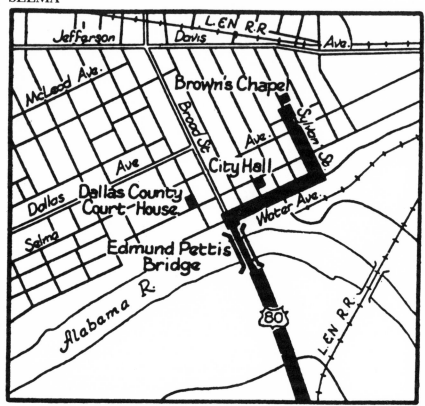

SELMA TO MONTGOMERY

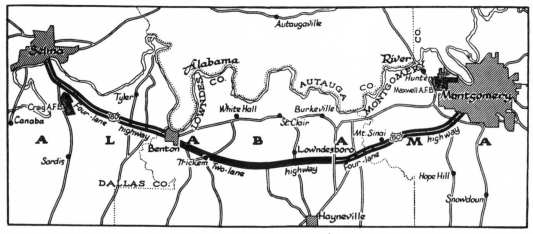

SELMA, 1965

The war is being lost in South Vietnam, and no
amount of power juggling in Saigon and no amount
of American military aid and advice has been able
to change that fact.
Indeed the question that may now have to be faced
is whether the war can be won at all—with or
without its escalation into a larger conflict and
fullscale United States involvement.

     —Don Oakley, "Editorially Speaking,"
     Selma Times-Journal, *January 1, 1965*

ONE. Even before the first kickoff, the 1965

Orange Bowl was one for the record books: more people were watching
it than had ever witnessed a football game before—72,647 of them
packed into the bulging stadium, with somewhere between twenty and
twenty-six million more waiting at the other end of their television sets.
It was the first bowl game played at night (this for the benefit of the
television cameras, as the big lights minimized shadows.) The star of
the evening, Alabama quarterback Joe Namath, was about to sign the
biggest contract in pro history for a rookie, with the New York Jets for
$400,000 plus benefits. And the Crimson Tide he led into the contest
had just been declared national champions by the wire services for the
second time in four years, having won ten straight games against the
toughest teams in the business.

  Perhaps no Americans in 1965 identified more with their state's
gridiron combat than did the citizens of Alabama. The game's importance was visibly confirmed on the front bumpers of thousands of cars
on every highway in the state; drivers were required to carry license
plates on only the rear of their automobiles, so front bumpers bore a
wide variety of messages and emblems. Among these designs, the only
one that came close to matching in frequency the stars and bars or the
sketch of a grizzled Confederate soldier shouting "Hell no, I Ain't
Forgettin!" was the one that said simply "Alabama" at the bottom,

with two footballs above it on either side of a big red numeral 1. Not infrequently the two kinds of plates, unrepentant rebel and national champion, were bolted one on top of the other on the same automobile.

It was probably fitting then, given the archetypal importance of the game in general and the epochal character of this particular contest that, as the last whistle blew and the crowds began filing out, the Alabama cause was lost. Namath, who had popped a knee cartilage for the third time just two days before, and was facing surgery on it as soon as the season was finished, didn't enter the game until the half, when the Longhorns of Texas had pulled strongly ahead 14–0. But even limping he outdid himself, completing 18 passes for 255 yards and bringing the Tide back to within striking distance of victory. Only the fanatic Texas defense stopped them, foiling a quarterback sneak on the one-foot line in the closing minutes to put the game away, 21–17. (Namath set an Orange Bowl record for completed passes and was selected Most Valuable Player.) The Crimson Tide went home that night the way the state's most revered heroes had before them: prouder in defeat than they could ever imagine being in victory.

Every Alabama public official of any importance was in Miami for the game, as well as many minor-league officeholders for whom being seen in the right places at the right time was important for their future ambitions. Among the latter was James G. Clark, the sheriff of Dallas County, who entertained hopes of running for statewide office some-day, perhaps soon. Clark had originally planned to be back in his county seat, Selma, by the next morning. But at the last minute he changed his mind and stayed over in Miami an extra day.

It was just as well that he didn't come back, because another, more personal defeat was facing him at home. Dr. Martin Luther King, Jr. was scheduled to have a mass meeting in Selma that Saturday after-noon, January second, to kick off a campaign aimed at winning the franchise for the black people of Selma and the South; and he was coming in announced defiance of an injunction prohibiting such mass meetings, an order issued the previous July by Clark's friend and men-tor, Circuit Judge James Hare. The sheriff had enforced the injunction throughout the autumn of 1964, and was widely rumored to have sworn that King would end up in the Dallas County jailhouse if he ventured into Clark's jurisdiction.

Sheriff Clark and his large band of possemen had traveled all over Alabama in the last few years to be on the scene of mass civil rights demonstrations and to take their stand with the forces of segregation. The sheriff, a large, tall man with a firm, square face, stood out among the lawmen with his grey and brown military-style uniform, complete with an officer's billed hat shiny with gold braid. And his tough, nononsense way of dealing with agitators and their marches in Dallas County had further made his name known around the state. He moved at will through the city of Selma, disregarding not only the municipal police but also the spate of federal court suits that attorneys from the Justice Department filed against him.

Judge Hare was Clark's most important supporter. The judge claimed to have made extensive researches into the African ethnic background of the black people of Dallas County, and he loved to talk about how these studies showed that most of them came from the Ibo tribes of what is now Nigeria, which was, he said, a distinctly limited, inferior stock. There were a few local blacks of a better Berber tribal descent, but that did not alter the larger picture. Predictably, Judge Hare believed completely in the segregationist portrait of civil rights organizations as more or less conscious tools of communist conspiracies based in Moscow, Havana and Peking, and he was bitterly hostile to "outside agitators."

Recently, however, a new municipal administration had been installed in Selma, and one of its first objectives had been to wrest away from the sheriff control over law enforcement inside the city limits. The new mayor, Joe T. Smitherman, had created the job of public safety director and appointed to it Wilson Baker, a former police captain in Selma. Baker had met with Clark and Hare several times during the fall to try to get them to accept the new city policy quietly, especially in its application to civil rights matters. The two men resisted, with Clark citing an old state statute designating the sheriff as the highest law enforcement official in the county. But Baker was adamant; that statute was old and irrelevant, he argued; the City Council had passed an ordinance giving him full police authority over the city, and he meant to carry out that mandate without any interference from anyone. At their last meeting before the New Year holiday, Baker made the application of this policy to the scheduled King mass meeting explicit: Judge Hare's injunction had been appealed to the federal courts by the civil rights groups involved; under the provisions of the Civil Rights Act of 1964, only those courts now had the authority to enforce it against anyone; consequently Clark had no powers of arrest under the injunction. On January second, Wilson Baker insisted, he would be in command of all law enforcement officers in the city; and that went not only for his policemen, but for Clark, his deputies and his posse as well. Baker made it clear he would assert this supremacy in public if necessary. So Clark stayed away, and for the moment Baker and Smitherman were free to deal with King and his "agitators" the way they wanted to; in Baker's words, to "meet nonviolence with nonviolence."

Dr. King and his Southern Christian Leadership Conference staff had threatened several times to mount a massive voting rights campaign in Alabama since their demonstrations in Birmingham in the spring of 1963 had brought that city and its segregationist leadership international notoriety. But not until several weeks before at a meeting in Birmingham did the SCLC executive staff make a firm decision to come to Selma, challenge Clark and his injunction, and organize from that city a movement that they hoped would force the United States Congress to pass legislation guaranteeing southern blacks the right to vote. Baker had learned of these plans soon after they were made, when a briefcase of Dr. King's was stolen in Anniston in north Alabama and its contents circulated widely among police officials in the state, and he set to work at once to counter them. Getting Sheriff Clark out of his path was only an initial part of his strategy.

One main reason for the city's new peaceful approach was economic: Joe Smitherman, a lean, nervous-looking appliance salesman who had ousted incumbent Mayor Chris Heinz with a pledge to "get Selma moving again," had as the main plank in his platform the attraction of new industry to Selma. Heinz had not sought to expand the city's industrial base, apparently out of distaste for the unsettling constellation of labor unions, northern ideas and federal regulations which usually trailed along with new factories. Smitherman was outwardly as orthodox a segregationist as Heinz, but was committed to new industry, problems or no. Local people working with him, and the interested company executives, all made it plain that the stability of the city was an important factor in their decision making about where to locate new plants. This translated to mean that they would not stand for any displays of the publicly sanctioned violence associated with Deep South resistance to desegregation. That meant containing Clark, who had met earlier civil rights demonstrations with mass arrests, beatings, and harassment of reporters. Smitherman got the message, as did Baker, who had taught law enforcement at the University of Alabama for six years after leaving the Selma police force, and who took his reputation as a professional very seriously. Moreover, with the Civil Rights Act of 1964 now on the books, the city faced some painful changes as the Justice Department moved in to force compliance on the Deep South's recalcitrant restaurant owners and school officials. Baker understood, as many of them did not, that by moving quietly and with the appearance of cooperation, those subject to the law could get by with the absolute minimum of compliance.

A visit by Martin Luther King, with the resulting publicity and disturbance it was bound to produce, would make this strategy, and the payoff in new industry, more difficult to achieve. Baker moved first to head King off: he flew to Washington in late November and made an appointment with Burke Marshall, head of the Civil Rights Division of the Justice Department. Retiring Attorney General Robert Kennedy sat in on the meeting, while Baker pleaded with them to intervene and persuade King to stay out of Selma until the next July. By that time, he pledged, he would get the Dallas County Board of Registrars to open up its procedures and register blacks in larger numbers, but without fanfare and without exposing themselves.

Baker is a serious-looking, soft-spoken man, without the air of drawling defiance affected by so many Black Belt lawmen in those years. The contrast in manner between him and Jim Clark was striking, and Marshall was impressed. He picked up his telephone and called King in Atlanta. They talked for twenty minutes, then Marshall hung up and turned to Baker, shaking his head. "The die is cast," he said. "They're coming to Selma in January. They've already put too much work in on the project to turn back now."

The meeting broke up a few minutes later. But as Baker was preparing to leave, Robert Kennedy spoke up. "You know," he said, "if you're smart enough, you can beat him at his own game."

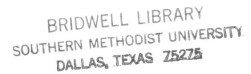

Baker nodded. If he couldn't keep King from coming, that was exactly what he intended to do.

Police cars were parked at both ends of Sylvan Street between Jeff Davis and Selma Avenues all afternoon Saturday, January 2, and white people couldn't get past them without proof that they were civil rights workers or bona fide reporters. But a steady stream of black people walked and drove by them unimpeded toward Brown Chapel African Methodist Episcopal Church, a red brick building with twin, short, tin-covered steeples, which stood in the center of the block. Inside, the freedom singing began early, and soon the worn brown benches were packed with people clapping and swaying to the music, which grew louder and more enthusiastic as the crowd grew steadily larger.

Black Selma had not had a mass meeting in six months, since a few days after the Civil Rights Act was passed. At that time several fights had broken out downtown when black youths had tried to enter the white sections of the Wilby Theater and the Thirsty Boy Drive-in. Judge Hare had used the violence as the pretext for issuing his order forbidding all the civil rights groups, as well as all the city's black activists individually, from gathering publicly in groups of more than three. The fact that the injunction also applied to extreme white groups like the National States Rights party, which had been holding meetings of steadily increasing numbers at the same time, did not mitigate the black resentment against it. The order had been appealed almost immediately, to the U.S. District Court in Mobile, but Judge Daniel H. Thomas there had dawdled through the rest of the year without rendering a decision, which was typical of his tepid concern for actions brought by black groups.

Workers from the Student Nonviolent Coordinating Committee had been in Selma for two years, and had led a fitful series of voting rights demonstrations to the steps of the Dallas County Courthouse. But not many of the marchers had ever gotten inside the greenstone building to fill out the lengthy voter application forms; and of those who did, even fewer managed to get registered. Barely more than three hundred blacks, of a county voting-age population of over fifteen thousand, were on the rolls, mostly schoolteachers, the few black professionals and business people.

But if the earlier demonstrations had not placed many new names on the voting list, they had succeeded in arousing many among the black population to a new level of discontent with their lot. After the enforced silence of the fall, almost every black man and woman of local prominence had welcomed the news that Dr. King, the civil rights movement's Moses, was ready to lead them personally out of their Black Belt Egypt. A Committee of Fifteen, representing every influential circle in the black community, was formed in late December under the auspices of the Dallas County Voters League to coordinate the voting rights campaign. The Voters League in turn had issued a formal invitation to Dr. King to come to Selma. Thus when he mounted the platform at Browns Chapel, after having arrived late, well after the meeting had formally begun, Dr. King was greeted not only by a noisy standing ovation but also by the strongest local coalition black Selma had ever seen.

Most of what he proceeded to tell them they knew only too well: that the county Board of Registrars was open for business only two days a month, took long lunch hours when it was, and if the members processed fifteen applications in a day, that was a lot. "At the rate they are letting us register now," he declared, "it will take a hundred and three years to register all of the fifteen thousand Negroes in Dallas County who are qualified to vote."

"That's right!" replied the people.

"But we don't *have* that *long* to wait!" he went on, the famous baritone rumbling through the church. At this they applauded again. He talked about the literacy test which had been made so complex that almost nobody, even highly educated white people, could pass it. He called it "a deliberate attempt to freeze voter registration at the present undemocratic levels."

But what fired the crowd the most was his declaration of intent: "Today marks the beginning of a determined, organized, mobilized campaign to get the right to vote everywhere in Alabama. If we are refused, we will appeal to Governor George Wallace. If he refuses to listen, we will appeal to the legislature. If *they* don't listen, we will appeal to the conscience of the Congress in another dramatic march on Washington." They were shouting now.

He took note of the fact that Selma was "attempting to change its image"; but he warned the new administration that "there will be no real community stability in Selma until democracy in Dallas County is a reality." To achieve the ballot, he added, "We must be ready to march; we must be willing to go to jail by the thousands." The city could save its reputation, but only if it heeded the rhythmic call which marked his peroration, and was echoed more loudly with each repetition by the responsive audience: "Our cry to the state of Alabama is a simple one," he shouted: *"Give us the ballot!"*

"When we get the right to vote," he said, "we will send to the statehouse not men who will stand in the doorways of universities to keep Negroes out, but men who will uphold the cause of justice: *give us the ballot!*

"And we will send to Congress men who will sign not a manifesto for segregation but a manifesto for justice; *give us the ballot!*

"We're not on our knees begging for the ballot," he said as he finished. *"We are demanding the ballot."*

He left them standing and cheering with an intensity that seemed to make the whole building tremble, promising to return again and again until the victory was theirs. Two deputy sheriffs and a lone state trooper who had sat through the service in the back row impassively taking notes left quickly after his finish, so they would not have to join the linking of arms that went along with the concluding singing of "We Shall Overcome."

Two hours later, Wilson Baker watched Dr. King leave the home of Mrs. Amelia Platts Boynton, where he had conducted a strategy session for the campaign, and drove off with his aides for Montgomery, followed by cars filled with FBI agents, sheriff's deputies and city police. His visit had gone smoothly enough, but only after the caravan was across the Edmund Pettus Bridge over the Alabama River and outside the city limits could Baker allow himself to relax. He had spent most of the day keeping Jim Clark's men away from the area around Brown Chapel; he had ordered the posse to assemble inside the courthouse several blocks away, to await his signal before venturing out to assist his uniformed policemen. The signal never came, of course, and by now the possemen all understood that they had been virtually in confinement during the meeting, and they weren't happy about their treatment.

The *Selma Times-Journal,* whose publisher, Roswell Falkenberry, was solidly in Baker's camp, played up in the next day's editions what it generously called the "cooperation" between the various law enforcement agencies involved, under Baker's supervision. And in an editorial, it firmly endorsed his strategy: "Often, other methods sometimes tend to provoke sporadic incidents of unlawful conduct. At least—basing our belief on the apparent success of the strategy employed in this instance —there is substantial reason to encourage continued use of these tactics for as long as they prove effective and practical in the positive maintenance of law and order in Selma and Dallas County."

Baker had won this opening round; the agitator had had his meeting and left town in one piece. But Jim Clark would be back by the end of the weekend. And King was coming back too; so the bout was by no means over.

*Moreover, there was the influence of the Southern
physical world—itself a sort of cosmic conspiracy
against reality in favor of romance. The country is
one of extravagant colors, of proliferating foliage
and bloom, of flooding yellow sunlight, and, above
all perhaps, of haze. Pale blue fogs hang above the
valleys in the morning, the atmosphere smokes
faintly at midday, and through the long slow
afternoon, cloud-stacks tower from the horizon and
the earth-heat quivers upward through the iridescent
air, blurring every outline and rendering every object
vague and problematical. I know that winter comes
to the land, certainly. I know that there are days
when the color and the haze are stripped away and
the real stands up in drab and depressing harshness.
But these things pass and are forgotten.*

—W. J. Cash, The Mind of the South

TWO.
Once during the 1830s, a rumor swept the Old Town area of rural Dallas County that the slaves in Selma had risen against their masters. Since there were thousands more slaves than whites in the town, such a rebellion could easily end in a horrible massacre. Major Benjamin Grumbles, commander of the battalion of militia in Old Town, rose immediately to the gravity of the occasion and called his men together out of their cotton fields. After rousing them with a long, patriotic speech, he persuaded two hundred to set out for the city at once, armed with muskets, hickory sticks and corn-stalks, whatever they had with them. It was many miles into town, however; soon night fell and the battalion made camp. But they were awakened by alarming flashes of light and rumbling noises coming through the darkness from the general direction of Selma, and again took march, only to be caught in a driving downpour and forced to struggle through knee-deep mud until they reached the city limits about noon the next day.

To the slime-spattered troops' astonishment, they found life in

Selma going on undisturbed; the slave uprising had been only a rumor, the noise and lights the harbingers of a thunder storm. The militia commander in Selma, General Shearer, gave the tired troops a good meal, thanked them for their vigilance, and sent them home. The men managed to keep reasonably good order until they got back across the Alabama River, but then they left their officers and scattered pell-mell for home.

The story of this "nigger insurrection" became a standing joke which followed Major Grumbles, called "Old Snort" by his men, all the rest of his days. And the local historian who recorded it added to his account that "This excited state of the public mind about insubordination of the negro population soon subsided, and very justly, for we think we are safe in saying, at no period of the world was there a greater fidelity exhibited on the part of a servile population towards their owners, than was on the part of the negro population and Dallas County generally, during all this great excitement. . . ." Nor was this judgment true only in ante-bellum times. The same writer said of the blacks of his own day, 1879, that he had "no hesitancy in asserting that no people have ever been more law-abiding and deserve more praise than the colored people of Selma. . . ."

There is little reason to think that this white Selmian was deceiving himself or attempting to fool his readers. The truth of slavery and segregation in the Black Belt of Alabama, and in Dallas County especially, is much more complex than most outsiders, particularly visitors from Yankee territory, ever suspect. And the fact that relations between the races there have been predominantly "peaceful" for over one hundred and fifty years is part of that paradoxical truth.

Many of the early settlers of the city were people of some substance, migrating west from older southern states. They were people among whom what was later to become the idealized aristocratic tradition of the legendary Old South had more substance than it did in most other places. Besides, the land was fruitful and the navigable Alabama River a ribbon of commerce, and soon enough some of them had the wealth needed to wrap their self-image in the mansions, clothing and stables full of thoroughbred racehorses which it presupposed. William Rufus King, who named Selma after the walled highland capital city of the

legendary Scottish Prince Fingal, was one such transplanted gentleman, and his career showed it. He became one of Alabama's first two
senators, and in 1852 was elected vice-president of the United States
under Franklin Pierce.

While he supported slavery to the hilt, to the end of his life King
was a strong Union man, and he frequently clashed with Alabama's
radical secessionists such as William Lowndes Yancey. Moreover, his
home county was never a particular hotbed of support for leaving the
Union, although as the struggle between North and South neared its
bloody culmination its white citizens were prepared to do their part in
defending their state and their peculiar institution. But many of Selma's men who joined the Confederate Army did so with heavy hearts;
unlike some others, they were not looking forward to the war, if only
because they had a great deal to lose.

Nor were these apprehensions to go unrealized. Several factories had
been built in Selma before the war broke out, and their facilities were
soon absorbed into what became the largest arsenal, munitions manu-
facturing center and supply depot in the South, employing the huge
total of ten thousand men within the city limits. In March 1865 the
Federal Army sent General J. H. Wilson to destroy this strategic target,
which he did, riding swiftly down from Tennessee with thirteen thousand crack troops and driving the spent forces of General Nathan
Bedford Forrest before him. The city was captured before the defend-
ers had had time to smash the large barrels of whiskey stored in one
of the warehouses; and when the Union soldiers found them, Selma was
soon at the mercy of a drunken, uncontrolled mob. For three nights
the city burned while the Union troops sacked houses, killed livestock
and terrorized the women. By the time the casks were emptied, the
"Pittsburgh of the South" lay almost completely in ruins.

Predictably, white Selma was bitter as it faced Reconstruction and
the impact of the Fifteenth Amendment. But among its residents were
a core of the Confederate generals and colonels around whom the myth
of the Lost Cause was rapidly crystallizing; these men had had their
fill of war, and were determined to resist and overthrow the carpetbag
governments through what were primarily political, rather than military, maneuvers. In 1869 and 1870 the Ku Klux Klan whipped and

lynched white and black alike only a few counties away, in Greene, Tuscaloosa, and as close as Marengo just to the west. But it never showed appreciable strength in Dallas County, because men like General Edmund Pettus doubted its real effectiveness and despised the class origins of most of its membership, and Pettus's opinion was authoritative in the county.

After the state had been "redeemed" by the Democrats in 1874, Negro suffrage became, rather than a threat to white supremacy in Dallas County, one of its main supports, as the stealing and manipulation of Freedmen's votes became practically an industry in the Black Belt, and made it one of the main poles of political power in the state. These "black" votes were one of the key weapons used to prevent the upstart Populists from translating their broad support elsewhere in the state into a rightful share of elective offices; as the saying went, "You can out vote us, but we can out count you." And when the state constitutional convention of 1901 moved to impose a poll tax, a grandfather clause, and a literacy test on blacks to deprive them of the ballot, the delegates from the Black Belt were apparently moved less by fear of black domination than by a desire to put an end to the need for their embarrassing and ungentlemanly habit of vote-stealing—and, of course, by a desire to disfranchise as well many poor whites in other counties, who usually voted against their interests.

In the ensuing decades, most blacks and whites rubbed elbows constantly in Selma as they had always done, and with the blacks both unable and apparently unwilling to challenge their subordination, the mentality of paternalism among the whites, and their ability to ignore the injustice of their segregated system, developed almost undisturbed. Blacks who stayed played their appointed roles with the ease of a lifetime's practice.

Beneath the surface of this careful structure, of course, there was the spreading tangle of personal relationships which often enough became much more intimate than the light of day could admit. Respectable people in the black community estimated that in 1965 fully 20 per cent of the city's black population were the direct offspring of unions between black and white citizens, and not a few of these mixed offspring were at least informally acknowledged by their white (and almost always male) progenitors. Nor was it unknown for a white woman of some standing to take a black husband and stay in Selma, in open defiance of the antimiscegenation laws, although such a woman was disgraced and ever after treated as if she was, and always had been, black herself.

Looked at more closely, then, what to northern eyes was a solid wall of segregation in Selma was actually more like a high picket fence, with not a few sags and gaps along its length. The white families loved and cherished, in their own way, the black maids they paid ten dollars and some old clothes for a long weeks' work, and the gnarled laborers bent in their fields with rarely a quarter to call their own. And the blacks, the ones who stayed, continued to use the deceptive carriage and vocabulary which could confirm their superiors' images even while it mocked and exploited them for the blacks' own purposes.

In this situation there was normally little need for organized, officially sanctioned violence. The system of segregation "worked." Problems were handled quietly, through economic and social pressures; or if a conflict went beyond that, it was settled individually, and usually kept out of court. Meanwhile, on the surface, during daylight hours, the blacks and whites followed the rules, smiled at each other, talked and joked as if everything was just as the whites believed it was and ought to be.

Against this canvas the positions of some of the people and forces in the city can be better understood as the civil rights movement embarked on an effort to change its pattern. Take Sheriff Jim Clark first of all: he was an outsider, from Coffee County in southeastern Alabama, an area where populist sentiment had long run deep against the Bosses and the Planters of the Black Belt. He had settled in Dallas County, and got into politics by managing the campaigns there of Governor James "Big Jim" Folsom, who was one of the Alabama populist tradition's most genuine representatives in the twentieth century. Part of Clark's duties included quiet overtures to the then very small but not insignificant block of black voters in the state. He did his work well; Folsom got the black votes, served two terms, and almost beat George Wallace in the 1962 primary. And when the sheriff of Dallas County died of a heart attack in 1957, Folsom did what he was supposed to do and appointed Clark to serve the remainder of the term.

By all reports Clark was a competent sheriff, popular especially with the smaller farmers and families in the rural areas outside Selma. But he was neither accepted nor trusted by the people from the old families in town, the people who had most of the money and the political clout. In the election of 1958 these traditional forces persuaded a captain in the Selma Police Department to oppose Clark in the Democratic primary. The captain's name was Wilson Baker.

It was a hard-fought campaign, one in which Clark employed his insurgent populist image for all it was worth. He played to the grumblings of the "county folks" against what he referred to as "that great big Buga-Boo, The Machine" inside the city limits. One of his deputies opposed him in the primary, and garnered just enough ballots to force a runoff. In the final race three events affected the outcome, how decisively depending on whose account one is listening to: First, Clark rehired his wayward deputy, announcing that they had settled their differences and he was too good a man to lose; and Clark's final tally increased by almost exactly the amount the deputy had polled. Second, Wilson Baker made the tactical mistake of appearing before a rally of the Ku Klux Klan outside of town in the closing days of the campaign. The Klan, remember, had little support and less respectability in Dallas County, and the appearance is said to have cost Baker the votes of the few hundred registered blacks as well as many among the better white people. Blacks in Selma insist to this day that this was what cost him the nomination. Finally, some strange things happened during the process of counting the votes, a process which was under the supervision of the sheriff's department; and Baker still believes the election was stolen someplace between the polling booths and the courthouse.

In any event, Jim Clark beat "The Machine," the old families and their supporters, and settled into his office at the courthouse with the prospect of a long tenure which most duly elected incumbents in the area rightly anticipated. Wilson Baker soon left the city police force for the University of Alabama, not to return for six years.

In the meantime, Clark again proved to be a capable enough sheriff, and opposition to him died down. But in February 1963 the defiant young organizers of the Student Nonviolent Coordinating Committee came to town and started talking to the blacks about voting, and integration, and something they called Freedom. When it came to dealing with these "agitators," the sheriff seemed to go more than a little crazy. The way he lashed out at the SNCC people and their small, tentative marches was more like what could have been expected in a city like Birmingham, where a half million transplanted poor whites lived, the kind who really *hated* niggers, the people who had made their Robert E. Lee Klavern of Ku Kluxers the largest and most brazen in the vast Invisible Empire of the 1920s. Clark's response might have been recognizable to a sociologist as not at all uncharacteristic of a populist segregationist threatened by stirrings among the black multitude; but it was out of place in Selma's calmer, more refined precincts, and the whites of breeding and influence in the city were offended and worried by his public displays of rage, his rough mass arrests, his surrounding of black mass meetings with his trashy possemen. They were also alarmed by the support he was getting from the angry and fearful lower-class whites.

Clark's conduct went unimpeded and even applauded by the administration of Mayor Chris Heinz, who was getting tired of the job after twelve years in office and wanted mainly to keep himself and his police force out of the federal court suits which soon began piling up against the sheriff and the county Board of Registrars. But the sheriff's role was a major, if unarticulated issue in the city election of 1964: Joe Smitherman, who had come up from a poor white background, had supported Clark in earlier years. But now, running only in the city, he promised equal, professional law enforcement, which meant he would try to put a leash on the sheriff; and to make good on the pledge, he brought back Baker, who had the confidence of the people who counted.

Baker not only had class, he was shrewd, as the most successful segregationists were always shrewd. Because of the civil rights laws, he warned the whites, "we're going to have to walk in the mud a little. I'd rather walk in the mud voluntarily of my own initiative with my head high rather than have some federal court force my face down into the mud without dignity." The words "a little" were key; Baker was also trying to tell them that the whites who maintained their dignity and stayed out of the federal courts were also the ones who would end up with the least mud to walk through.

Thus when Dr. King came on January second and Baker faced down the deputies and the possemen, he did so as the representative of traditional, conservative Selma. It was Clark who was different, who was the agitator. Baker hoped to duplicate the performance of Chief Laurie Pritchett of Albany Georgia in his dealings with King two years before. Pritchett had met Albany's civil rights marches with quick, efficient arrests that involved no beatings or official outbursts; and his policy had sucked the momentum and publicity out of the movement the way corn bread sops up gravy. Pritchett was always careful to speak courteously and "moderately" to the out-of-town reporters: "I realize I'm living in a changing world," he told the man from the *New York Times*. "You've got to adapt yourself to the situation. We are not in the same old school." He emphasized to all and sundry his overriding professionalism: "It's not a matter of whether I'm a segregationist or an integrationist," he insisted. "I'm a duly constituted law-enforce-ment officer, dedicated to the enforcement of the law." But, as he later admitted, he never forgot what he was really after: "We, the duly constituted authorities and the citizens of this city, met 'nonviolence' with 'nonviolence' and we are, indeed, proud of the outcome." His success was appreciated by other city officials. "We killed them with kindness," said one with visible satisfaction. "Apparently it was a condi-tion M. L. King and the other outsiders had never encountered before."

Albany was not only a place where good southern manners were observed in the course of repression; it was also the most complete defeat Dr. King and his Southern Christian Leadership Conference had suffered up to that time. Pritchett had outsmarted the enemies of white supremacy, the way the best southerners had done ever since it became clear they couldn't outgun them.

How deep this style of social control ran is also evident in the case of the Dallas County Citizens Council, the first in the state. That the Alabama councils began in Selma was usually pointed to, by Yankee commentators who came through town, as proof positive of the city's commitment to massive resistance to desegregation by fair means or foul. But this interpretation was vastly off the mark. At the end of 1964, while the council was able to claim to be one of the largest in the state, with every influential white person in the county enrolled as a charter member, the more revealing facts about it were that it had no membership list, no regular newsletter or communication with its members, no procedure for the election of officers, and no separate activities beyond a fish fry or barbecue held more or less semiannually. Perhaps more important, it was committed to opposing integration through strictly legal means, and what this came down to was mostly a lot of wind. A look at issues of the council's national magazine the *Citizen* published in these years shows them to be filled mainly with the most patent kind of joiner-trivia, spiced only occasionally with more substance than the house organ of some innocuous service club.

In sum, the Dallas County Citizens Council was more than anything else a co-optative device, aimed at giving nervous whites something to join *other than* the Klan, or the National States Rights party, or some other "extreme" and unrespectable group; and at this function it was largely successful. Beyond that, it seemed designed to be little more than a cheering section for whichever politician, like Governor George Wallace, was able to make the best use of it. To further underline the inactivity and irrelevance of the local group, the Dallas County Council membership also encompassed people whose real sentiments were actually opposed to segregation. Among these were members of Selma's old, affluent and respected Jewish congregation, who had a special interest in keeping the group's rhetoric miles away from the anti-Semitism that affected the Klan.

This set of contrasts should not be overdrawn. As the early months of 1965 unfolded, the dialectic of old and new in white Selma was to become complex almost beyond recognition. Faced with the first important challenge to their supremacy since Reconstruction a century before, white responses strained tradition: the Citizens Council was to spring into at least the appearance of life; the kind of mob action for which the despised Klan was best known would come to Dallas County; and to meet this threat, the forces of tradition would ultimately have to make use of what the blacks set out to accomplish. There was also irony and dialectic aplenty on the black side; but that will not come into focus until a little later. The interplay among the white protagonists, which resumed and intensified almost as soon as Dr. King's car disappeared into the night on January second, was to make the most difference in the early weeks of 1965.

In the past few years, while travelling over much of the United States, I have made this observation: the colored people of our area actually have been the happiest of any others to be found anywhere. They really have enjoyed their own nice churches, fine schools and club meetings. The colored in the country declare Saturday a special day for themselves. They come into town, meet with each other, and really have a wonderful time.

> —Celeste Bruce, letter to the
> Selma Times-Journal,
> *February 22, 1965*

THREE.
One successful mass meeting does not make a movement. The SNCC and SCLC staff people in Selma knew that from long experience. There were thousands more blacks out in the city who hadn't attended, and the whites would be early at work spreading rumors, lies and threats among them to keep them away from the campaign. Selma had no black newspaper, and fully half the blacks couldn't read anyway; so there was only one way to make sure the people knew what the visit of Dr. King really meant: hit the streets.

The staff divided among the city's five wards, and fanned out into them with leaflets announcing that ward meetings would be held on Thursday, January 7. The workers were hard to miss in their blue overalls or walking in mixed black and white pairs down the dusty, rutted dirt streets. And if their knock on the shabby doors of the houses and shacks often produced smiles of hope and a pledge of "I'll be there," it more often was met by expressions that were cautious or downright fearful. It was the old, the sick and the permanently unemployed who were most likely to be at home during the day; and it was these who, being most dependent, were most vulnerable to reprisal for cooperating with these strangers, and who were likely to know the least about them and their mission.

One ancient, wrinkled woman told a canvassing worker solemnly that she didn't know what voting was. Her eyes widened when it was explained to her. Oh no, she insisted, she couldn't go down to that courthouse; if she did she would have to carry her coffin with her, because the white man was sure to hit her over the head and she just wouldn't be able to stand it. There were two places she just couldn't stand, she repeated, and that was the courthouse and the jailhouse. No, she couldn't go down and register.

A black preacher in a worn blue suit told another canvasser with affected dignity that he just wasn't interested in politics. Yes, he agreed that politics are good to have around. And he had nothing against people that do vote. But no, he didn't care for voting.

There were many others, sitting on the weathered porches taking the weak January sun, who simply nodded and looked away, or mumbled "Yeh, I'll be on," by reflex, unconvincingly. It was here along the Selma streets, going block by block, that the greenhorns among the civil rights workers, especially the whites from the North and West, got their first close look at the effects of segregation on actual, individual people. The cumulative impression was one they did not forget easily.

At the first ward meetings that Thursday night, the workers had a similar problem even with those who were brave enough to attend. Ward Three, for instance, met in the basement of Tabernacle Baptist Church on Broad Street, and the meeting was conducted by big James Orange, a tall black SCLC worker. Orange explained to the small, subdued crowd that what a ward meeting was for was so people could talk about conditions in their neighborhoods and how to go about getting the things they needed. "You're the people who live here," he concluded, "and now it's your turn to speak up for yourselves."

The room fell silent. Orange looked around expectantly, wordlessly coaxing them to talk. At length an old, thin woman stood up hesitantly. "Well," she said quietly and slowly, "they . . . they don't hardly ever pick up the garbage along my street."

"That's right," murmured a man in the next row, looking around at her. Others nodded.

"Right now," the woman continued, still speaking slowly, "there are still big piles of leaves from the fall around. And when it rains they clog the drains and the mud is awful."

"That's *right,*" the man repeated, as if he had just realized the fact. The heads nodded more vigorously now.

Orange asked if anyone else wanted to talk about the garbage on their street. Someone did; and so it went. The discussion that evening did not get much further than the garbage, the mud, and the lack of street lights, but it represented a watershed experience for the people present. It is unlikely that any of them had ever dared stand up in such a relatively public place and speak openly against the conditions under which they had to live. As the meeting ended Orange told them the ward would meet again early next week, to select its own resident ward captain and to begin talking about how to relate to the activities which the Voters League, SNCC and SCLC were planning for the next registration day, January 18, which he said was really going to be Freedom Day.

Wilson Baker was out of town most of that week, visiting relatives in North Carolina. But before he left he had met again with Sheriff Clark, Judge Hare and City Attorney McLean Pitts, trying to maintain some semblance of cooperation in anticipation of King's return and the expected beginning of demonstrations. Baker told them that his jurisdiction covered everything in the city except the Dallas County Courthouse, including the sidewalks around the court building. The others disagreed. This was an important point, because the Board of Registrars met in the courthouse and any demonstrations would be certain to attract crowds on the outside sidewalks. Baker said this meant it was his job to supervise the portion of any voting registration line that extended out beyond the courthouse steps; Clark contested this also.

Pitts supported Clark, even though he was the city's lawyer. This was not surprising because most of his practice was before Judge Hare, and he had to keep in good standing with him. But Baker bridled at Pitts's position and warned Pitts he would not let anyone interfere with him doing his duty; if Pitts got in his way, Baker swore he would arrest him like anyone else.

Pitts was shocked; the city attorney, he protested, was immune from arrest by city police. Baker, who knew the law, challenged him to find any such grant of immunity in the city ordinances, and repeated the warning. The meeting ended with Hare and Clark admitting grudgingly that the public safety director *had* handled King's first appearance reasonably well, but without agreement as to what would happen next. Pitts left the meeting shaken by the fierceness of Baker's insistence. Clark was not so easily intimidated.

With Baker gone for much of the rest of the week, Clark's men moved around the city largely unhampered. They followed the workers canvassing the wards and sent deputies into three of the first ward meetings Thursday night. But at one, the Ward Four meeting held in the back of Brown Chapel, they got a reception they hadn't bargained for from an SCLC staff member named James Bevel. Bevel was on Dr. King's executive staff, and was in charge of the SCLC workers in the city; although short and unimposing in appearance, he was one of King's most eloquent and fiery spokesmen, known especially for the vigor and force of his denunciations of racism. He also knew of the maneuvering going on among the city's whites, and was ready to play on it. Before a small, dumbfounded audience, Bevel stood up and ordered the deputies to leave. One of them raised a camera to take his picture, and he angrily told him to stop and repeated the order for them to leave. The deputies were wary of getting involved in an incident in such surroundings, and they left. The news of this unprecedented act of defiance quickly spread around the city.

That same day the *Selma Times-Journal* felt it necessary to explicitly coax the sheriff to go along with the city policy: in an editorial entitled "Facing up to reality" Assistant Editor Arthur Capell wrote: "Certainly this performance on the occasion of Martin Luther King's visit here must be as reassuring and welcome to Sheriff James G. Clark as it was to this newspaper and as we believe it is to the entire community. ... The spirit of cooperation evidenced by our county leaders in rallying behind the city's realistic leadership to meet the Saturday challenge of King's visit here gives real reason to feel optimism that it is proceeding along this course."

This was mostly whistling in the dark, as editor Capell learned firsthand the following day. He met with Clark and Hare all afternoon, trying his hand at persuading them that the city's policy was not only the safest but also potentially the most effective antidote to King's noxious agitation. He got nowhere.

This jockeying for position reached a climax of sorts the following week. Dr. King returned to Selma and announced at a mass meeting that he would lead a march to the courthouse on Monday, January 18, when the Board of Registrars would again be open. Squads of people would also be sent out, he said, to test the readiness of Selma restaurants and hotelkeepers to comply with the public accommodations sections of the Civil Rights Act. That law had been on the books for seven months, but there had been virtually no successful integration of the city's cafes and inns. Several proprietors had privately expressed willingness to comply, but all were afraid to do so unless everyone else did so as well. They were now waiting for a federal injunction to come down ordering them by name to comply so they could give in involuntarily under tyrannical federal pressure. Dr. King declared that as part of the testing he and his party would register Monday at the Hotel Albert, Selma's ante-bellum pride, a copy of the Doge's palace in Venice begun before the Civil War and built largely with slave labor.

But Wilson Baker knew that January 18 was crucial for more than one reason. The campaign scenario King was following called for demonstrations to begin in several other places in the Black Belt, with the main focus to be on wherever the most visible opposition developed. If Selma didn't provide the needed action, and it hadn't so far, King and his minions would move on, leaving only a token force in Dallas County and taking the limelight with them. So it was imperative that January 18 go quietly, especially at the courthouse. After another intense round of negotiations, he got Clark's reluctant assent to this view.

When Dr. King arrived at the Dallas County Courthouse Monday morning, at the head of a line of four hundred blacks, he was met not only by Baker, Clark and a horde of newspeople, but also by George Lincoln Rockwell, the fuehrer of the American Nazi party, and Jimmy George Robinson of the National States Rights party. The NSRP, along with the Klan, had held meetings in Selma the previous summer, and when the Civil Rights Act passed and fighting began downtown, the groups began attracting some interest and support among some of the poorer whites who felt especially threatened by what they believed was about to happen. And when Judge Hare issued his injunction, he included the Klan and the NSRP under the ban on meetings. Now that King and his agitators were back and had successfully defied the order, these groups began emerging from the shadows as well.

Clark immediately ordered the reporters across the street, so they didn't hear much of the dialogue between Rockwell, Robinson and King. The nazi, wearing a trench coat and chewing on the end of a corncob pipe which was his trademark, accused King of being a Communist, and dared him to let him speak to the mass meeting that night and present his segregation-is-best-for-black-people case direct to the people in an open debate. Rockwell loved to debate, and had once appeared on the same platform with Black Muslims, to express solidarity with their campaign for a separate Afro-American nation. King hesitated, then said certainly, Rockwell and Robinson could each have fifteen minutes.

Then, however, as the marchers turned their attention to an effort to get into the building, Robinson spoke up, not to King but to Rockwell, taunting him about his Nazi affectations. Immediately the two began heckling each other, as members of the two groups usually did whenever they got the chance, and the crowd passed them by. Rockwell, in the wake of their earlier quarrels, had in fact sued the NSRP for conspiracy, libel, and slander; the action, still pending as they met, asked $550,000 in damages for what Rockwell called the NSRP's attempts to deprive him and his tiny band of Nazis of financial support and the friendship of potential members.

So far everything was going according to plan for Wilson Baker. He had stopped King a block from Brown Chapel earlier and directed him to break the march down into ranks of three and four, so that it would not constitute a parade, for which a permit was necessary; and the group had complied, walking on the sidewalks and obeying traffic signals. Baker and the sheriff posed for a picture together as the marchers arrived at the courthouse and their "supervision" passed into the county officials' hands. The leaders announced their intention to register, and Clark told them to come in through the entrance on the north side of the building along Lauderdale Street. But instead of stopping at the registrars' office, he led them straight across the hall and out the back door into an alleyway, ordered them to line up there, and strung a rope across the alley to emphasize just where they were supposed to stay. He passed out numbered cards to the people in line, and told them to wait until called before entering the office to complete the application. A moment later the blacks in front saw a dozen whites going up into the office. The board was especially slow processing these early applications, and took a leisurely lunch break at midday. None of the blacks waiting in the alley where the quarantined reporters couldn't see them got inside the building again, not even those who stood there all day.

The testing went more successfully. The evening before, the city restaurant owners association had met in a secret emergency session and a majority agreed to comply without further resistance. Monday morning, dittoed sheets were passed out to regular customers advising them of the restaurateurs' intentions of submitting to the law of the land. A few still held out; of these, most closed their doors. Only one owner, Harmon Carter who ran Carter's Drugstore on Alabama Avenue, actually refused to serve a black testing team and ordered them to leave his premises. And there was at least one establishment, the Silver Moon Cafe on Franklin Street, that stayed open but went undisturbed, because the blacks familiar with the attitudes of many of its regular clientele were not ready to face their reaction without protection.

At the Selma Del, an expensive establishment on Broad Street, an integrated group was served resentfully but quietly, though not before a bizarre incident had marred the genteel atmosphere of the place. A local reporter noticed a stranger huddling in the darkness of a telephone booth, and asked if he was waiting for someone. "Yes," came the muffled reply. "I'm waiting to have lunch with Martin Luther *Coon*."

"Where is Rockwell?" the reporter asked, guessing the man's sympathies.

"Oh, wherever he is, he's up to no good. No good for the niggers, that is."

The reporter noticed a large doll at the man's feet. "Is that your doll?"

"Yes." The man turned around, and his face was made up minstrel style, black greasepaint with a wide, white band around the lips. "That's my lunch," he said.

"You must be a cannibal."

"Yes."

The man turned out to be Robert Alison Lloyd of Arlington, Virginia, one of Rockwell's close associates. Lloyd had caught the spotlight only two weeks before in Washington, when the Mississippi Freedom Democratic party was challenging the right of the lily-white congressional delegation from Mississippi to take their seats in the new House of Representatives when the mass of the state's 45 per cent black population had been excluded from the process of their election. During the debate over the challenge, Lloyd—again in minstrel blackface —had slipped past the House doorkeepers and raced onto the floor shouting "Heah I is, I'ze the Mississippi delegation!" until he was dragged out. He produced more than a few chuckles from the congressmen, who went on to sidetrack and later kill the challenge.

But Lloyd was now on different turf, and Wilson Baker was in no mood for jokes. As soon as he heard about it, Lloyd was arrested, charged with disorderly conduct, and forced to wash off the greasepaint before being arraigned in city court.

At the Albert, Dr. King and ten of his staff were registered without fanfare. And the change their presence represented was less stark than it might have been, because the Albert was Selma's quality watering place, and King and his group were all thoroughly bourgeois in their tastes and knew how to act in such surroundings. The only trouble came from the NSRP's Robinson, who followed them in looking for a chance to get his moment of attention. He walked into the lobby toward King, who asked him, "Are you going to be able to come to the meeting tonight?"

"I'm afraid not," Robinson replied. "Could you step over here for just a minute?"

King moved toward him, and as soon as he was within range Robinson hit him on the temple with his fist and kicked him in the groin. King doubled over, and at the opposite end of the lobby a white woman jumped up on a chair and started shrieking "Get him! Get him!"

Wilson Baker, standing several feet away, moved at once. Striding across the lobby he grabbed Robinson by both lapels of his jacket, almost right where the NSRP thunderbolt insignia were, and lifted him right off the floor. "What are you doing in here anyhow," he demanded gruffly, as he dragged the segregationist out the door and put him in a police car. Robinson was charged with assault and disturbing the peace.

At the mass meeting that night, Rev. Frederick D. Reese, the president of the Dallas County Voters League, spoke about the breadth of support their voting rights campaign was developing in the black community of Selma, Alabama. Reese, a tall, very dark and handsome man, was the top local black leader, an instructor at the all-black R. B. Hudson High School and the pastor of two small rural Baptist churches. He spoke with an accent strongly formed by the Black Belt's soft sibilants; the overflow crowd, recognizing him as one of their own, listened attentively. So complete was the support, he insisted, that before long even the Negro *teachers* were going to be marching. They would march, Reese said, because most of them, the people who were charged with training the coming generation in the mechanisms of government and the responsibilities of citizenship, couldn't exercise these responsibilities themselves because they weren't registered to vote, despite their educational attainments. And they were fed up with this situation, so fed up that they were going to march downtown and demand to be registered.

None of the civil rights workers present permitted him or her self to scoff openly at Reese's declaration; but they didn't believe any such thing would happen. The longer they had worked in the movement, the more firmly they had been convinced that of all the Uncle Tom strata of southern Negro communities, the teachers were the most incorrigible. Many of the SNCC and SCLC staff people had begun their careers as fulltime organizers after being expelled from black high schools and colleges by fearful, compromised black administrators. And they had been tossed off one campus after another across the South as they tried to bring their message about smashing segregation to the youth of the region. Of course Reese was a teacher himself, and the past president of the Selma Negro teachers association. But he was also a preacher, and in any case a man of unusual leadership skills, so he wasn't representative.

The workers were more interested in knowing what tactical plans would come out of the private staff meeting held by Dr. King and his circle at the Albert after the mass meeting. Baker had held things closely in check today, and his success had to be taken into account. He had even kept the visiting Nazis from cashing in on Dr. King's pledge of speaking time and using it to antagonize the people with their racist oratory. He had done this by stopping them when they approached the church, and arresting Rockwell and his two henchmen when they demanded to be let in. This happened in the outer darkness so that no one knew of it until later, and it underlined Baker's determination to keep things quiet, even if it meant letting Rockwell cool his heels in the city jail for the night.

At the staff meeting, held about midnight, Baker's success in keeping a leash on Clark and his friends was discussed extensively. The press could not be expected to stay around and give the movement the national exposure it must have unless there was some action to photograph and write about. The consensus was that they would try another march the following morning; and if it too went quietly, they would begin shifting their activities to another location; perhaps Marion, in Perry County to the northwest; or Camden, in Wilcox County to the south. They should find some action in one or the other of them. Not a single black was registered in Wilcox County, for instance, even though the population was 80 per cent nonwhite. And on a huge plantation in Millers Ferry, in Wilcox, lived six hundred black families who never saw United States currency; the owners had their own coinage, octagonal tin coins, for use at the plantation commissary, just the way they had in ante-bellum days. Yes, there were many places in the Black Belt where the campaign might get some action.

Wilson Baker had a spy in the meeting, and was gratified to hear of the decision. With a little luck, he would have King out of town for good without firing a shot or making a single arrest. In fact, the Smitherman administration might come out ahead: the reporters were already filing stories about Selma's "progressive new look."

But his satisfaction was shortlived. The mayor called; Jim Clark wanted to see them at the county jail immediately. When Baker arrived Clark was in a wild rage, swearing that he'd arrest "every goddam one of them that comes down there tomorrow!" Apparently the militants among the possemen he had deployed around the courthouse during the day had been after him, complaining that Baker was giving the city away to the niggers, and demanding to have some of the kind of law enforcement they were accustomed to. He paid no attention to the entreaties of Baker and Smitherman to hold off just a little longer.

FOUR.

But Dr. King's staff had its spies as well, and when the people gathered at Brown Chapel for the following morning's march, they asked for fifty volunteers who were ready to go to jail. Fifty hands were raised at once; and after a lesson in nonviolent self-defense they set off grimly in the direction of the courthouse, again following Baker's order to split up into small, widely spaced groups.

At the courthouse the line stopped, not at the door on the Lauderdale Street entrance, but around the corner at the Alabama Avenue entrance on the east end of the building. This, they told Clark, was the front door to the courthouse, and this was the door they were going to enter. And they weren't going to wait in any alley either.

Clark wasted little time in arresting them; and one of the first he grabbed was Mrs. Amelia Boynton. Mrs. Boynton was not only a veteran local civil rights activist; she was also a registered voter, and was on hand to serve as one of the two enrolled voters required by the law to vouch for the truthfulness of each of the numerous declarations all applicants were required to make. Mrs. Boynton is a tall, aristocratic-looking woman, not inclined to take any guff from James Clark or his trashy possemen. And when she didn't move fast enough to please the sheriff, his temper flared. He grabbed her by the back of her collar and pushed her stumbling halfway down the block to a sheriff's car, in full view of the reporters and the astonished black marchers. The others

33

were led into the courthouse, held for several hours and finally arraigned on a charge of "Failing to leave the place of an unlawful assembly after being warned to disperse by a public officer." For this violation they could be sentenced to a five hundred dollar fine and a six-month stretch on the county chain gang.

Attorneys from the NAACP Legal Defense Fund arrived in Selma that afternoon to assist with the expected legal workload, and they succeeded in getting all the sixty-seven people arrested released on bail by nightfall. The group got out in time to eat dinner and be presented to that night's mass meeting. At the meeting Rev. Ralph Abernathy, who was Dr. King's closest companion, proposed that the Dallas County Voters League accept Jim Clark into honorary membership for his sterling service in bringing the plight of black people in Selma to the attention of the nation. The crowd shouted and laughed its approval.

Afterward there was another staff strategy session. Having succeeded in bringing Clark's brutality into the open, it was agreed to step up the pace the next day. There was something obsessive about Clark's response to the sight of a line of black faces ringing his green marble courthouse; he may have thought he was acting for some calculated end, but he looked and carried on like he couldn't stop himself from striking out at them. It was as if he was caught on the stage of a drama in which he was unable to step out of his role. But this only made the sheriff that much more important to the movement. If his campaign was to be carried through the news media to the nation at large and get a meaningful response from Congress, Dr. King had to have someone like Clark to do in public, before the cameras, what whites had done to blacks for three hundred years and more largely without notice. His whole strategy was aimed at bringing this violence to the surface, where the light of day could begin to dry up the diseased attitudes that underlay it.

Wilson Baker was not pleased with this news. He had done all right in his own bailiwick during the day, bringing George Lincoln Rockwell into court and having him declare that he had had it with the opposition of the city authorities. "They cut my heart out with this harassment, so I'm going to leave and let Martin Luther Coon take over your city," he said, to no one's regret. That declaration would be on the front page of the *Times-Journal* the next afternoon, and would look good to the Yankee reporters and the local powers at the same time. Jimmy Robinson had been convicted of assault and fined one hundred dollars, and he also indicated plans to leave town. But these counted for little now that Clark had begun his antics. The focus was on him, and he knew it.

The situation got worse, however, even faster than Baker had anticipated. The blacks sent three waves of fifty up Sylvan Street to Alabama Avenue Wednesday morning, and they headed straight down it toward the disputed "front" entrance of the courthouse. Clark was there, in a fine temper. He towered over John Lewis, the quiet chairman of SNCC, and let him know what he thought: "You are here to cause trouble, that's what you are doing. You don't live here. You are an agitator, and that is the lowest form of humanity." He looked beyond Lewis to the rest of the people lined up, still refusing to follow his directions to the alley where they had waited Monday. "If you do not disperse in one minute or go in as I have directed you, you will be under arrest for unlawful assembly." He looked down at his watch and counted off the seconds. But the people didn't move. He had them led off back down Alabama Avenue to City Hall, where the county jail occupied the third floor.

The second wave of fifty came and was arrested, and then the third. As this latter group crossed Lauderdale Street they bunched up on the corner at the courthouse. Clark siezed the chance to draw Baker, who had been watching the display with obvious distaste from a few yards away, into the process. *"Captain* Baker," he shouted, knowing the reference to his old rank would needle the public safety director, "they are blocking the sidewalk. Will you clear it?"

But Baker would not bite. He walked over and told the blacks to line up outside the Alabama Avenue entrance so that the sidewalk was unobstructed; they complied. Clark stopped them as they approached: this door was his turf and they were not coming in. An impasse was developing, and two plainclothesmen stepped in, moving back and forth between the sheriff and the public safety director. Clark ordered the helmeted possemen who were lined up around the steps to push the crowd off the sidewalk into the street. Then, calling out that they were blocking the street, he asked Baker again to arrest them. Baker told them to line back up on the sidewalk, in a single file along the edge so there would be no doubt about its passability.

Finally Clark abandoned the game and angrily grabbed a bullhorn. "You have one minute to disperse or get in the voter registration line," he announced, "or you will be under arrest." The line stood silently, looking at him. "You are under arrest," he said.

Mayor Smitherman could still tell reporters the next day that Baker and Clark were in agreement, and do it with a straight face. And the *Times-Journal* published, in a box on the front page a joint declaration of the City Council and the county Board of Revenue which argued that "However strong the provocation, calmness and self-restraint by each of us is the greatest protection for all concerned in this time of crisis." But the façade was rapidly wearing out, and the black community was about to bring this out unmistakably into the open. For on Friday, the teachers—defying all their history and the skepticism of every civil rights worker on the scene—the Negro teachers of Selma were going to march.

They had planned to be at the courthouse at three o'clock Friday afternoon, but at twenty minutes till, when Rev. Reese arrived at the elementary school where they were to gather, only two cars were parked outside. The time had been picked carefully: it gave the elementary schoolteachers time to finish their classes at two-thirty, so as not to miss time from work. They chose Friday so that, if Clark arrested them, their lawyers would have ample time to get them all bonded out before classes started Monday morning.

Reese had worked long and hard for this gathering, and in a few minutes his apprehensions eased as cars began crowding into the lot. It is hard to know just what impelled the teachers to move that day, jeopardizing their jobs and the fragile middle-class status they afforded. Reese's efforts, which included preaching to the group at their association meetings and waving the long voting application in their faces as he shamed them, one colleague to another, about their acquiescence in their disfranchisement, were undoubtedly a key factor. Probably more important was the fact of the spirit and energy which the voting rights campaign had catalyzed and focused in the black community. Dr. King's staff members often paused to look at each other during these days and remark, "Brother, we got a *move*-ment goin' *on* in *Selma!*" with an inflection that was half exultation and half astonishment. The community had developed its own momentum, and their struggle a legitimacy of its own. Few groups within it failed to sense the current; and the teachers, like the others, were eventually swept up in it.

By three o'clock practically every black teacher in the city was sitting in the school auditorium, listening as Reese went down a list of their names, taking roll. Only a few were permitted to indulge their fears and stay behind: the very aged, the seriously infirm, and one member of a couple if both spouses were teachers and there were young children at home. More than a hundred still remained, and they left the building a few moments later, walking in widely spaced pairs past Wilson Baker's watchful officers toward downtown.

Outside the courthouse, a large contingent of possemen stood around the Alabama Avenue steps waiting and making quiet, nervous jokes. The only standard uniform item they wore was a small hexagonal silver decal, worn on their headgear, on which was lettered in black "Sheriff's posse"; beyond that their dress was a study in motley: helmets whose origin varied from construction sites to motorcycle shops and military surplus stores, with only a few of the genuine police variety; faded khaki GI shirts and pants, or work clothes; some wore big six-shooters in pendulous leather holsters, and most hefted hand-turned unpainted hardwood billy sticks. Most also carried cattle prods, metal tubes filled with batteries, a hand grip at one end and two electrodes at the other. The prods varied in length and charge; a few were more than two feet long, and could put out a jolt the recipient would not soon forget. Overall the possemen were not a classy-looking outfit, and their shabby appearance made them seem a little uncomfortable at the prospect of facing an assembly of schoolteachers.

The gaggle of reporters was again exiled across the street, and city policemen kept them moving along slowly, in a kind of circle, to comply technically with the various prohibitions against loitering, walking on the grass, blocking the sidewalk, unlawfully assembling, etc., which were being so strictly observed. Around them the downtown area was unusually quiet, with few people coming and going in the surrounding stores. If any group was likely to make its protest nonviolently it was this one; yet the tension was almost palpable; and it increased as Reese, walking with the teachers association's incumbent president, A. J. Durgan, hove into view coming past City Hall, leading the quiet columns.

Jim Clark came out of the courthouse onto the steps, dangling a long billy club from one wrist. His tailored uniform was crisp and natty, but its very design stamped the sheriff as being of the same rough stock as the posse, especially in contrast to Wilson Baker's never-varying wardrobe of dark conservative business suits and a gray felt hat. Looking up the street toward the teachers, Clark untied the knot in the thong on the club, then tried to retie it; and even from across the street the reporters could see his hands trembling. Finally he grabbed the club with his free hand, turned and walked back inside, as a black reporter, standing in a phone booth on the opposite corner, caught his first glimpse of Reese and Durgan, then scooped up the phone and shouted into it: "I can't believe it! This is bigger than Lyndon Johnson coming to town!"

The teachers were dressed in their Sabbath-day best, high heels, flowery hats and gloves on the ladies, somber-colored suits, hats and shiny shoes on the men. Their starched, sharply creased carriage and deliberately slow steps only seemed to heighten the silence and the tension. Reese was solemn, nodding occasionally to the few speechless blacks that he passed, not breaking his long stride as he reached out to pump briefly on a few outstretched hands. And then they were across Lauderdale Street, closing ranks at the foot of the Alabama Avenue steps.

The superintendent of schools, J. A. Pickard, and the president of the School Board, Edgar Stewart, were waiting to greet them. By turns they pleaded with the teachers to leave, reminding them graciously that they had always had "good relations" with their white counterparts, but that these could be destroyed by such unprofessional displays, and insisting that if they would only ask, the school board would gladly give them time off from school to come down during registration days and file their applications.

Reese just as graciously demurred. He said they had simply come to see if the board office was open, and if it was not, to walk past it through the Lauderdale Street exit, as a sign of their concern over the way registration proceedings were handled. Surely that would not disrupt the county business unduly.

Stewart went inside to advise Clark of the plan and, the teachers thought, to urge him to let them walk through unmolested. But Clark pushed past him through the door. "You're trying to make a plaything out of this conversation," he told Reese. "You have one minute to get off these steps or I'll move you."

Reese stood fast, and soon Clark motioned to his deputies and began shoving the teachers down and away from the steps with the flat of his club. Reese and those nearest behind him stumbled to the sidewalk, recoiled from Clark's continued jabs, but quickly regained their balance. With quiet glances at each other they reformed their pairs and again advanced on the steps. Clark pushed them off a second time. And once more they returned.

Now the sheriff was shaking with anger. "You have one minute to get off these steps or you will all be under arrest," he shouted.

Still they stood silently, the cautious formality of their presence a mockery of Clark's panicky tone as he began ticking off the seconds. Beneath their subdued elegance, each of them carried a toothbrush, a small tube of toothpaste, and a supply of any necessary pills secreted in pocket or purse. Now it looked like they would need them.

But then the circuit solicitor, Blanchard McLeod, stepped between the glass doors and pulled the sheriff back behind them, where he whispered intently in his ear for what seemed like a long time. Clark paused for a moment, then rushed back out, signaled to the deputies and once more pushed the teachers off the steps.

That was enough. Reese waited another minute or so at the foot of the steps, then turned and, with a pace as slow and deliberate as before, crossed the street and led the group back down Alabama Avenue, past the department stores, past City Hall, to Sylvan Street and Brown Chapel, leaving Clark in momentary, ludicrous command of his marble citadel.

A youth mass meeting was in progress at Brown Chapel, and a large crowd of students, having heard the astounding news, was waiting expectantly for the teachers to return. Reese led them up the steps and down the aisle in the same slow, solemn pairs; but around them the place erupted into a tumultuous cacophony of cheers and applause, an ovation that continued until the last of the hundred-plus had assembled around the pulpit. Behind them veteran civil rights workers broke down and wept at the spectacle and teachers and students both joined them, the teachers overcome by a wave of self-respect and unrestrained admiration from their students that they had never experienced before.

Something very important was happening in black Selma now; if there had ever been any doubt of it, there wasn't anymore. The church broke out into the freedom song "Aint Gonna Let Nobody Turn Me Round," and it was clear that these people really meant it.

*(To be filled in by the applicant in the presence of
the board of registrars without assistance.)*

*I _____, do hereby apply to the
board of registrars of _____ County, State of
Alabama, to register as an elector under the
constitution and laws of the State of Alabama and
do herewith submit my answers to the interrogatories
propounded to me by the board. . . .*

*I hereby certify that I have received no assistance
in the completion of this citizenship and literacy
test, that I was allowed the time I desired to
complete it, and that I waive any right existing to
demand a copy of the same. (If for any reason the
applicant does not wish to sign this, he must discuss
the matter with the board of registrars.)*

Signed:_____

(Applicant)

—*From the Alabama voter
registration application, 1965*

FIVE. The following morning a restraining order

was issued against the county officials by Judge Daniel Thomas of the
U.S. District Court in Mobile. The Justice Department had sought the
order after a series of SNCC-led demonstrations at the courthouse the
previous summer had been met by Clark and the posse with even more
vicious responses than the current ones. Dr. King had originally agreed
to have SCLC join SNCC in leading those marches, but later changed
his plans and went instead to St. Augustine, Florida. Without King to
attract the big national media, Clark was able to harass the SNCC
workers and brutalize the marchers into paralysis, and clamp Judge
Hare's injunction against mass meetings on them as a kind of final blow
without producing the national reaction he was later to elicit.

The case had been tried in Selma in early December, and the public
exposure of their tactics had been embarrassing to the defendants,
Clark, Judge Hare, Solicitor McLeod, and Probate Judge Bernard Reynolds; but they weren't particularly apprehensive about the outcome.
Judge Thomas was a native of Autauga County, which adjoined Dallas

on the northeast, and he had always shown a great solicitude for the sensibilities and problems of those he referred to as "his people" in the area, at least the public officials who kept having troubles with the Justice Department. In 1964, for instance, after considerable litigation, he had finally agreed to appoint a federal voting referee in Perry County, just to the north of Dallas, where the percentage of blacks versus the number on the rolls was about the same as in Selma, and the registrars' monkey business with black applications was even more blatant. But the referee mechanism was slow and cumbersome, and Thomas had done nothing to speed up the process. Thus in Perry County the referee's presence, which was the "victorious" outcome of years of legal struggle by the Justice Department, made little difference to the mass of blacks, who still could not get registered.

But so tepid was the judge's commitment to upholding the rights of black citizens that even such Pyrrhic victories were rare for civil rights attorneys who practiced before him. In fact, Judge Thomas's record of reversals on appeal in civil rights cases was so bad that the section in the 1964 Civil Rights Act that provided for cases under its titles to be heard by special panels of three federal judges was referred to by knowledgeable federal attorneys as "The Thomas Amendment," because it had been designed specifically to bracket men like him with other less prejudiced judges on the circuit, among whom Thomas would be outnumbered even in the Deep South.

Predictably then, the order, while agreeing with the Justice Department's copiously proven allegation that the defendants had been acting to harass, intimidate and coerce Selma's black citizens in an attempt to deny them the right to vote as guaranteed by the Fifteenth Amendment, still managed only a mild rebuke. Judge Thomas directed them not to interfere with "the orderly process of voter registration," adding that "under the guise of [law] enforcement there was to be no intimidation, harassment or the like of citizens of Dallas County legitimately attempting to vote. . . ." The judge also allowed that the process of registration was probably too slow, but warned outsiders, those not eligible to register in Dallas County, not to meddle with the registration line either.

There was little clarity in the order about the points that had been at issue in the demonstrations during the previous week: whether the blacks could have the same access to the building as whites, where they could wait, and in what numbers. Nor was there anything more about the registration process beyond the tut-tutting over its languid pace.

The first response the order produced was a tack to the right by supporters of the city officials who had not been involved in the suit. The *Selma Times-Journal* sounded a strange new note that Sunday as it editorialized against "the unprincipled directives laid out in the evilly conceived plans by professional civil rights agitators," leading to "acts of provocation through the hypocritical harangues of Martin L. King and his lieutenants," through which "Negroes have managed to disrupt the normal routine of this community, and have created an atmosphere of disunity among many of our white citizens, who have unsuspectingly fallen into the trap deliberately triggered to ensnare them." The rhetoric was a little forced and artificial, as if editor Capell was using a vocabulary he wasn't accustomed to. The concern behind it was real enough, however: the editorial mentioned "finger pointing, whisper campaigns, impulsive accusations and obviously warped propaganda handouts. . . . Both the city and county officers performed their duties as prescribed. It was undesirable . . . to make any arrests: but since there was no alternative, it is deplorable that some citizens have seen fit to exploit the act as a means to create a rift between our two law enforcement agencies." It was a manly attempt to paper over the rift, but one that didn't have much chance of success.

In the black community the order was regarded as a setback rather than a victory for the campaign. James Bevel, who had tossed the deputies out of a ward meeting, was the main preacher at the mass meeting that night, and he was in a combative mood: The order, he said, "may make it more difficult for us to do some of the things we have done before, and we might be cited for contempt of court. But I don't mind being cited for contempt because Negroes were born under an injunction in Alabama. If Judge Thomas plans to connive around with letters of the law in order to deny us our rights, he has a bad dream coming. . . . We mean to vote and have representation in government and we will settle for nothing less. I'm saying here and now," he finished, "that we must be prepared to fight and die for everything that is ours. And there is going to be rabble-rousing all over Alabama until we get the right to vote."

When a march left the church Monday morning for the courthouse, the line was routinely stopped by Wilson Baker; but he was suddenly more curt and strict in his directives than he had been previously. He told the marchers to break up in pairs spaced several yards apart, as the teachers had done, and not to bunch up at corners waiting for traffic lights. Staff workers had to station themselves at intersections on the route downtown to pace the group and keep them in the acceptable formation. Baker, like the *Times-Journal,* was apparently reacting to white sentiment which was supporting Clark against the interference of the federal courts, and was under pressure to get tougher with the renewed demonstrations.

At the courthouse Clark was in full regalia and taking personal charge of the line as it formed at the door, walking up and down to see that the sidewalk stayed clear, and shoving people who didn't move fast enough out of his way with his billy club. Down at the far end of the line, where the courthouse adjoined Ted Gentry's Chevrolet dealership, Wilson Baker kept a stern eye on the scene, ordering the staff workers to keep away from the line.

One black worker, Willie McRae of SNCC, didn't move fast enough when Baker told him to. The public safety director walked over and told him to go into the alley between the courthouse and the auto showroom; McRae refused. Baker grabbed him by the shoulder and barked, "You're under arrest," at which McRae went limp and collapsed at his feet. Two policemen dragged McRae across Lauderdale Street to a police car, while the blacks in the line turned to watch.

Mrs. Annie Lee Cooper, a woman standing about halfway up the line, heard the commotion behind her and turned to see what was going on, stepping a few paces away from her place at the edge of the sidewalk to get a better view. Just then the sheriff came up behind her, elbowing people roughly back into the line. He shoved Mrs. Cooper hard, so that she lost her balance.

It was one push too many: with a curse under her breath, she turned around and slugged Clark near the left eye with her fist. She was a tall, powerfully built woman, and Clark staggered to his knees under the blow; as he did, she hit him again.

Two deputies rushed at her, and one threw his arms around her from behind, trying to push her down. But she stomped on his foot and jammed her elbows into his belly; as his grip slackened she broke loose, ran over to the sheriff, who had not yet regained his footing, and socked him a third time. Now three deputies grabbed her, and wrestled her to the ground; the sheriff got up, lifted his billy club, and struck at her head. But she grabbed the club and hung on, knocking Clark's white helmet off as they struggled over the club in the grass. Finally he wrenched it free, his hands trembling visibly, and cracked her on the head with it before the deputies hauled her off in the direction of their cars.

Baker had watched the altercation in astonished silence, but now he felt compelled to move. He approached the rear of the line and ordered everyone who did not have one of the hundred numbered cards to reform into their pairs and get out of the area, if they didn't want to receive the same treatment.

Mrs. Cooper was no stranger to the long lines at the courthouse. In November of 1963 she had organized a group of her fellow employees at the white-owned Dunn Rest Home to join one of the early SNCC marches and try to register. But Mr. Dunn came by while they were waiting, identified her, and threw a fit. He fired her and the others as soon as they returned to the Home, and got so angry at one woman he lost his temper and chased her down a hallway brandishing a long stick, trying to chastise her physically for her arrogance. At this all the black employees on that shift, some forty in all, walked off their posts in protest, and were likewise fired for insubordination. After that there were continual rumors of a blacklist against the forty women, and Mrs. Cooper was unemployed until she found work at a black-owned motel.

Thus her outburst, while an obvious violation of nonviolent discipline, was accepted sympathetically by the audience when it was mentioned at the mass meeting that night. Even Dr. King, who had been watching from across the street, said that the sheriff had provoked her. There was also comment about Wilson Baker's new hard line, and calls to defiance by Dr. King's aides. Ralph Abernathy carried this theme the furthest, and struck back at Baker directly. He pointed to an antenna-like device attached to the pulpit which had appeared several days earlier and told the people he had been warned to watch what he said because the city police had placed a "doohickey" in the church that transmitted every word outside so they could hear.

With that, Abernathy set his jowly face into a resolute expression. "But they forgot something when they said that," he announced. "They forgot that Ralph Abernathy isn't afraid of any white man, or any white man's doohickey either. In fact, I'm not afraid to talk to it *man to man.*" He reached down and grabbed the antenna device, lifting it up for all to see, then addressed it directly: "Doohickey, hear me well!" The people laughed with delight. Abernathy had a droll, earthy humor in his speeches which had quickly become so popular that they looked forward to his comic relief with more anticipation than they did the ponderous eloquence of Dr. King himself. He was in fine form that night, too, preaching at length to the "doohickey" about the evils of segregation and the futility of trying to impede their movement. He told it what he thought of it's master's new policy. "We don't have to spread out when we go down to that courthouse, doohickey," he scolded. "And the next time we go we're going to walk *together,* we're not going to go two together twenty feet apart. We're not going to have a parade, we're just going to walk down to the courthouse. When we want to have a *parade,* doohickey, we'll get the R. B. Hudson High School Band and take over the town!"

The whole audience was convulsed with laughter at this perfor- mance. People held their sides and wiped their eyes; they had never seen anything to match it. Abernathy wound up with a line and a mock-sentimental tone borrowed from his funeral preaching: "Fare- well, doohickey, I must leave you now. But as I go, I just want to say to you, may these few words, find you well." With exaggerated care he replaced the antenna on the edge of the pulpit.

When the meeting ended, two city policemen came in and took the "doohickey" out, and it was not seen again.

The next two days saw business as usual at the courthouse. The people marched down, and Baker sent back all those beyond the hun- dred who got the numbered cards. The workers sent them back again, insisting that Clark was violating the order, and sixty were arrested. But there was a new element in the situation: Abernathy's "doohickey" speech had angered and embarrased Baker and Smitherman. And the mayor, fearing that mass parades without benefit of permit were in the offing, yielded to Clark's insistence that outside help was needed, and called on Col. Al Lingo of the state police. This was the outfit that had

changed its name to state troopers when George Wallace ascended to
the governorship. The next morning a line of their big, ominous-
looking two-tone blue Fords, each with the stars and bars emblazoned
on the front bumper, was drawn up around the armory on Franklin
Street, and Lingo himself was on hand to oversee the situation.

Baker didn't like having the troopers around. Their reputation for
unprovoked violence against black demonstrators was as bad as that of
Clark's posse, even if they were attired in more snappy, professional-
looking uniforms. So he kept them close to the armory awaiting his call
for help, and a local reporter commented the next day that Lingo was
under as much surveillance in Selma as were any of the black agitators.
The arrests on Tuesday and Wednesday went relatively quietly, however, and by Wednesday afternoon most of the troopers were back at
their regular duty posts.

But the troopers' appearance, even on a leash, was a red flag to the
movement. Wednesday night Dr. King was in Atlanta, the guest of
honor at a gala banquet attended by most of the city's white elite in
a rather tardy, grudging recognition of his selection as winner of the
Nobel Peace Prize three months before. King noted graciously that the
occasion was "quite a contrast to what I face almost every day under
the threat of death and it's a fine contrast to have people say nice
things. I wish I could stay on the mountain," he added, "but the valley
calls me. I must return to the valley." At a special executive staff
meeting on Thursday, January 28, the shape of that return became
clear: it was time for him to get arrested in Selma.

A few days later a reporter from Birmingham would somehow come
upon a copy of a memo written by a second-level SCLC staff person
about the Alabama Project, and publish excerpts from it as an exposé
of King's advance "master plan" for the campaign in Selma. In point
of fact, the relation between what was happening in the city and the
scenario in the memo was tangential at best, and the "exposé" failed
to get much attention. But one of its recommendations had been
accepted: Dr. King was to court arrest during the campaign, and once
behind bars he was to issue a "Letter from a Selma Jail," which he
hoped would galvanize northern support the way his lengthy, eloquent,
letter from the jail in Birmingham had done two years before. The staff
agreed at the January 28 meeting that the "tension point" was ap-

proaching in Selma, and the time for him to move was at hand. February first was chosen as the date; it was the next regularly scheduled registration day, the crowd would be large, and the media present in force. The word went out to the field staff to mobilize the largest possible turnout, including high school students if necessary.

Again, the Selma authorities knew of the decision quickly enough from their intelligence sources, and countermoves began immediately. One of the first responses was that Judge Thomas suddenly yielded to the pleas of civil rights attorneys and clarified his restraining order. The registration line could not be limited to the first hundred to arrive, he decided, nor could civil rights workers be prevented from approaching the line to encourage and advise people in it, as long as this was done in a quiet and orderly way. This was apparently intended to take the wind out of King's charges that the order was being used against the people, and to deprive him of the chance to get arrested at the courthouse simply for being there.

Next the *Times-Journal* unwound its "outside agitator" tape again, in an editorial entitled "The Path of the Judas Goat," which excoriated "premeditated displays of obvious defiance to local state and federal authority. Many otherwise responsible colored citizens have been coerced into participating in the commission of unlawful acts by the intemperate harangues of professional 'hatchetmen' employed by hypocritical civil rights organizations." It linked King and the Nazis, denounced "mobocracy," but warned that violent opposition to black civil disobedience would not be tolerated by "respectable" whites.

The main issue here most likely revolved around the question of who was going to do the arresting: Clark wanted to make Baker do it, so that he would lose some of his "moderate" image, and maybe his cool as well. Baker wanted to avoid making the arrests for just those reasons. Clark was said to have the ear of Judge Thomas, and may have obtained the clarification of the restraining order to give him more leeway in maneuvering against Baker. High-ranking state troopers who were sympathetic with the sheriff also visited the city quietly at the end of the week, and were reported to be putting intense pressure on Baker to enforce the parade ordinance strictly if King tried to march en masse.

The city was getting pressure from another direction as well: Mayor Smitherman's industrial development efforts had paid off and the

Hammermill Paper Company of Erie, Pennsylvania, was set to an-
nounce on Wednesday, February third, its intention to build a huge
plant in the city. It would be extremely embarrassing to have the
announcement made while the city was filling up its jails with people
who would likely end up working in the plant.

But Dr. King and his staff had their own set of considerations. They
were afraid of what Clark might do to King once he got him out of
sight away from the press. King himself was beyond concern for his
personal safety; but his inner circle worried about it for him, and they
wanted to minimize the risks involved. Besides, the more pressure that
could be brought on the city because of the coming of Hammermill,
the better. So their preference was that Baker do the arresting, and they
knew exactly how to force him to do it. His own scrupulously enforced
parade ordinance provided a trap he couldn't avoid.

The people were clearly ready: They were on their feet shouting and
cheering when King told them Sunday night that they were going to
march on the courthouse by the hundreds, because "whatever it takes
to get the right to vote in this state we're going to follow that course
. . . if it takes filling up the jails . . . if it takes marching in the streets
of this city day after day . . . if it takes marching to state capitol en
masse and standing before the governor to demand our rights." The
time had come.

It went exactly according to plan. When two hundred and fifty
people walked out of Brown Chapel behind their leaders that cold
Monday morning, down Sylvan Street toward the intersection where
the public safety director sat glumly in his official car, they were walking
all together, in a brazen, though very orderly, flouting of his earlier
restrictions. Baker climbed out of the car and met them. He had
laryngitis, and could hardly talk. "This is a deliberate attempt to violate
the parade ordinance which you have obeyed for three weeks," he told
King angrily. "If you don't break up the line into small groups, I'll have
to arrest you."

King said they felt they had a right to march, and that the ordinance
violated their constitutional right of peaceable assembly. Then the line
moved forward again, leaving Baker standing to one side. He didn't

attempt to stop them for another two blocks. But they had him; he could not let them march right past him defiantly like that through the downtown area to arrive in a mob in front of the posse. He drove up to the head of the line, stopped it again, and told them they were under arrest.

King immediately asked if they could kneel and pray, and Baker let them. It wasn't hard to imagine that some of the staff workers were thanking God for their good fortune to be going to jail on schedule without falling into the hands of the sheriff. After they had finished, Baker marched them the two remaining blocks to City Hall, and assembled the crowd in the parking lot behind it.

*"When the King of Norway participated in
awarding the Nobel Peace Prize to me he surely did
not think that in less than 60 days I would be in
jail. He, and almost all world opinion, will be
shocked because they are little aware of the
unfinished business in the South."*

—Dr. Martin Luther King, Jr.
"Letter From a Selma Jail"

*"It may interest you to know that before the Selma
outbreak word was passed to the world of the
massive campaign. Before he was ever jailed in
Selma for breaking the law, the perpetrator of the
violence had an ad prepared to run in the* New
York Times *asking for funds to finance more
demonstrations. Before he was jailed in Selma he
had stationery printed giving his address as the
Selma jail. He went to Selma with the set purpose
of breaking the law so that he would be arrested.
His love of publicity is above the sacredness of the
laws of our land—not only the laws of Alabama,
but of the whole nation, the laws of your state."*

—Alabama Congressman James Martin,
February 10, 1965

SIX.
It took hours for all the demonstrators to be
booked and taken upstairs to the county jail, which was the only facility
large enough to hold them. Before long the people waiting to be
processed began playing little tricks that drove the city policemen on
duty up the wall: lining up obstinately at the white water fountain,
switching the "white" and "colored" signs on the bathrooms, and
generally acting considerably less than intimidated.

Baker kept Dr. King and Abernathy to the last, hoping they would
post bond and be off his hands. He knew about the planned "Letter
from a Selma Jail," and still hoped somehow to head it off. But of
course King refused to post bond, and Baker couldn't just let him walk
out; he had no choice but to send him upstairs with the rest of the men,

who were jammed into the county jail's dayroom and had been shaking the cellblock's steel walls and floor all afternoon with their spirited freedom singing.

The men were in a bay about eighteen feet by ninety feet, with gray steel walls and floor, its only furniture a pair of bolted down large metal tables and several old mattresses strewn about the floor. The dozen or so regular black county prisoners watched in amazement from their cells across a catwalk, and all broke out in thunderous applause when King and Abernathy finally came through the clanging gate. King immediately took charge, but didn't want to make a speech, and suggested that the group have a "Quaker-type meeting," letting those inclined to speak or pray or sing do so as the spirit moved them.

The spirit was indeed moving, oddly enough in almost a direct hierarchical procession down from Dr. King. The first to speak was Abernathy, who produced a small Bible from an inside pocket and began with a reading from Psalm 27:

> The Lord is my light and my salvation;
>   whom shall I fear?
> The Lord is the strength of my life;
>   of whom shall I be afraid?

The passage summed up the mood perfectly. After Abernathy, Reese spoke, then a few other preachers and a white civil rights worker. The speeches were interspersed with more exultant, rhythmic freedom songs, and with the windows shut against the February chill, the room quickly became like a sauna bath, hot and extremely humid from the excited respiration of over a hundred men. But no one minded, and the meeting continued for more than an hour before breaking up into smaller groups, in which the men continued talking exuberantly, many now hoarse from their continuous singing.

Dr. King moved to the bars along the catwalk, and went down its length greeting the county prisoners in their cells and listening to the circumstances of their cases. He heard a series of depressing tales: One man said he had been there almost two years awaiting trial, with no opportunity for bail; another had been there twenty-seven months, after being snatched off the street one Saturday night and beaten up.

He wasn't even sure what the charge against him was, though he had heard it was rape of a white woman. The others' stories were mostly similar, though they hadn't been in as long. These grim results of Black Belt justice left their hearers feeling depressed and helpless, but more determined to make their own confinement count. Their spirits held up even when Baker appeared a little later to spirit King and all the other staff workers among them out to the smaller city cells downstairs.

Almost five hundred more people were arrested that day, most of them students who had stayed out of school to observe what the staff workers told them was a Freedom Holiday. There was something about the involvement of these teenagers that especially galled the whites. They regarded it as proof positive of King's evil, manipulative intentions, his disregard for the real welfare of the local black community. This was probably based on their traditional view of education and "self-improvement" as the legitimate, one-at-a-time route for black advancement, even though the white practice consistently contradicted this profession (which it did even in their jokes: "What do you call a colored man with a Ph.D.?" ran a current jest. "Nigger" was the emphatic answer.) But by then the entry of the young people hardly amounted to manipulation on the civil rights groups' part; with all the action in town centered on the courthouse, and after their own teachers had marched, the students had actually been restrained from leaving their campus en masse until today.

The student marchers managed to make it all the way to the courthouse before being stopped, arrested and put on buses. Their singing and stomping made the vehicles rock and jerk strangely all the way to the armory, a long, low, white building where they were taken to be processed. Inside, Probate Judge Bernard Reynolds was holding court on the dirt floor of the field house section, bringing the students one by one before him to state their name, age, school and parents' names; then they were released in the custody of their parents and warned not to come back. Many of them refused to cooperate with him, however, and they were taken back out to the buses and hauled away to Camp Selma, a state-run prison camp several miles west of the city.

Mass arrests continued Tuesday and Wednesday, and jail facilities all around that part of the state were soon full to bursting. Judge Hare was outraged by the presence of singing crowds around his courthouse, and had groups of them hauled before his bench to face charges of contempt of court. Attorney Peter Hall, a black Legal Defense Fund lawyer, managed to get into one such proceeding and made a game effort at defending them. He pointed out that the court had been in recess when the alleged contempt had occurred; that the defendants had not even been inside the building when their alleged contempt was committed; and he made mincemeat of the deputy who was called to identify the defendants, showing that he didn't know one from another unless they first said their names, and that he had no evidence whatever that anyone present had been involved in the actions which had so offended the judge.

But Hare was unimpressed. His contempt power, designed to assure his control over the courtroom, was not subject to appeal or delay, and he quickly sentenced the group, and succeeding ones, to the maximum penalty: five days and fifty dollars, with the fine to be worked off at the rate of three dollars per day if they could not pay it. On Wednesday he issued an injunction banning demonstrations in the vicinity of the courthouse while the Circuit was in session, and Sheriff Clark read the order to more gatherings of marchers before hauling them off.

There were also large demonstrations and then mass arrests in Marion, the seat of Perry County thirty miles northwest, during this week. Dr. King had assigned only a few organizers to that area, but they had found the people receptive, and soon had a full house of people at the Morning Star Baptist Church ready to spill out its old battered doors and march around the columned white courthouse which was just down the street in the center of the little town square. Local authorities let them march on Monday, but by Wednesday their jails were full as well, and ringing with the inmates' noisy music.

Sheriff Clark and his men had more of their kind of action with the coming of the mass arrests. The possemen pushed people around and made liberal use of their cattle prods, which left no scars, as they marched people off to the buses. And once in confinement, the prisoners had to put up with Clark's version of hospitality. One group was taken to a prison camp only to find their compound stripped of beds and bedding, the floor covered with water, and the heat off. They spent the night standing huddled in corners, trying to keep warm. A group taken to Camp Selma after being arrested later that week found similar conditions: they walked past piles of mattresses and blankets in the hallways, and found their rectangular compound bare of any furniture except a tub of water with a single dipper, and a stopped up toilet with no seat. There was nothing to sleep on but the smooth concrete floor. The windows were stuck open to the cold February air, and outside they could see their bedframes on the grass, rusting newly from the mist and serving as novel perches for the camp's flock of poultry.

The food was not much better. The authorities were given standard allotments for provisions, but left to disburse them in the most economical manner they could devise; and the less that was spent actually feeding a prisoner, the more was left to pocket. Someone around Selma was making a lot of money in that business: at the Dallas county jail, the standard fare was half a cup of blackeyed peas and a square of cornbread twice a day, a routine broken only once or twice by grits and syrup or, on special occasions, a boiled chicken neck. At Camp Selma the inmates were served beans and somewhat larger sections of cornbread, perhaps because the regular prisoners there had to put in a full day's work.

For Dr. King, of course, going to jail was like a vacation, a blessed respite from the punishing nineteen and twenty-hour days he put in outside, and he and Abernathy set about making the most of it once they were in the quieter quarters of the city jail. The two had been to jail together almost every time they had been arrested, and had long since developed a routine for passing the time constructively. This was a concept they had borrowed from Gandhi; it included an initial two-day fast and a regimen of prayer, meditation, hymn-singing, exercise and rest, punctuated by conferences with aides and lawyers who were let in at intervals by city authorities. They were perfectly safe, and except for the fact that the bedding was lumpy and uncomfortable, in no hurry to end their interlude. Both stayed in jail until Friday.

Despite the demonstrations life went on in Selma that week, marked by two events which otherwise would have dominated local consciousness completely. On Wednesday Hammermill made its long-awaited announcement: their new plant would be located a few miles east of Selma; it would cost almost thirty million dollars, produce four hundred tons of bleached kraft pulp a day, and provide two hundred and fifty permanent jobs. Speaking at the luncheon held to celebrate the announcement, the president of the Chamber of Commerce, J. M. Gaston, articulated the general feeling: "What this thing means to me," he said, "I can hear the cash registers ringing in my grocery store." Others looked forward to a second bridge across the Alabama River, and called the plant a major breakthrough in the development of the area.

The night before the announcement Governor George Wallace had come to town, to speak to a massive crowd from which all out-of-town reporters were barred. Wallace's popularity was such that every official of any local consequence was on hand, with the single exception of Wilson Baker, who was over on Sylvan Street keeping an eye on the mass meeting at Brown Chapel.

But the crowd didn't hear what it expected from their self-proclaimed super-segregationist chief executive. Martin Luther King was in their jailhouse, five hundred more black people had been arrested in their streets that day, but Wallace's theme of "Selma's Bustin' Out All Over" was related to those events only by unconscious irony. The governor talked instead about his program of industrial expansion in the state; he bragged of having brought some four hundred million dollars worth of new plant investment to Alabama in 1964; he praised Selma and Dallas County as outstanding partners in this crusade among areas of comparable size; and he predicted even greater heights would be reached as the plans for opening the Alabama River to deepwater traffic were completed. But he never mentioned segregation or demonstrations, not even law and order. There was, there had to be a message in his very silence on the subject; but he didn't pause to let the people draw him out about what it might be.

On Thursday there was a sudden pause in the demonstrations. One reason for the lull was that Judge Thomas was set to issue an injunction against the Dallas County Board of Registrars in response to another Justice Department suit and the black leaders wanted time to see just what tactical implications its provisions might have for their campaign. But another and possibly more telling consideration was the arrival in Selma that morning of Malcolm X.

Malcolm had been at Tuskegee seventy-five miles east for a speech

the night before, and some of the SNCC staff people had gone over
to listen and invite him to bring his black nationalist message to their
city as well. Malcolm had been anxious to come; he was interested in
talking to Dr. King, whom he had met only once before very briefly.
He arrived at Brown Chapel Thursday morning to find several hundred
people assembled, awaiting marching orders for the day.

But Malcolm's coming had some SCLC workers in a panic; they
were afraid he might live up to his reputation as a fire-eating opponent
of nonviolence if he was permitted to speak to the crowd of predominantly young people, and leave the workers with a situation they could
not control. But the SNCC workers were insistent in their demand that
he be permitted to speak, and the SCLC workers reluctantly gave in.

Malcolm was rather restrained in his remarks: "The white people,"
he told them, "should thank Dr. King for holding people in check, for
there are others who do not believe in these measures. But I'm not
going to try to stir you up and make you do something you would have
done anyway." He urged them to take their case to the White House,
and remind President Johnson that 97 per cent of the black people had
voted for him. If they got no response there, he said they should carry
their grievances to the United Nations, and put American racism on
trial before the world.

This was a new line for the people, but they knew a powerful speaker
when they heard one and the response was warm. Outside, the SCLC
workers were becoming more and more worried. Just then, it seemed,
Providence intervened: a car pulled up carrying Mrs. Coretta Scott
King and Mrs. Juanita Abernathy, in town to pay a call on their
incarcerated husbands. Andrew Young, the senior SCLC staff member
present rushed up to Mrs. King and said, "You're going to have to come
inside and greet the people, because Malcolm X is here and he's really
roused them. They want to hear from you."

"Andy," Mrs. King replied, "I'm just not in a speaking mood."

"You must do it," Young insisted. "By the time you get inside, you'll
feel like it."

The two women went in, and were greeted with a loud ovation. Mrs.
Abernathy spoke first, followed by Coretta, and both emphasized the
importance of perseverance in nonviolence to the movement's chances
for success. Afterward Mrs. King was introduced to Malcolm, and he

told her, "Mrs. King, will you tell Dr. King that I had planned to visit with him in jail? I won't get a chance now because I've got to leave to get to New York in time to catch a plane for London where I'm to address the African Students' Conference. I want Dr. King to know that I didn't come to Selma to make his job difficult. I really did come thinking that I could make it easier. If the white people realize what the alternative is, perhaps they will be more willing to hear Dr. King."

Malcolm then left the church and drove off toward Montgomery. Mrs. King was impressed with his sincerity, and passed the message on when she saw her husband briefly later in the day. And if Malcolm's appearance failed to make the hoped-for impression on the local whites, neither did it leave the SCLC chieftains with a howling mob to restrain. Their fears had proved to be exaggerated, and Malcolm, dead less than three weeks later with a chestful of assassins' bullets, never got the chance he wanted to meet Dr. King and talk further about their different, yet perhaps not incompatible, perspectives.

Judge Thomas issued his order at about the same time Thursday that Malcolm was leaving. The injunction was carefully drawn, reportedly with the help of the county officials subject to its provisions. The Board of Registrars was ordered to process at least one hundred applications per registration day if that many people showed up, and to make provisions for eight people to fill out applications at the same time. He also directed them to stop using the Alabama literacy test, which had been challenged just a few days before in a Justice Department suit that sought to kill it in the whole state. Thomas also ordered the board to act on all applications submitted by June 1, 1965, before the end of that month; if that deadline were not met, he said, he would appoint a federal referee. And in the meantime any rejected applicant could appeal the board's decision directly to him for review.

The injunction represented a major attempt by the white leadership to head off the demonstrations in Selma. It contained what seemed to be real concessions which would open up the voting rolls to larger numbers of black citizens. Even the SCLC workers weren't sure at first what its impact would be; Andy Young told the people at Brown Chapel, when they heard it was imminent that "In every battle there are many rounds, and this round may have come to an end. We may have a little breather." There were other murmurs about the possibility that things might be worked out.

Reportedly Clark had helped draft the order, in order to get himself off the hook with his more militant supporters. He could freely denounce the order as another example of tyrannical federal trampling on states rights, even while edging himself toward the periphery of the scene in apparently reluctant compliance. The strain of facing the demonstrations and struggling with the conflicting pressures in the white community was clearly taking its toll on him, as it was on everyone else involved.

But after looking it over closely, the civil rights workers decided that the injunction was not enough to meet even their minimal demands. Their main objection was that it did not order the board to meet more often. There were only eight more sessions set before June first, which meant that the board would process a maximum of eight hundred applications, most of which would probably be rejected. A significant portion of those people rejected by the board could hope that Thomas would order them registered on appeal; but that meant more time and trouble. With fifteen thousand eligible black people in Dallas County, what the process set up by the order amounted to was several more years' delay in getting them registered, several more years in which the whites could apply their quiet, mostly nonviolent forms of coercion and intimidation, at which they were so experienced, to keep people out of the courthouse and off the rolls.

Thus on Friday, February fifth, the movement went back into the streets and back to jail, bringing the total number of arrests for the week to more than three thousand. The hopes of those who had written the order for a break in the turmoil in their city vanished. Moreover, that afternoon Dr. King posted bond and left the jail to meet with a group of fifteen northern congressmen who had come to Selma for a firsthand look at what was happening there, as part of their own efforts to get new federal legislation passed to assure southern blacks the right to vote. The congressmen took depositions from several local blacks, listened to Mayor Smitherman tell them to mind their own business, and returned to the capitol with their commitment to federal action intensified.

Dr. King soon followed them to Washington; he had appointments made on the next Monday to see Vice-President Hubert Humphrey, Attorney General Nicholas Katzenbach, and, he hoped, the president himself about voting legislation.

But after he arrived the meetings were abruptly cancelled, because of the press of news from Vietnam: Communist guerillas had attacked several American bases there on Saturday, February sixth; the airfield at Pleiku was hit hardest, and eight men were dead, over a hundred wounded. Retaliatory raids were mounted at once against bases in North Vietnam, by forty-nine Navy jets. "I've had enough of this," an angry president told a special meeting of the National Security Council that weekend. Holding the casualty list from Pleiku in his hand he said "The worst thing we could possibly do would be to let this thing go by. It would be a big mistake."

"We are doing something we do not want to do in making the appearance book immediately available for persons to sign. But after evaluating all aspects of the local situation, we feel that in making it available we are acting in the best interests of the community. It is vitally important to both white and Negro citizens of Selma that the racial disorders of recent weeks be terminated immediately. And the board feels that the opening of the appearance book provides a reasonable basis on which Negro leaders can and should remove demonstrators from the street."

—*Victor B. Atkins, Chairman of the Dallas County Board of Registrars, in the* Selma Times-Journal, *February 8, 1965*

SEVEN. President Lyndon Johnson had

mentioned a need for a new law to protect the voting rights of black people in his 1965 State of the Union message to Congress. But the reference was brief and unspecific, and no concrete proposal followed it to Capitol Hill. In fact Johnson had no intention of submitting any voting rights legislation to the new Eighty-Ninth Congress; there was opposition to the idea inside the administration, and the president himself reportedly felt that the nation, and especially the South, had plenty to digest in the titles of the Civil Rights Act of 1964, which were not yet all fully operative.

At the same time, however, the president understood that the civil rights leaders' charges of mass disfranchisement in the Deep South were not exaggerated. And he was prepared, in his own good time, to do something about it: even before the 1964 election, he directed Deputy Attorney General Nicholas Katzenbach, who was to succeed Robert Kennedy as head of the Justice Department a few months later, to begin work on a bill designed to put a stop to literacy test discrimination. But he ordered Katzenbach to keep the project a secret, in order to avoid giving Republican presidential nominee Senator Barry Goldwater any further ammunition in wooing southern white votes, and to permit the president to maintain his freedom of timing on its submission. Also, as Katzenbach began work, it became evident that the bill had to thread a careful constitutional path, because the Constitution clearly gives states the authority to set voting requirements. Katzenbach was thus uncertain as to whether the bill should be in the form of a law or as an amendment to the Constitution.

This was how the matter stood in February 1965 when Martin Luther King came to Washington to confer with the new attorney general. The demonstrations in Selma had gained a good deal of national press coverage, and had even produced a few sympathy demonstrations, including a sit-in by SNCC supporters at the U.S. Attorney's office in New York City. There had also been a growing number of statements by liberal congressmen and senators of both parties urging the administration to add a voting rights bill to the batch of messages it was sending to the hill. In response to these pressures, the proposal that Katzenbach had been working on was allowed to surface, and while King was in jail the president told a press conference that he intended to see that the right to vote was secured "for all our citizens." The same day George Meany, president of the AFL-CIO, added his gravelly voice to the chorus calling on the White House for a response to the conditions being dramatized by the full jails of the Alabama Black Belt.

But there was still no clarity about just what the administration would propose, and this was what King planned to discuss with Katzenbach, Vice-President Humphrey, and possibly Johnson himself. King wanted to urge them against sending a constitutional amendment, because the process of approval for such a measure—two thirds votes of each house of Congress and ratification by the legislatures of three-quarters of the states—was so tortuous that the proposal would be an easy target for the South's master parliamentary sharpshooters in Congress. Besides, even if successful, it would take years. King also wanted to argue that the bill must contain provisions for the appointment of federal registrars, to take the enrolling of black voters completely out of the hands of the boards, which had for so many decades excelled at evading and frustrating every outside intervention on behalf of black citizens. Finally, he wanted them to finish and submit the legislation soon, right now if possible. The crowded streets of Selma were a signal that his people had waited long enough.

The White House did not cancel the meeting with him lightly. The president, increasingly preoccupied with the darkening situation in Southeast Asia, was on the threshold of the key decisions which would commit him and his administration irrevocably to direct involvement in the war. The attacks at Pleiku, the long casualty list he carried with him that weekend—these may well have been the events which sent him teetering over the edge. Lyndon Johnson was not unmindful or indifferent about the matters Dr. King wanted to raise; but King could wait. Vietnam could not.

Dr. King took the setback philosophically, and flew back to Montgomery on Monday to address a mass meeting there. The campaign was spreading widely out from Selma now, and Montgomery was where it would probably culminate. So he called on the enthusiastic crowd which greeted him there to join him the following morning for a march "by the thousands" on the Montgomery County offices to demand that they be opened to free black political participation. In Birmingham, other associates were planning a similar march and rally for a week hence.

But on Tuesday morning, scarcely two hundred people appeared for the scheduled massive march. And as if that was not bad enough, when the skimpy crowd arrived at the courthouse, they found that the Board of Registrars had thrown open its doors to them, and even hired extra clerks to make sure all applications would be processed with dispatch. In fact, the hundred or so in the march who had actually come to apply were in and out of the office, their forms complete, inside of an hour.

The cap on the day's humiliation was that county officials had even set aside a hospitality room for the visiting reporters. When it was over there was nothing for Dr. King to do but make some comments about how many southern blacks "have been denied the vote so long, many of them have lost the motivation." The only good news came from Washington: the decks had been cleared after the weekend flurry about Vietnam, and the officials were ready to keep their appointments, if he was available. Dr. King boarded the next plane for Washington, and by day's end had made his case to Katzenbach and Humphrey, and had

504

6444

4O4K。3

even been whisked into the Oval Office for a fifteen-minute chat with the president.

In Selma, Jim Clark was now trying hard to follow Wilson Baker's lead in dealing with the continuing demonstrations, probably because King's lawyers were already trying to have him cited for contempt of Judge Thomas's January order. Over the weekend there were quiet negotiations between black and white leaders over the use of an "appearance book" at the Board of Registrars; Judge Thomas's order to the board directed it to make such a book available within two weeks, for people to sign while the board was not in official session. Those who signed would be given numbers, and they would have precedence for filling applications on regular registration days. A number of the local leaders, including Rev. Reese, were momentarily persuaded that the opening of the appearance book a week early would constitute an important sign of good faith on the part of the whites; and the whites believed that the black leaders had agreed to end demonstrations once it became available.

But things didn't work out as the whites had hoped. The SCLC staff in the city, particularly James Bevel, argued vehemently that the appearance book was just another white man's trick, a delaying tactic like so many others and no concession at all. On Monday morning, February eighth, they held a press conference to denounce it, and to call for the opening of the board office six days a week, the holding of registration in other locations as well, the appointment of deputy registrars, some of whom would be black, and the elimination of all voting requirements except age and residence. Bevel said he would lead a group to the courthouse to make explicit their boycott of the book.

The word hadn't spread quite fast enough, though, and by the time Bevel's sixty marchers arrived at the courthouse a dozen or so blacks had already signed the appearance book. Filing in through the Lauderdale Street entrance, Bevel and the others each walked by the office and ostentatiously declined to sign the book. Jim Clark was watching; and he did his best to restrain himself. Members of the board were in the office, processing applications on their own time to stay on the good

side of Judge Thomas's directives. The chairman, a rough-faced man
with a white crewcut named Victor Atkins, came out and asked the
people if they wanted to sign the appearance book. They said no, they
had come to register. Atkins pointed to a hand-lettered sign on the wall,
indicating that the next regular registration day was the following
Monday, February 15. "Can you read that sign, old man?" he snapped
at one.

"No, sir," came the reply.

"Can you read at all?" Atkins sneered.

"No, sir."

"Now isn't that nice," Atkins announced loudly. "You can't read
and yet you want to vote. Move along."

Finally Jim Clark had had all he could take. "You're making a
mockery of this!" he shouted at them. "If you don't want to sign the
book get out!" He called to his deputies and together they pushed the
group out the door and down the steps, cattle prods pulsing freely. The
people defiantly re-formed and made a line outside the entrance. The
sheriff warned them of the injunction forbidding demonstrations in the
area; and when that didn't move them he took them up to Judge Hare's
courtroom, for trial on contempt. Among those arrested were three
visiting whites: Rev.'s Ira Blalock and Gordon Gibson, both Unitarian
ministers from Boston, and James Richardson, a lay Catholic theolo-
gian from New York City.

While this group was still inside the building, however, about two
hundred youngsters showed up outside, ringed the courthouse and
produced small handmade signs denouncing segregation. They stood
silently for about half an hour, shifting their feet uneasily while the
possemen looked on with menacing expressions. Finally, nothing having happened, they turned to leave; but deputies stopped them. At this
point Wilson Baker, disgusted at the thought of what was about to take
place, went into the courthouse and huddled with the sheriff. When
he came out the deputies and his policemen walked down the line
confiscating the signs. Then they let the young people go.

Tuesday went more quietly. About a hundred young people assembled at the courthouse with small signs; after a half hour, all law
enforcement officers were withdrawn from the area, leaving them alone

and looking very unthreatening in the absence of all the uniforms and firepower. They stayed about two hours, then left. The only thing worth taking note of was the sheriff's attempt to block the reporters' view of them by parking two large yellow schoolbuses in the street between their line and the cameras.

This was the kind of response Baker and the city administration had been begging Clark for; and it seemed to be getting results. The demonstrations were steadily decreasing in size, and they were made up more and more of students off on a lark from school. If they could contain the sheriff and keep it up, King might end up in the same humiliating position he had been in in the Montgomery demonstration.

But holding Jim Clark back proved to be tougher than expected. The next day, when two hundred young marchers showed up at the courthouse and pulled out signs reading, among other messages, "Jim Clark Is a Cracker," and "Wallace Must Go," the situation took a bizarre turn. Clark again tried his maneuver of pulling up the schoolbuses between them and the press. But the kids were ready for him this time, and immediately walked around to the other side of the courthouse, where they were once more in plain sight of the reporters. Clark then ordered the buses to drive around the block and pull up behind them again. He stationed a phalanx of possemen shoulder-to-shoulder across the sidewalk at the head of the line to keep them from slipping out into view again. By lunchtime they showed no signs of leaving, and Clark walked around passing out fried chicken to the possemen hoping hunger pangs would encourage their departure.

The appearance of a relief column of marchers approaching the downtown area seemed to make the sheriff feel it was time to do something. But what? Inside the courthouse he ran into City Attorney Pitts, and asked him if he thought it would be a violation of Judge Thomas's order to run the students away from the courthouse area. Pitts allowed that in his opinion this would not violate the order, and besides it "might relieve some of their steam." Clark didn't need much more coaxing. He walked back out to the line and said, "All right, come on."

The buses pulled away, and the possemen closed in with their cattle

prods. A few jolts and the group was walking and then running, but
not back to the church. They were directed down Water Avenue along
the curve of the river. Deputies closed in behind them in their cars,
blocking side routes and taking turns running alongside to give a few
electric jabs of encouragement. "You wanted to march, didn't you?"
they shouted. *"Now march!* Close up that line! Move on!" They
likewise slowed down the carloads of astonished reporters who were
trying vainly to get within camera range.

The strange parade continued past the city limits, the youths screaming and panting, the possemen prodding and bopping them and having
a hell of a time. At a small bridge two miles from town Clark had cars
pull up and form a blockade, beyond which no reporters were allowed.
And after a run of more than a mile farther down River Road southeast
of the city, the lawmen finally abandoned the chase as the students
began stumbling into the ditches, vomiting up their exhaustion and
terror, and scattering into the surrounding fields of a black-owned farm.

Clark explained with a sneer to the blockaded reporters that he had
arrested the group for truancy, and was removing them to the Fraternal
Order of Police lodge some six miles out of town on River Road, taking
them there because all other confinement facilities in the area were full.
"No, I didn't say you're under arrest, but I told them the equivalent
of that," he told a questioner. "When a man in uniform says 'Come
on,' anybody knows what that means. But they all broke loose and
escaped. We tried to catch 'em, but they're a bunch of kids and we
couldn't run as fast as they could. . . . Cattle prods? I didn't see any."

A little later Wilson Baker drove out past the bridge to the farm
where the students had regrouped to wait for a way to get back to town.
Slumped down in the back of the public safety director's car were two
SNCC workers, who took over coordination of the stream of battered
black taxicabs which responded to their call. All Baker would say to the
reporters who asked why he had carried the agitators in his own vehicle
was, "I'm human too."

The reaction wasn't long in coming. That night the mass meeting
at Brown Chapel was packed, and rang with cries for federal troops to
be sent to protect the black community; a telegram to that effect was
approved to be sent forthwith to the president. A second mass meeting

for youth was held at First Baptist Church, down the street from Brown Chapel, and Dr. King made it back to town just in time to stop by there and preach hard to the youths about the importance of nonviolence in the face of provocation. Then he moved to the adult meeting, to report on his conversation with the president, made more pointed remarks about nonviolence, and urged a massive turnout at the registration line next Monday, "in numbers that will let the nation, the world, Governor George Wallace and Sheriff Clark know that we do not intend to stop until we can register without any obstacles. We want all our rights and we want them here and now!"

In white Selma, too, important people had had enough. Thursday's *Times-Journal* featured a front-page editorial, "A Time for Decision," denouncing the sheriff's shenanigans, without mentioning him by name: "The comedy of errors that has been in continuous performance in the vicinity of the Dallas County Courthouse during recent weeks," it harrumphed, "has reached the point that responsible community opinion demands the curtain be rung down." The forced march "represented . . . a sharp departure from the script . . . followed . . . prior to Wednesday's impromptu walk." It pleaded once more for those involved to leave the marchers alone; if only they were left unmolested and unnoticed, they would go away. But pleading alone would no longer suffice. "The time has come—like it or not—when the citizens of this community must take a stand in determining the course that is to be followed if this city and county are to return to the status of dignity, respectability and decency which they have always known."

Pretty strong stuff for those pages, and it had an effect almost at once. When four hundred black people surrounded the courthouse that afternoon, again with handmade anti-Clark signs, the sheriff stayed inside. Wilson Baker went in and conferred with him for almost an hour while they waited, and finally all the deputies were pulled out of the area. The group finally marched once around the block and then left.

On Friday the sheriff entered Vaughan Memorial Hospital, complaining of chest pains. "The niggers are givin' me a heart attack," he told one reporter. They didn't let up because of his confinement: as soon as word of his hospitalization reached Sylvan Street, two hundred youths set off through a drizzle for the courthouse. There they knelt, with the cameras rolling for once undisturbed, and prayed for their adversary's full recovery—in mind and body, they were careful to add.

The forced march incident clearly perked up the campaign's local momentum. Dr. King "postponed" the planned march in Birmingham, in order, he said, to focus attention more clearly on Selma and the Black Belt. And on Monday, February 15, the largest crowd so far was lined up for almost ten blocks along Lauderdale Street when the Board of Registrars opened up for business. Nor was the response confined only to Selma; there were hundreds more in Marion, and even a crowd in Camden, forty miles south, the crossroads seat of Wilcox County.

There had been more private meetings between blacks and whites in Selma over the weekend, in which the city had agreed to grant a permit for Monday's march. The permit helped the organizers bring out the largest possible crowd by guaranteeing that there would be no arrests. In return, the blacks told the students to go back to their classrooms, and the long line was made up almost entirely of adults. They also abandoned their boycott of the appearance book; Reese in particular felt they should take advantage of any procedure through which more blacks might get registered, even as they continued to press for more sweeping measures. More than five hundred names were added to the book that day, while Jim Clark, now out of the hospital, watched sullenly but without interfering.

But if the turnout was gratifying, the speakers at that night's mass meeting didn't treat it as a victory. "We're just about as far from freedom tonight as we were last night," said Hosea Williams of SCLC, speaking in place of a hoarse Dr. King. "I'm not happy at all. I don't see anything to rejoice about." At a staff meeting later that night the consensus was that the pressure on Selma should be stepped up, not decreased, even as the organizing spread to other counties as well.

Heat it up they did, too. The next day C. T. Vivian, a tall, highly articulate member of Dr. King's executive staff, led twenty-five people downtown to challenge the now-revived sheriff, who was permitting only six people at a time inside to sign the appearance book. It began to rain as they got there, and Vivian led them around to the Alabama

Avenue entrance, which had a small roof above it. Clark saw them coming and locked the door; they crowded under the small cover and sang freedom songs. Clark's office was right next to the entrance, and the music must have rankled him, because a few minutes later deputies pushed the door open and he stuck his head out far enough so the blacks could hear him, and began reading Judge Hare's injunction against demonstrations around the courthouse.

Vivian interrupted him several times during the reading, demanding that he let them stand inside out of the rain. Clark, getting angrier by the second, ordered them to leave twice, and Vivian again loudly refused. The deputies pushed them roughly off the steps with their clubs, knocking several to the ground. Vivian turned toward the reporters across the street who were unlimbering their cameras, shouting: "If we're wrong arrest us, but don't force us to leave! We don't mind being beaten and going to jail for democracy! I know you want to beat me!"

A cameraman nearby switched on a spotlight to get a sharper shot of the action. Clark whirled and cried "Turn out that light or I'll shoot it out!" It was hurriedly switched off again. The sheriff went back inside and the party returned to the steps, with Vivian loudly berating him for acting in such a brutal and un-Christian manner. Clark's temper couldn't stand any more of this baiting; with deputies trying vainly to hold him back, he reached between the glass doors and smashed Vivian in the mouth with his full force. Vivian went flying, and the deputies dragged him off, blood running from his lips.

This encounter made vivid television, and sent waves of anger through the black community. Rev. Reese told a friend that night he was ready to call the young people back out of school if necessary, and that a boycott of white-owned businesses, especially those that employed members of Clark's posse, would be announced Wednesday night. He also swore they would march any time they wanted to. And that included marching at night.

Sure enough, Dr. King told Wednesday's mass meeting in no uncertain terms that "Selma still isn't right." The registration process was still too slow, and the harassment more than could be tolerated. "We must engage in broader civil disobedience measures to bring the attention of the nation on Dallas County," he declared. "It may well be we might have to march out of this church at night. . . . We may have to fill the jails of Selma and Dallas County."

Night marches represented a sharp escalation in risk for the movement, and a quantum jump in the problems confronting Wilson Baker. He had less than thirty policemen; and once the sun was down every shadow could become a hideout for some crazy person with a gun, leaving his forces hopelessly outnumbered. There were crazy people around, too, just waiting for their chance. These agitators needed martyrs for their publicity campaign, damn them; and night marches were a perfect way to get them.

*"CHAIRMAN POLAND: In your judgement . . .
what class of men composed the bands that
committed these outrages?*

*"GENERAL EDMUND PETTUS: Well sir; I have no
reason to believe that there were any that would be
properly called 'bands' in our county . . . and my
impression is that at first there were some
substantial, good citizens in them; but like all other
men who undertake to regulate society by mob law,
the better class of men discovered that they could
not control the bold and bad element associated
with them, and they left the organization in the
hands of turbulent, bad men who . . . used it, or
their influence in it, for extremely bad purposes."*

> —Testimony Before the Joint Select
> Committee on Ku Klux Klan in
> Alabama, July 6, 1871.

EIGHT.

The white community of Marion thirty miles northwest of Selma had been undergoing strains similar to those experienced in Selma during the past month, since George Best of SNCC and SCLC's big James Orange, the worker who coaxed the people into talking at Ward Three's first meeting in Selma, had moved into Perry County. These agitators had quickly turned out the schools, set the people to marching around the courthouse square, filling up the registration line, and crowding into the white restrooms in the courthouse. But here the conflict was in a different, much more rural setting; and when a large white strategy session was held on February 17, the forces arguing for a policy of ignoring the agitators till they went away were overwhelmed by people who wanted blood. In fact, two important whites were physically assaulted for suggesting that it might be worthwhile to negotiate with the blacks, and that pretty much settled the question.

The next morning James Orange was arrested for contributing to the delinquency of minors, and the sinister blue Fords of Al Lingo's state troopers began looming into Marion, with the colonel at their head. C.

T. Vivian, having been released from jail in Selma Wednesday after
Judge Thomas removed his case to federal jurisdiction, was sent to
Marion to address Thursday's mass meeting at Zion's Chapel Methodist Church, a weathered clapboard structure which stood on the
southeast corner of the courthouse square. The scene in Selma being
quiet for the moment, a squad of reporters followed Vivian to Perry
County.

The climax of the meeting was to be a night march. It wasn't going
to be a long walk, just out the church and down the sidewalk a hundred
yards or so in the direction of the jail. If they were stopped, the plan
was to kneel for a prayer, then return to the church and call it a night.
They would do about the same thing if they got all the way to the jail.

But when the preachers at the head of the line came out the door,
the sidewalk was lined with helmeted state troopers, long, black billy
clubs at the ready, and they were stopped less than half a block down.
"This is an unlawful assembly," the police chief announced over a
public address system. "You are hereby ordered to disperse. Go home
or go back to the church."

Just then all the street lights around the square went out, and the
troopers began clubbing the Rev. James Dobynes, a black minister at
the front of the line. Dobynes, who had been chosen to lead the group
prayer, began imploring his God in a loud, terrified voice, as the
troopers dragged him away, still beating him.

The reporters had been kept in a group back at the corner, and could
not see what was happening at the head of the line. But when they
saw clubs swinging and the people screaming and running back toward
the church, they started out into the street to get a better look. At that
moment they too were attacked, by a group of whites that had been
standing around the corner. Richard Valeriani of NBC News was
clubbed to the ground and left bleeding from a large head wound. A
UPI photographer, Pete Fisher, was knocked down by one man while
two others grabbed his camera and trampled it to pieces. Other photographers' equipment was splattered with black paint amid shouted orders to get the hell out of there.

The panicked crowd tried to get back into the church, but the doors
were jammed full and the people spilled around it, down a side street,
taking cover wherever they could. The troopers came after them, clubs

swinging, splitting scalps and smashing ribs as they advanced. Two or three dozen people rushed through the doors of Mack's Cafe, a few doors down, seeking refuge in its crowded, dark interior. Among them were Jimmie Lee Jackson, a young man twenty-six years old, his mother Viola and his grandfather, Cager Lee, eighty-two. The old man had already been caught and beaten behind the church, and was bleeding. His grandson was helping him out the door to get medical attention when a squad of troopers came toward them, chasing and beating people before them, and forced the two men back into the cafe. The troopers came inside, smashed all the lights within reach and began clubbing the people indiscriminately. When one hit Viola Jackson and knocked her screaming to the floor, Jimmie Lee lunged at him. The trooper struck him across the face, and young Jackson went careening into the floor himself. Then a trooper picked him up and slammed him against a cigarette machine while another trooper, a man named Fowler, drew his pistol and calmly shot Jackson point blank in the stomach.

Jackson didn't realize he had been shot until a few moments later, because the troopers continued beating him and the others unmercifully. Pulling himself up again from the floor, he ran blindly out the door of the cafe, clutching his stomach, headed back up the street past the church toward the bus station, where his car was parked. But more troopers were waiting outside, and he was struck again and again along the way, until he finally collapsed bleeding on the sidewalk.

Someone finally picked him up and carried him to the Perry County Hospital. There the duty physician ordered that he be transferred to Good Samaritan Hospital, a Catholic mission facility in Selma, because Perry County had no facilities available for blood transfusions. As ambulances sped off through the darkness down Highway 14 toward Dallas County carrying Jackson and the half-dozen others who required hospitalization from their beatings, trooper cars were still cruising through the unlit Marion streets looking for more blacks to attack.

Awhile earlier, someone had noticed Jim Clark, dressed in civilian clothes but carrying his billy stick, standing near the courthouse square. "Don't you have enough trouble of your own in Selma?" he was asked.

"Things got a little too quiet for me over in Selma tonight," the sheriff answered with a smirk. "It made me nervous."

For the state troopers the action in Marion was like a shot of amphetamine to a speed freak. Twenty carloads had been loose in the town Thursday night, and following the scent of more excitement a similar convoy converged on the Dallas County Courthouse the next day. There was no holding them back now, and the complaints of the roughed-up reporters—NBC featured Richard Valeriani in his hospital bed, head stitched up and speech still slow from sedatives, on its evening news Friday—only made the adventure that much more heady.

Such attacks were normally either completely ignored or massively downplayed by the local media, as part of the sealed-lips defensive policy most of the white South had followed ever since Reconstruction. It was part of the cloak of silent acquiescence needed while white supremacy was being re-established by any means necessary. The custom went as far back as when Confederate General Nathan Bedford Forrest, the defender of Selma and the founder of the Ku Klux Klan, solemnly swore to a congressional investigating committee in 1871 that no such terrorist body did or ever had existed. Down South they called it "lying like a gentleman." Selma's Confederate general, Edmund Pettus, gave similar testimony in his turn.

The mayor of Marion, Mr. R. L. Pegues, spoke out of this tradition when he was interviewed the next day about the troopers' assault on the march. "Actually," he said, "very little went on, and what did go on was by the church. It all happened in a very short time—about three minutes." He blamed "outside leadership from Selma" for the trouble, adding, "they were determined to take over the town. They wanted a night march, and of course, we can't have that. Quite frankly, it wasn't much of a battle." Governor Wallace's press secretary said he had information that Jimmie Lee Jackson had gone after the trooper who shot him with a bottle.

People like Pegues, Clark, Lingo and many others thus despised the reporters, who broadcast the crudities of their expression, exposed their lies and revealed the violence of their behavior, almost as much as they despised the black agitators. This went especially for the Yankees among them, but did not stop there: even the *Selma Times-Journal* received a steady stream of hate mail for paying so much attention to the "agitators." It gave the troopers and their cohorts a special satisfaction to have kicked some of the reporters' well-dressed electrified Yankee asses.

The only practical difference between Selma and Perry County as night fell Friday and the mass meetings began with the pounding, piercing freedom songs, was in the person of Wilson Baker. With the troopers unleashed in his streets and the news of Marion broadcast, he had word that Klansmen and other violent trash were infiltrating the city to get their share of what they thought would be an even better second round. His one chance to prevent it was to keep the blacks inside their part of town, if possible within the confines of the George Washington Carver Homes, a federal housing project that surrounded Brown Chapel, away from the troopers and possemen. As the crowd inside, whipped to a fever pitch by Hosea Williams of SCLC, rose to walk out the old wooden doors, he prepared to do just that.

The people knew they were taking a big risk. Before leaving, Williams had asked that everyone give up any weapons they were carrying, to insure the nonviolent discipline of the march. A large pile of knives and other arms was collected. Then Williams led the way out, to confront Baker only a few feet off the church's broad steps. Baker had his policemen lined up across the sidewalk, and for the first time they were wearing white helmets and held clubs ready; and the public safety director spoke to the marchers through a bullhorn, also for the first time.

"We're not going to have a night march in Selma," he declared into the speaker. "We've come too far in Selma to have any trouble now. Every place on earth you've tried night marches someone has been seriously injured. I do not want this in Selma and I will do everything I can to prevent it."

There were defiant shouts of "We're gonna march!" from the crowd. Baker paused and glared at the people. Behind him, downtown, trooper cars were lined up on Lauderdale Street for the whole length of the block beside the courthouse. Al Lingo and Jim Clark were there, as was the posse, and God knew who else in the shadows, anxious to greet the group: these niggers were crazy. Baker looked at Hosea Williams, and asked him to take the people back inside. Williams refused.

Baker then told Williams he was under arrest, and put him in his car, while he pleaded with the crowd to abandon their plan. "Jimmie

Lee Jackson is near death tonight after a night march," he reminded them. "You say you are nonviolent people, so go back into the church." He told the ministers who had followed Williams he would let him go if they would take the people back in. Faced with what looked like a solid wall of his police, they reluctantly agreed to do so, and the line filed sullenly back into the church.

Baker then told Williams he could rejoin them. "This is dirty pool," Williams complained to Baker inside his car. "If you're going to arrest me take me down to the jail; don't just hold me here and then let me out. It don't look right." But he had no choice but to get out and follow the people back in.

That left the problem of keeping them off the streets. A short while later, Baker went into the office in the back of Brown Chapel, and told the workers there he was ready to reopen negotiations for the city about their various demands. The local leaders were called back from the podium, and an impromptu conference went on for over an hour. It ended with Baker accepting a list of community demands, which he pledged to convey to the proper authorities, in hope of having a concrete response to report by Monday. The blacks agreed to call off their demonstrations in the interim. Baker told a reporter later that the demands included nothing new, and that in any event he was just a cop and had no other authority. So his visit was apparently mainly a device to gain a breathing spell, in hopes the situation would cool off and he could perhaps bring Clark and Lingo back into line.

Governor Wallace took quick advantage of the truce to issue a ban on night marches on Saturday, February 20, with the declaration that "Mass demonstrations in the nighttime led by career and professional agitators with pro-Communist affiliations and associations is [sic] not in the interest of any citizen of this state, black or white." And Baker stretched the lull as far as it would go, urging the blacks to give him more time to try and persuade county officials to adopt the registration approach Montgomery officials had used when King led his march there.

But on Monday, when no one in charge had actually made any concessions, the maneuver ran out of gas. Dr. King returned from a weekend in bed fighting a fever, led a morning march to the courthouse, and went to pray with Jimmie Lee Jackson in the hospital. And the plan for the evening was to close the mass meeting with a march in defiance of the Wallace ban, courting arrest if necessary.

But no march developed that night, though not because of any brave bluster from Wilson Baker. As the mass meeting heated up in Brown Chapel, the telephone in the rear office rang. On the line were officials from the Justice Department and FBI, warning that they had solid evidence of a plot to murder King if he marched that night. The conspirators planned to have one group attack the line in the middle as a diversion to draw the police away, then in the ensuing confusion the death squad would go for King at the front. There was no way they could guarantee King's protection in the darkness, the officials said; so they implored him not to march.

King made them no commitments. Death threats were an everyday matter for him, and if he arranged his schedule to avoid them he would end up doing nothing. Several whites had been ready to shoot him in Marion on February fifteenth, he had recently learned, and were frustrated only because in the crush of people around him they could not get a clear chance to aim. During a trip to California he would make the following weekend, threats would be made that the podium where he was to speak would be dynamited, and police would arrest a man who turned out to have a huge arsenal in his home. So this telephone call was a matter of routine to him. It was the other people in the room who were terrified by the threat, and took the telephone plea seriously. King himself had long since come to terms with whatever terrors the prospect of a violent death held for him, and had vanquished them utterly. As far as he was concerned, the meeting would continue, and the march was to go ahead.

But the telephone rang again a few minutes later. This time Attorney General Nicholas Katzenbach himself was at the other end, upset despite his reputation for unflappability. The threat was genuine, he said, and his men were hopelessly outnumbered. King *had* to cancel the march. King's aides begged him not to go, and he reluctantly yielded to their pleas, emerging to tell the people that while Governor Wallace's ban was clearly unconstitutional, they would not defy it that night. "We have a right to march at night," he told them, "but in our own good time we will make clear that we cannot abide by the order."

Across town, the Dallas County Citizens Council was coming into

ominous life that same evening. It had a new chairman, former Mayor
Chris Heinz, and a new target: the soft policies of the new mayor and
his public safety director. Two thousand people were on hand, including the mayor, the sheriff, and all the other important people in the
area except Baker, to hear Ross Barnett, the former governor of Mississippi, who had become a national figure of sorts with his defiance of
federal attempts to enroll James Meredith at "his" state university in
1962.

Barnett was an orator of the backwoods type, who grew red of face
and hoarse of voice before he was far into his harangue. Shaking a fist
in the air, he told the cheering crowd that "The purpose of our enemies
is to diffuse our blood, confuse our minds and degrade our character
as a people." They applauded again as he insisted that they faced
"absolute extinction of all we hold dear unless we are victorious." It was
a good speech to have heard before going out to murder Martin Luther
King.

Even without the night march, it was touch and go around Sylvan
Street that night. As Dr. King's car pulled out of the parking lot next
to Brown Chapel it was stopped by a state investigator named Robert
Godwin, who ordered King to roll down the window, and then berated
him for permitting his officers, who had been inside the meeting, to
be asked for their credentials. Godwin was angry, and his halting of
King's car attracted the attention of blacks standing around the entrance to the church. Word spread instantly that King was in the hands
of a cop, and people started pushing out through the doors to see what
was happening. At this a force of state troopers stationed down the
street jumped out of their cars and began forming up.

King told Godwin with perfect candor that he knew nothing of the
policy which had so bothered the investigator, and suggested that he
discuss it with Brown Chapel's pastor, Rev. P. H. Lewis. Godwin then
looked around and became aware that he was about to become the
center of a dangerous incident, and let King go. As King's car moved
away, the people relaxed, and so did the troopers.

King's decision not to march had left some of the people a little
itchy: they still wanted to defy Wallace's ban in one way or another.
John Lewis, the chairman of SNCC, accommodated a group of them
the next evening and led a twilight march down Sylvan Street. Baker

stopped them just around the corner of Alabama Avenue, near the Coca-Cola bottling plant, on which a sign hung describing Selma as "progressive and friendly." The troopers and posse were still at the ready down at the courthouse, and Baker was not going to let them get their hands on the march. Nor would he give Lewis the satisfaction of getting arrested. He just held them there while they sang, prayed, and finally decided to go back.

After Tuesday, however, the night march idea was quietly abandoned. The next Monday was March first, another registration day and thus another occasion for mobilizing large crowds. This meant a return to canvassing, making the widespread personal contacts that alone could assure another strong turnout. Moreover, the campaign was still expanding its scope: James Orange, out of jail in Marion at last, moved on up Highway 14 to Greensboro in Hale County. James Bevel and others had just made contacts to the east in Lowndes County, which like Wilcox to the south was 80 per cent black but without a single Negro voter. Workers were also sent out to Demopolis, fifty miles west in Marengo County, the home of the Alabama Grand Dragon of the Ku Klux Klan and two active Klaverns. In Selma on Wednesday, Mrs. Amelia Boynton announced that the Committee of Fifteen, the local campaign strategy group, had voted to impose a complete boycott on white businesses, and would also ask blacks to quit riding the city buses, on which they were still expected to sit in the rear.

In Montgomery, the Alabama state senate, which was meeting in special session to consider Governor Wallace's controversial plan to provide free textbooks for all the state's schoolchildren, paused in its deliberations Tuesday to pass a resolution supporting the state troopers actions in Marion of the eighteenth. The resolution declared that the charges which had been made by news organizations whose reporters had been injured that the troopers had not done their best to protect people were "baseless and irresponsible." According to senate sources, this statement had been watered down from an earlier version which called the allegations "false and unfounded."

Col. Al Lingo, anticipating this support, had served Jimmie Lee Jackson in the hospital with a warrant charging him with assault and battery with intent to murder one of his officers. This only served to keep Jackson's shooting and the need to protest official brutality on the mind of Dr. King's tacticians. King had promised the people on Monday night, as he announced that they would not march, that there would be a large demonstration in Montgomery soon, to take their case and their demands direct to the foot of the capitol steps. On Thursday night, James Bevel spent some time walking around alone outside the Torch Motel where he was staying, agonizing over his own problems and the problems of the movement, especially those involved in making their cries for justice and protection from state-sanctioned brutality more vivid and inescapable for the watching nation. Suddenly he had an idea that he felt sure would bring home the situation as nothing they had tried before had: they would not only march *in* Montgomery, they would march *to* Montgomery, starting in Marion where Jackson had been shot, through Selma where Clark had jailed them, and down U.S. Highway 80, through Lowndes County where no blacks were registered at all, fifty miles to the state capitol itself, where Wallace would be unable to ignore them. That was it; Bevel felt it was just the right response to the present situation and the mood of the people. Bevel could hardly sleep for excitement at his inspiration.

That same night Jimmie Lee Jackson began having difficulty breathing, and soon slipped into shock. After midnight doctors opened up his stomach cavity to see what was wrong and found a massive, overwhelming infection. They worked feverishly for four hours trying to clean it up, without success. By morning Jackson was dead.

> *"Not all of Washington these days is trying to
> figure out solutions to Vietnam. There are enough
> civil servants left over to look after many other
> matters, including how much of peanut butter
> should consist of peanuts.*
>
> *"The government in its majesty proposes a floor
> of 90 per cent. Those who make peanut butter
> would rather have the matter left to their own
> judgement. For some years now they have been
> changing the recipes around, trying to find out what
> the public likes best. . . .*
>
> *"Nobody in the capital is contending that peanut
> butter mixers are putting in things you wouldn't
> want to eat. It just seems that Washington is
> uneasy about any situation it finds to be uncovered
> in its rule books. Few are uncovered anymore,
> either."*
>
> —*Lead editorial, "Goobernment,"*
> Selma Times-Journal, *March 1, 1965.*

NINE. All that L. C. Crocker, Jim Clark's chief
deputy, had to say about Jimmie Lee Jackson was this: "I believe they
wanted him to die. They wanted to make a martyr out of him and they
did." That was a lie, of course, notwithstanding the fact that everyone
on the SNCC and SCLC staffs knew that it was only a matter of time
until someone got hurt badly in the demonstrations. But that was
because of the reality of what they were protesting, not some self-
serving design for publicity. In fact it was only luck and the unrelenting
efforts of Wilson Baker and his beleaguered police officers that had
kept the casualty list as low as it was. No one with a dark skin in these
counties needed to be reminded that their marches were dangerous;
and with Jackson's death, their anger and determination in the face of
repression only increased.

Zion's Chapel Methodist Church in Marion was packed solid on
Sunday, February 28, for the first of several memorials for Jackson. The
people were treated to a brilliant and outraged sermon by James Bevel,
who was laying the groundwork for his new idea of a march all the way

to the state capitol. He preached from two texts: The first was from Acts 12, verses 2 and 3: "Herod killed James, the brother of John, with a sword; and when he saw that it pleased the Jews, he proceeded to arrest Peter also."

"I'm not worried about James anymore," Bevel shouted; "I'm concerned about Peter, who is still with us. James has found release from the indignities of being a Negro in Alabama, and no longer can he be cowed and coerced and deprived of his rights as a man. James knows the peace this world cannot give and lives eternally the life we all hope someday to share.

"I'm not worried about James; I'm concerned with Peter, who must continue to be cowed and coerced and beaten and even murdered."

What could be done to save Peter? Bevel turned to the second text, from Esther 4, verse 4: "Also Mordecai gave Hetach the copy of the writing of the decree that was given at Shushan to destroy the Jews, to show it unto Esther, and to declare it unto her, and to charge her that *she should go unto the king, to make supplication unto him, and to make request before him for her people.*"

There was a decree of destruction against black people in Alabama, Bevel went on, but they could not stand by any longer to see it implemented. "I must go see the king!" he cried, again and again, and the answering shouts from the people grew to a full-throated chorus of approval. His intuition about their readiness was correct: *"We must go to Montgomery and see the king!"*

Monday, another Freedom Day, found Dr. King mostly in a car racing madly across four counties, careening down slippery roads, touching base with crowds lined up outside the courthouses in Perry, Dallas, Lowndes and Wilcox counties, some standing where none of their kind in living memory had stood before. It rained hard all day, and King asked Jim Clark when he arrived at the Dallas County Courthouse to let the three hundred people with him come inside. Clark refused "in the name of common sense," and began calling the numbers of people who had signed the appearance book, but in a low voice so that few people could hear. A signer who did not answer after their number had been called twice, he or she lost his place and had to sign again and await another registration day. The local leaders quickly responded by setting up a relay system, with people stationed all along the line to listen for the numbers and pass them on. This irritated the sheriff, who began calling the numbers faster and jumbling them together. King left the line and drove to Lowndes County.

At the county seat, Hayneville, only twelve blacks had braved the rain and their history to appear at the decrepit courthouse in the square and become the first blacks in sixty years to ask for registration forms. Registrar Carl Golson, tall and bespectacled, angrily told them that applications were being taken at the jailhouse, which was two miles away. The group trudged through the downpour to the jail, only to be told there that they had been misinformed; voting business was done at the courthouse after all. When they got back, Golson told them registration had closed for the day.

Dr. King arrived while they were still standing there, and asked to speak to the glowering registrar. Golson replied angrily that unless he was a prospective voter in Lowndes County he didn't want to see him.

"We don't understand," said King mildly.

"You are damned dumb then if you don't understand," Golson shouted. "If you are not a prospective voter applicant, it is none of your business what is going on here."

King asked one more question: "Are you a Christian?"

"Yes, I am a Methodist," was the reply. "But what has Christianity to do with the vote?"

From there King drove to Wilcox.County, where two hundred people, drenched to the skin, were waiting around a rundown red-brick building, once a jail, inside which the registrars were taking a few leisurely applications. Here, however, the blacks had a special problem, which they would also encounter in Lowndes: with no registered black voters, there was no one to vouch for the new applicants as required by state law. No whites had stepped forward to fill the gap, and the obstacle seemed insuperable. Fifty state troopers, blue helmets and ready billy clubs dripping with rain, stood not far away, eyeing the line threateningly. But King spoke encouragingly to the people, assuring them that they would get the ballot, and leading them in the responsive chant: "What do you want?" *"Freedom!"* "When do you want it?" *"Now!"*

The rain had not let up by Wednesday, when Jimmie Lee Jackson was to be buried. Two funerals were planned, the first in Selma and the other in Marion, followed by interment in a tiny rural black cemetery. At Brown Chapel a long white banner with the handprinted legend "Racism killed our brother" was hung over the arched brick entrances, and the building was overflowing by midmorning. Hudson High School was practically empty that day, and by the time the service started as many as two thousand people were standing in the muddy street around the church, waiting to file past the coffin.

The crowd was equally large in Marion. Ralph Abernathy told them that "Jimmy Jackson has joined the ranks of the many martyrs who have fallen along the way in building this great nation and in bringing us to this hour. We are gathered around the bier of the first casualty of the Black Belt demonstrations. Who knows but what before it's over you and I may take our rightful places beside him."

"Our Father," intoned Rev. J. T. Johnson of Marion, "we pray for the policemen of this town and this state, who would rather see blood in the streets and a man shot down than sit down and talk."

The people's emotion was spilling over into open sobs by the time Dr. King rose. Jackson's mother Viola, still bearing her bruises, wept quietly. King meditated on the question, "Who killed him?"

He was murdered by the brutality of every sheriff who practiced lawlessness in the name of law.

He was murdered by the irresponsibility of every politician from governors on down who has fed his constituents the stale bread of hatred and the spoiled meat of racism.

He was murdered by the timidity of a Federal Government that is willing to spend millions of dollars a day to defend freedom in Vietnam but cannot protect the rights of its citizens at home. . . .

And he was murdered by the cowardice of every Negro who passively accepts the evils of segregation and stands on the sidelines in the struggle for justice.

Jimmie Lee Jackson's death says to us that we must work passionately and unrelentingly to make the American dream a reality. His death must prove that unmerited suffering does not go unredeemed. We must not be bitter and we must not harbor ideas of retaliating with violence. We must not lose faith in our white brothers.

Soon it was over and the pallbearers filed out into the rain, placing the coffin on a hearse which moved off slowly past the ramshackle cafe where its passenger had been shot. The crowd followed behind, walking down the incline to Highway 183 under a moving forest of umbrellas. The procession stretched out fully a half mile behind the hearse, and kept up its solemn pace all the way out to the Heard cemetery, which was little more than a grassy clearing in the piney woods where Jimmie Lee Jackson had earned his meager living as a pulpcutter. After the final prayers at the graveside his lodge brothers donned their symbolically embroidered caps and aprons and went awkwardly through their rituals, then helped lower the casket into the grave dug in the bright red soil.

Dr. King confirmed later that day that Bevel's plan for a march to Montgomery had become official, to begin from Selma the next Sunday, March seventh; it would, he said, proceed across the Edmund Pettus Bridge and down Route 80. The people were ready to go.

It is not certain that any of the black leaders, even Bevel, really thought the march would get very far, at least on the first try. The preparations made for it during the latter part of the week were scanty, haphazard. In the white community, however, their announcement had set off some of the most intense and involved interplay yet seen, maneuvering which went on until the moment of confrontation.

Governor Wallace met with Al Lingo on Thursday, to discuss "problems of traffic control" during the march. By the end of the day, and probably at that meeting, Wallace's scenario for stopping the march was laid out; its details are unclear, but there is every indication that he intended it to be carried out as peacefully as could be expected from the troopers. His plans were conveyed to county and city officials in Selma, and Joe Smitherman, assured by high aides to Wallace that there would be no violence, pledged the full cooperation of city police in the effort. Jim Clark said about the same thing, but it is evident that he, and Lingo too, were quietly developing plans of their own.

Fatefully, Wilson Baker was out of town just then, hiding out somewhere in Louisiana for a few days trying to get some rest. When he returned the next day and learned of what the mayor had committed his men to do, he was furious. Smitherman was crazy, and so was Wallace, Baker said, to believe that Lingo and Clark would let the blacks march into their clutches and then just permit them to turn back unscathed. The troopers had been hanging around for two weeks waiting for their chance, and missing out on it only because Baker kept the marches quarantined inside the housing project. If the city had to be involved, he argued, let his men arrest the marchers when they started and not let the group get within range of the troopers. Or on the other hand, get the troopers out of there and just let them alone completely; the blacks weren't ready to march, and the thing would break up in confusion before it got to Lowndes County. King would be sorry he ever agreed to the idea.

But Smitherman was reassured, when he asked Wallace people he trusted, that everything was under control and he had nothing to worry about, so he put Baker off. Saturday morning Sheriff Clark left town for Washington, to appear on a television interview show, and that gave rise to hope that his influence might be eliminated from the confrontation entirely, as it had been on January second.

This debate was interrupted early Saturday afternoon by a march of white people to the courthouse. The group, calling itself Concerned White Citizens of Alabama, was marching in support of the voting rights campaign, and was a unique gathering in the state's civil rights struggle. A Lutheran minister from Birmingham, Rev. Joseph Ellwanger, was at the head of the column of about seventy people; the others were mostly university professors, liberal ministers, and their wives. Their plan was to walk to the courthouse and read a declaration denouncing brutality and intimidation, and calling for the registration of all eligible voters without discrimination.

Baker had conferred with Chief Deputy Crocker, and had no difficulty getting him to agree to ignore the march completely; thus when Ellwanger mounted the steps to begin reading his declaration, no officers were around to restrain—or to protect—him: "We, as white citizens of Alabama," he read, "have come to Selma today to tell the nation that there are white people in Alabama who will speak out against the events which have recently occurred in this and neighboring cities and towns."

On this occasion Baker's policy turned out to be a miscalculation: this was Saturday afternoon, when people came to town. As the march came into downtown, local whites began following it, and a large crowd was soon gathered around it at the courthouse. Across Alabama Avenue on the lawn in front of the federal building a large body of curious blacks was likewise collecting; and the mix was an obviously volatile one.

"We consider it a shocking injustice," Ellwanger continued, "that there are still counties in Alabama where there are no Negroes registered to vote." Now he was being drowned out as the hostile whites began singing "Dixie." Their singing became louder when Ellwanger finished and had his people strike up "America." Across the street, the blacks responded with a chorus of "We Shall Overcome"; but the musical confrontation was clearly only an overture to a physical one. Among the hostile whites was Jimmy George Robinson, late of the assault on Dr. King in the Albert Hotel, in town again to get in on the action to come. He swaggered around pushing the concerned citizens roughly out of his path, being egged on by other angry whites.

Wilson Baker got word of the tension developing around the courthouse and hurried down to the building accompanied only by his chief lieutenant, Robert "Cotton" Nichols. The two pushed through the roiling mob, and asked the concerned whites to hurry up and get it over with. Ellwanger and his friends, thoroughly shaken by their brush with disaster, filed away down Lauderdale Street back to the black Reformed Presbyterian Church where they had started. Then Baker crossed the street and told the now angry black crowd to disperse as well.

Jimmy Robinson wasn't finished, however. Walking down Alabama Avenue away from the courthouse he spotted a SNCC photographer, ran over and slugged him. The photographer tried to flee, but Robinson grabbed him again. Two other whites leaped to join him, and they beat the SNCCer to the sidewalk. The young man writhed away from them, jumped to his feet and dived into a car parked along the curb, locking the doors against them. Robinson and the others now gathered around the automobile and began rocking it from side to side, trying to turn it over.

They had two wheels high in the air by the time the city police arrived. Robinson was arrested, and the others dispersed. Baker himself had stopped another beating nearer the courthouse, and if he needed any further confirmation of his belief that the mood of the city as the time of the Sunday march approached was ugly and dangerous, he now had it.

At the Reformed Presbyterian Church the rattled concerned citizens were cheered by a warm reception from SCLC leaders. James Bevel even made them laugh, by allowing that when he had learned that *white* citizens of Alabama were marching in Selma in support of voting rights for blacks, he had decided that the kingdom must be coming right today. Bevel and C. T. Vivian also talked about the march to Montgomery, and the announcement which had just come over the radio: that Governor Wallace had declared that the march would not be permitted. Wallace had said the march "is not conducive to the orderly flow of traffic and commerce within and through the state of Alabama. The additional hazard placed on highway travel by any such actions cannot be countenanced. Such a march cannot and will not be tolerated." Bevel said the march was on regardless.

Mayor Smitherman told the *Times-Journal* that afternoon he was in complete agreement with Wallace's decision, and repeated that the city police would cooperate fully with the plan. But he had yet to hear from his own public safety director about this policy. That evening Baker told him that under no circumstances would he order his men to take part in what he was sure would turn into a bloodbath. The mayor insisted the die was cast. In that case, Baker said, he was resigning forthwith. Someone else could give the order.

Word of this confrontation spread quickly among the city's influential whites; and several members of the city council met hastily with Baker and then the mayor to try to forestall the split. After a long, heated conference that night, it was agreed that the city would post only two men across the Pettus Bridge, where the troopers were to gather, and that they would stay inside their patrol car. Baker again urged that he be allowed to arrest the group as it left Brown Chapel. The mayor, however, still believed the governor's pledge of a peaceful confrontation. He had met with Clark and Lingo himself before the sheriff left for Washington, and they had repeated again their assurances that these were their orders, and that they intended to carry them out.

"You asked me
to tell you what I saw
that gray sunday morning. . . .

"there was that pile
of rolled-up blankets
taken off beds and wrapped up
with belts, or old ties, or string.

"there they were
in the corner by the altar—
a patchwork mountain of rolled-up trust.

" 'we are going'
'WE ARE GOING'
spoke that patchwork mountain
in its unvalued dignity. . . . "

—*"Crumpled Notes (found in a raincoat)*
on Selma," Maria Varela

TEN. Sunday morning Baker met with Deputy

Crocker and Major John Cloud, who would be in command of the
troopers once they took their positions on the highway. They agreed
with Baker that there should not be violence that afternoon, and that
there might well not be any arrests. Baker was also told that Col. Lingo
would meet Jim Clark at the Montgomery airport later when he returned from Washington, and keep him busy there until the whole
thing was over. It was further agreed that the city police would supervise the march until it crossed the bridge, and would take charge again
once it had turned around and was back inside the city limits.

If Baker's apprehensions were mollified by this meeting, it was probably not for long. Within a few hours his men had disarmed several
carloads of whites who were circling around the city like sparrowhawks
eyeing a kill. These people acted like they knew something more than
a quiet mass arrest scene was in the offing. The troopers were also
limbering up, as a black man named John Carter Lewis learned that
morning to his regret. Lewis, who worked as a dishwasher, was stopped
by two troopers on his way home. The troopers differed about what to
do with him; one said Lewis was all right, but the other insisted, "Let's

beat him up anyway." This trooper ended the discussion by hitting Lewis on the head with his night stick.

"I staggered," Lewis recalled, "and he hit me again. I dropped my billfold on the road. I bent over to try to pick up the billfold and he hit me again. And then when I tried another time to pick up the billfold he hit me again." The troopers left him with a broken arm and head injuries.

At Brown Chapel, the mood was subdued, much more so than for the earlier demonstrations. The people could sense the violence in the air, and their mood was one of dogged determination rather than defiance or even exuberance as it often had been before. The somber atmosphere deepened as word came that tear gas had been issued to the troopers, and Dr. Alfred Moldavan of New York, a volunteer with the Medical Committee for Human Rights (MCHR) conducted impromptu workshops in the church about how to minimize gas effects by keeping low, walking into the fumes, and not rubbing one's eyes.

Dr. King had told an audience in New York on Thursday that he would lead the march himself; but he also had obligations at home in Atlanta to fill first. Arrangements were made for a small charter airplane to fly him from Atlanta to Selma's tiny municipal airstrip as soon as he had finished preaching his first sermon in weeks to his home congregation in Atlanta. But this time, as on the evening of the night march plot, it was the people close to him who persuaded him to stay away. It appears they may actually have finessed him away from it, assuring him that the march would be a cakewalk which would be stopped without either violence or much public impact, and that he could just as well spend the day resting at home and preparing himself for the second try, which would probably be more eventful. From that distance, having been gone several days, King probably was unaware of the atmosphere of tension that had enveloped Dallas County and shown itself the day before when the whites marched. So he allowed himself to be dissuaded from coming.

Meeting in the parsonage next to Brown Chapel, the SCLC staff was divided into two groups, on the expectation that if the first set of marchers was arrested a second, and possibly a third wave would follow them. James Bevel, Andrew Young and Hosea Williams flipped coins to see which of them would represent Dr. King at the head of the first wave. Williams lost, and went back into the church for a final pep talk and a chorus of one of his favorite gospel songs, "God Will Take Care of You," which he reserved for occasions like this. Then he and SNCC's John Lewis led the six hundred people out of the church and up Sylvan Street in a column of twos, singing. Four ambulances carrying MCHR first aid teams followed them toward downtown.

Across the bridge, Highway 80 was being closed to traffic, and a long line of cars began backing up. A crowd of whites was lining up in front of the small markets and gas stations along the road, and they were in a reckless, volatile mood. Reporters were ordered by the troopers to assemble in a small area near Lehmann's Pontiac showroom, and two troopers were assigned to keep them there. And just as the column appeared over the crest of the long steel bridge, a car pulled up alongside the troopers. In it were Al Lingo and Jim Clark.

As they reached the high point of the Edmund Pettus Bridge, Williams and Lewis saw the blue line of troopers, spread for nearly a hundred yards shoulder to shoulder across the highway's four lanes, waiting with their billy sticks held in front of them and their bulky gas masks hanging at their waists. Williams whispered hoarsely to Lewis: "John, can you swim?"

"No."

"I can't either," Williams said, "and I'm sure we're gonna end up in that river."

Then the column fell silent as it proceeded down the bridge's grade toward the waiting troopers. Major Cloud was standing out in front of the line, and when the blacks came within a hundred yards he directed the men to put on their masks. A few fumbling rubber noises were still being heard when he ordered the marchers to halt. They would go no farther, he told them, and must disperse within two minutes.

"May we have a word with you, Major?" Williams asked.

Cloud was already counting. "There is no word to be had," he replied tersely, then he called: "Troopers, advance!"

The line moved forward into the column, billy clubs held with both hands. Williams and Lewis stumbled backward into the pair behind them and went down, with troopers in turn falling on top of them. As the column dissolved in panic, the troopers broke ranks and began running after the blacks, clubs swinging wildly. The younger men and those women who could run fastest got out of the way first, fleeing for cover between the stores and down toward the riverbank. Behind them the older people were surrounded by eddies of violence. One after another of them was knocked to the pavement, screaming in pain and terror, the wooden clubs thudding into their flesh. From the sidelines a shrill cheer went up from the watching whites.

After a sweep down the column, the troopers fell back and re-formed their lines, pulling out their tear gas canisters and flipping off the safety rings. The blacks who had run began circling back to pick up their fallen comrades, and those still conscious knelt to pray. They were still on their knees when the troopers struck again, spraying the gas before them in a thick white cloud and clubbing everyone they could reach. Mrs. Amelia Platts Boynton, who was standing tall only a few ranks from the front a moment before, had been one of the first to fall, clubbed into unconsciousness. As she fell to the pavement, a creased plastic rainhat that someone had given her slipped down over her face. A trooper came up and dropped a tear gas canister right in front of her, and as the piercing liquid and fumes sprayed out, only the wrinkled sheet of plastic kept it from drenching her eyes and going straight into her lungs.

Now from between nearby buildings a line of horses emerged at the gallop, their riders wearing the possemen's irregular uniform and armed with bullwhips, ropes, and lengths of rubber tubing wrapped with barbed wire. They rode into the melee with wild rebel yells, while behind them the cheers of the spectators grew even louder. "Get those god-damned niggers!" came Jim Clark's voice, "And get those god-damned white niggers!"

Across the bridge city police stepped out of their places on Water Street and stopped the ambulances at the foot of the ramp. People were running now, choking and crying, up the other side away from the fumes, with the horsemen in angry pursuit, swinging their whips and ropes. Soon they came in view fleeing down the downtown side, only to be met by another group with clubs. The mounted possemen had harassed them away from the wounded, and most of these lay helpless in the lingering, stifling gas.

All through downtown the pursuit and beating continued, up Water Street to Franklin, down Franklin to Alabama, out Alabama to Sylvan and into the project itself. Wilson Baker watched helplessly as the bloody mob swept past, unable to move even when one of his own men lost his cool and began beating a black who passed nearby.

As one group of marchers came running down Franklin Street past City Hall with the mounted possemen in hot pursuit, a bold, enraged black man named Clarence Williams, who was sitting on the side of the street in his automobile, decided to act. He pulled his car around sideways across the roadway, cutting off the horsemen just long enough to give their victims a sufficient lead to get back into the black housing project ahead of them. Then he pulled away, and the possemen, really feeling their strength, turned on those black bystanders farther down the street who had been watching terrified from their cars. They began banging their billy clubs on the car hoods, shouting: "Get the hell out of town! Go on, I mean it! We want all the niggers off the streets!" The blacks left in a hurry, running over curbs and bumping fenders to get out of there. In a few moments the downtown area was deserted except for the rampaging lawmen.

As Clark approached the project Baker confronted him, told him it was evident that there was no further threat from the march and said he would take charge again, as they had agreed. Clark elbowed past him, declaring "I've already waited a month too damn long about moving in!" Baker then ordered his men to leave the area, to avoid being caught in any more mayhem. Troopers and possemen roamed through the lines of boxy red-brick apartments for half an hour, chasing anyone they saw and throwing tear gas into one home where Clark thought he saw something suspicious. Another squad of possemen rushed into the First Baptist Church at the far end of the project, grabbed a black youth they found there and threw him through a stained glass window depicting Jesus as The Good Shepherd.

Now the black people, back in their own territory, had recovered enough to begin feeling their anger, and bricks and bottles were soon flying after the marauding police forces. Clark himself was nicked by a rock, and this heated him up even further. The civil rights workers who had not been on the march and were thus not gasping to regain their breath and sight worked frantically around the doors of Brown Chapel, pleading with people to go inside and pushing them back through the doors. It was hard work; the air inside the church was acrid with burning gas droplets shaken off the marchers' clothes; and more than a few were hysterical with terror, pain and rage.

Other blacks were coming in with more focused feelings to express. After blocking the possemen with his car downtown, Clarence Williams had driven home and packed his two guns into his car. Then he came back to the church, full of cold fury and ready for anything. Two workers spotted him and pulled him back to the church office, where they preached to him about staying nonviolent until he decided to leave. Williams couldn't go along with their nonresistance ideas, but respecting their commitment he felt the only right thing to do was get back in his car and drive home with his weapons.

As the field cleared outside, Clark, his possemen and the troopers began slowing down. Baker then ventured back with his men up Sylvan Street, more aggressively now. "All right now," he told Clark gruffly, "get your cowboys the hell out of here." He posted his men in a cordon around the church area in a show of force of his own. Inside, Hosea Williams had flushed the fumes from his eyes, and with his face still dripping wet began preaching the crowd into a semblance of defiant but approximately rational anger, denouncing Baker's neutral stance as hypocrisy and insisting he had never seen anything so brutal even when he was captured by the Germans in World War Two. John Lewis, his skull fractured, refused to go to the hospital until he had told the audience, "I don't see how President Johnson can send troops to Vietnam. I don't see how he can send troops to the Congo . . . and can't send troops to Selma, Alabama. Next time we march, we may have to keep going when we get to Montgomery. We may have to go on to Washington."

More than fifty people were taken to the Good Samaritan Hospital, as well as Burwell Infirmary, once the police relented and let the Medical Committee ambulances cross the bridges and begin picking up the wounded. At Burwell, more a ramshackle nursing home in the dilapidated style of separate but equal than a real hospital, all but one of the beds were already full, so the floor was soon littered with bleed-ing, choking people, as the staff raced around with bandages and an oxygen tank. At Good Samaritan there was more space and profession-alism, and the bloodstains were quickly wiped up from the floor around the emergency room door. Several of the victims were hospitalized for days.

The SCLC leaders assembled again in the parsonage and got on the phone to Dr. King in Atlanta. He was shocked at what had happened, and immediately issued a statement to that effect. But what was to come next? A heated discussion raged for almost an hour among those on the extensions in the parsonage and those at the other end. Should Dr. King come to Selma at once and lead another march tomorrow morning, while calling for help from sympathetic northerners, or should he call for help first and not march until Tuesday? And what about federal court action to restrain Wallace and Clark from interfer-ing with the next attempt?

It was finally decided that Dr. King would send out telegrams to northerners that night asking them to come to Selma, that his attorneys would be in court in Montgomery Monday morning to ask for a restraining order against the officials, and that the next march attempt would not be made until Tuesday, to give the outside supporters a chance to arrive.

In a few hours the first of several hundred telegrams was flashing across the country from SCLC headquarters on Auburn Avenue in Atlanta, signed by Dr. King and addressed to every prominent church person known to be sympathetic whose address SCLC's program direc-tor, Randolph Blackwell, could lay his hands on. The messages read, in part:

> In the vicious maltreatment of defenseless citizens of Selma, where old women and young children were gassed and clubbed at random, we have witnessed an eruption of the disease of racism which seeks to destroy all America. No American is without responsibility. . . . The people of Selma will struggle on for the

soul of the nation, but it is fitting that all Americans help to bear the burden. I call therefore, on clergy of all faiths . . . to join me in Selma for a ministers march to Montgomery on Tuesday morning, March ninth.

The reporters who had captured almost the entire attack on their telephoto lenses, had been busy during these hours as well. The Sunday night movie on ABC television was interrupted for a long film report of the assault on Highway 80, a sequence which showed clearly the quiet column, the flailing clubs, the stampeding horses, the jeering crowd and the stricken, fleeing blacks. The movie was *Judgement at Nuremburg,* starring Spencer Tracy as the American war crimes judge, and Burt Lancaster as an accused Nazi magistrate.

1. *U.S. Highway 80,
Lowndes County Alabama,
looking west toward Selma*

2. *Roadsigns near the
city limits*

3. The earliest known, anonymous painting of the Alabama River near Selma, looking south; circa 1830

OPPOSITE, TOP: 5. The Alabama River, 1973; a view similar to that in the 1830 painting

4. General Edmund Winston Pettus

6. *The bridge from Selma, spanning the Alabama River*

7. *A street in black Selma*

8. *Rev. Frederick Reese, right, joins Dr. King at the head of a march; Ralph Abernathy is behind King, with Rev. L. L. Anderson at his left.*

9. *Rev. Reese, leading the teachers, confronts School Board President Edgar Stewart at the Courthouse, while school Superintendent J. A. Pickard stands by, January 22, 1965.*

10. *Sheriff Jim Clark and his possemen at the Alabama entrance to the Dallas County Courthouse*

11. With his deputy Robert "Cotton" Nichols at his right, Selma Public Safety Director Wilson Baker (in light raincoat) awaits a group of marchers near Brown Chapel.

12. Mrs. Amelia Platts Boynton Billups being carried from the Pettus Bridge, March 7, 1965, after being felled by clubs and tear gas

13. State troopers massed on Sylvan Street

14. Jimmie Lee Jackson

15. James Reeb, in glasses
at far left, joins the
second march to the bridge,
March 9, 1965.

"HE DIDN'T COME.

and they went without him.
Picked up their bedrolls,
umbrellas (we had laughed about
what 'de lawd' would do
if it rained)
and brown paper sacks with toothbrushes.

"I wonder would it have been differenthad he been
there?

"but no matter . . .
a man is allowed his weak moments
and other christs always seem to rise up
to take their place.
many hundreds did that day."

> —*"Crumpled Notes (found in a raincoat)*
> *on Selma", Maria Varela*

ELEVEN.

The national impact of the attack on the march, which was featured again on the television news shows Monday, was little less than seismic. In Washington every politician who could get a reporter to listen denounced it and demanded some sort of federal action. A dozen prominent blacks trooped into Attorney General Katzenbach's office at the Justice Department at lunchtime, to harangue him about the necessity for sending a force of federal marshals into Alabama at once. Their spokesman, Rev. Jefferson Rogers, said when he emerged that "I frankly do not think the marshals will be sent. We've got to apply all the pressure we can on this man to make him understand the situation. I believe the Attorney General is sympathetic, but sympathy just won't help."

Further pressure was not long in coming. Three young people from Washington SNCC soon appeared in the hallway and tried to get into Katzenbach's office to mount a sit-in. It took four guards to haul one of them, a huge fellow named Dale Smith, out of the building as he chanted "Freedom, buddy, Freedom!" They were replaced not long after by twenty more, who camped around the attorney general's door and refused to move until they had been assured the marshals would be sent.

After closing time they were still there, and the attorney general stepped out briefly to speak to them. He said he wouldn't be swayed by their presence. "I have responsibilities to fulfill and decisions to make . . . that will not be influenced one way or another just because you're going to sit here all night." When they still hadn't left by ten o'clock, Chief Marshal James McShane was sent out to deal with them. "You've had your chance to talk," he told them. Their response was to drop to the floor; some rolled into defensive balls. "This is a public building and it closes at 6:00 P.M.," McShane went on as other marshals wrestled with the wriggling bodies. "We've made a decision that you must leave, and now you must decide how." The protesters chose to be dragged out, resisting all the way.

A few blocks down the street in front of the White House, a large, noisy picket line had appeared, with placards calling for troops, marshals, new laws, and other things, and it kept up its singing and walking all that night. Before dark, a planeload of well-known Washington religious figures was on its way to Dannelly Field in Montgomery, which itself was already jammed with pilgrims headed for Selma. One of those from Washington, Methodist Bishop John Wesley Lord, explained his coming emotionally: "I heard that Dr. Martin Luther King was calling for white ministers to come and march, and I am a white minister. You can say that I heard the Macedonian call. We heard the call of God from Selma and we came."

Carloads of supporters, most of them white, continued to arrive all evening at the marathon mass meeting which had been going on in Brown Chapel practically all day; among them were Rev. Malcolm Boyd, Dr. George Docherty, pastor of the historic New York Avenue Presbyterian Church in Washington, and Father Geno Baroni, the first of a parade of activist Catholics. There was Mrs. Charles Tobey, the widow of a New Hampshire senator, and Mrs. Harold Ickes, whose husband was once secretary of the Interior. And scores more.

Dr. King and others had been preaching hard all day about the importance of maintaining nonviolence in the face of violence, to a not unanimously agreeing audience. But the appearance of these growing numbers of well-dressed, determined white outsiders ready to join them in facing whatever lay ahead left the people gaping in astonishment and then applauding with renewed confidence each new batch as it arrived. Come Tuesday morning, they would be ready.

During the day Monday Governor Wallace had summoned Mayor Smitherman and Sheriff Clark to a meeting in his office, where he had chewed them out angrily for allowing Sunday's violence to happen. He warned them that he would not tolerate a repeat on Tuesday, and had told the troopers so as well. But just as the meeting began, one of the governor's closest aides had pulled Smitherman aside and whispered to him not to get upset by the chief executive's tongue-lashing; it was really directed at Clark, and Wallace had called Smitherman on the carpet too just for the sake of appearing evenhanded.

Dr. King's attorneys were at work in Montgomery on Monday according to plan, petitioning U.S. District Judge Frank M. Johnson to restrain the state and county officials and permit the Tuesday march to proceed. Johnson was one of the most independent, highly regarded jurists on the southern federal bench. He had had many run-ins with George Wallace, who had referred to him as a "carpetbagging, scala-wagging, integrating liar"; and his record on civil rights cases was such that his home was guarded each night by a federal marshal.

Thus the lawyers' hopes for favorable action were high. But Johnson didn't go along with their scenario. The judge asked them to wait until he could hold a hearing. Dr. King first agreed to delay the march; but when he saw the magnitude and intensity of the response to his plea for help, he changed his mind. Frank Johnson didn't take kindly to the rebuff however, and early Tuesday morning turned his request into an order: "This court does not see from the complaint . . ." he wrote, "any justification for issuing a temporary restraining order without notice to the defendants and without a hearing. There will be no irreparable harm if the plaintiffs will await a judicial determination of the matters involved." The plaintiffs were enjoined against proceeding with the march until the hearing was held, beginning Wednesday, March 10.

Thus was created Dr. King's most famous dilemma. The federal courts had almost always been a refuge for him and his movements in the South, and Judge Johnson's record was one of the best. That was why he had been willing initially to go along with his request for a delay. But now the church was more than full, the airport was crowded, the routes to Montgomery and the Black Belt were teeming with people converging on Selma, all of them ready and determined to march Tuesday and face any eventuality. Perhaps the only eventuality they had not considered was being in contempt of a federal court order.

Dr. King and his circle, augmented with visiting figures like James Farmer of the Congress of Racial Equality and James Forman, the executive secretary of SNCC, met through the night at the home of a black dentist, Dr. Sullivan Jackson, and argued about what to do. Ultimately Dr. King became firm in his intention to go ahead. He told this to the attorney general when he called him well after midnight; and Nicholas Katzenbach was unable to budge him with an hour's pleading. The White House then sent the head of the Community Relations Service, former Florida Governor Leroy Collins, to Selma on a government jet to try to head it off. Meeting with King not long after sunup Tuesday, Collins repeated the plea for a delay, adding that this was the president's wish as well. But by then Dr. King was immovable. When the president's press secretary, George Reedy, announced later that morning that the president had asked that the march be postponed in compliance with the order, the die had already been cast.

Failing to stop the march, Collins worked frantically to keep the confrontation it would inevitably produce peaceful. He met secretly with Clark and Lingo in the back of a used car dealership, and got them to agree to leave the line alone if it stopped when ordered to and then returned to the church. There is uncertainty as to whether Dr. King explicitly agreed to go along with this plan or not, but it appears that he did.

Even if an agreement was made, the situation was about as unpredictable as it could get. Clark had made agreements before, as had Lingo. Whites who knew Clark well were sure there would be many people dead by nightfall. Inside Brown Chapel throughout the morning there was more preaching of nonviolence as the crowd waited fretfully to learn whether the leader was going to defy a federal judge or not. James Bevel, who wanted to march, told the crowd that "Any man who has the urge to hit a posseman or a state trooper with a pop bottle is a fool. That is just what they want you to do. Then they can call you a mob and beat you to death." Practically all of the three thousand people milling around Sylvan Street wanted to march and were preparing themselves for the worst.

Finally Dr. King appeared about 10:30 A.M. to insist that "Nothing will stop us, not the threat of death itself. The only way we can get our freedom is to have no fear of death. We must show them that if they beat one Negro, they are going to have to beat a hundred, and if they beat a hundred, they are going to have to beat a thousand. We will not be turned around. The world must know that we are determined to be free."

That settled it, although it took more than three more hours of milling around before things got organized enough for the march to begin. Once formed the line took up all available space in front of the church and beyond it down the sidewalk and back into a large playground behind it. Few of the people could even hear Dr. King's final words, but his sentiments were unanimously shared: "We have the right to walk the highways, and we have the right to walk to Montgomery if our feet will get us there. I have no alternative but to lead a march from this spot to carry our grievances to the seat of government. I have made my choice. I have got to march. I do not know what lies ahead of us. There may be beatings, jailings, tear gas. But I would rather die on the highways of Alabama than make a butchery of my conscience."

Then the line set off, with the front ranks loaded down with religious celebrities. Hundreds of priests, rabbis and ministers followed, raising their voices in continuing choruses of "Aint Gonna Let Nobody Turn Me Round." They passed groups of state troopers stationed in the center and at the corners of each block, up Sylvan Street to Water Avenue, then along the riverbank to Broad Street and the bridge.

At the foot of the bridge a U.S. marshal, H. Stanley Fountain, was waiting with a copy of Judge Johnson's order. King stopped the line when Fountain stepped in front of him, and listened gravely as he read them the order. Then Dr. King said "I am aware of the order," but insisted he was going ahead. "I am not going to interfere with this march," Fountain said. "Let them go." There were only a few city policemen on hand, and they stepped back to the curb with Fountain, while the long line began rolling past them.

The afternoon was cool but very clear, with bright sunlight making everything—the turgid river, the steel bridge girders, the people's faces —look especially vivid. The contrast in the atmosphere with that of the first march was marked; Sunday had been overcast, gray, gloomy and cold, befitting the occasion. Now as the front ranks reached the crest of the bridge, they could see the troopers' blue plastic helmets gleaming in the sun; the veterans noticed with relief that there were no gas masks dangling from their belts. Still the line fell silent again at the sight of well over a hundred men standing two deep under the heedless changing traffic signals, their clubs once more at the ready, all across the highway and along both sides for a hundred feet, forming a long, ominous cul-de-sac for the first dozen ranks. Major John Cloud was again in command, and he let King get within fifty feet before speaking through his bullhorn: "You are ordered to stop and stand where you are. This march will not continue."

"We have a right to march," Dr. King replied. "There is also a right to march to Montgomery."

Cloud repeated his order. King then asked if they could pray. "You can have your prayer," Cloud said, "and then you must return to your church."

Dr. King asked the marchers to kneel, and the line, stretching back up the ramp to the bridge for almost a mile, sank down. Prayers were offered, by Bishop Lord, Dr. George Docherty, and Rabbi Richard G. Hirsch of the Union of American Hebrew Congregations. The worship was quiet but fervent.

As the group finished and rose to its feet, Major Cloud abruptly turned and ordered the troopers to clear the road. If there was a secret script for the confrontation, the state then violated the agreement. The highway to Montgomery stood before the marchers, wide open.

What would have happened if Dr. King had tried to lead the march through this unanticipated breach? They had not been given permission to proceed, and who could tell what the troopers would have done if King had started forward? Apparently Wallace had either wanted to entice him into a clear violation of the federal court order or to make him look timid in the eyes of the more militant marchers. Or was there a more dangerous possibility—was it a trap? A federal official standing near the pavement was told by a high trooper officer a moment later that the withdrawal order came direct from the governor's office, where a second-by-second account was being monitored over an amplified telephone. In Washington, the attorney general sat in his office chain-smoking and listening to a similarly audible description from attorney John Doar, his representative at the scene.

Dr. King, if he hesitated at all, paused only a few seconds before directing the line to turn and march back across the bridge to Brown Chapel. Those behind him moved forward to the place where the leaders had been stopped before making their turn, each rank wheeling around and trudging up the ramp. Occasional verses of "Aint Gonna Let Nobody Turn Me Round" could still be heard, although the song was now a little ironical.

There were those in the march who were disappointed at this outcome, and they were to make their dissatisfaction noisily evident when the march was over; but they were a small minority. Most of those who walked over the bridge were simply relieved that, after nerving themselves to face death itself, they were in one piece, walking back through downtown Selma singing and smiling. Most of the others were reassured by the explanation Dr. King offered at Tuesday night's mass meeting. He told them that the presence of the white clergy had made the police restrain themselves, and the racism revealed by this difference in treatment was one of the things he had hoped the march would dramatize. More important, by marching to the site of the Sunday assault in such massive and distinguished numbers, they had communicated to the country the magnitude of the oppression in the Black Belt. King said he understood that many in the audience had come prepared to carry the cross and felt they had ended up carrying only a toothpick; but the march had been a real victory, and their role was crucially important just as it had turned out. Finally, he pledged that they would get to Montgomery, no matter how long it took.

As large as the Selma march was, it was only a small speck among the crowds who were in the streets elsewhere supporting the black cause that day. The picket line outside the White House grew to more than seven hundred people, circling slowly on the broad sidewalk along the high black iron fence, pushing baby strollers, waving their signs and singing. The congressmen from Alabama insisted that Martin Luther King and his outside agitators were to blame for everything, and if his misguided supporters would go home everybody would be better off, but the only people who heard them were reporters for papers in their home districts. Everyone else was crying, even louder as the second march crossed the bridge into who knew what dangers, for federal marshals, federal troops and at the least a federal voting rights law. President Johnson told reporters he deplored the brutality and had urged all involved to maintain respect for law and order. But most importantly, he announced that he had committed the administration to submitting a voting bill to Congress within a week's time.

More vigillers gathered outside Nicholas Katzenbach's office at the Justice Department Tuesday, and their numbers grew steadily until at closing time there were almost two hundred. The marshals took a gentle approach during most of the siege, even sending out lunches for them at noon. But again they had to drag them away when they decided it was time for them to leave, and it took thirty marshals to do it.

But Washington's demonstrations were not the largest or most disruptive: in New York hundreds of people mobilized outside the Manhattan FBI office, snarling traffic at Sixty-ninth Street and Third Avenue for four hours. In Chicago fifty people rushed out and sat down on the pavement at State and Madison, jamming traffic there until police hauled them away and arrested twenty-four of them. There were marches in Boston, Cleveland, Oakland, Syracuse, New Haven, even across the border in Toronto. The largest was in Detroit, where Republican Governor George Romney joined Democratic Mayor Jerome Cavanaugh at the head of a crowd of ten thousand that marched around the federal building five times.

Even the *Selma Times-Journal*, editorially expressing "Our Considered Opinion," admitted that "even after two days of attempting to analyze the almost unbelievable events of Sunday afternoon, we are still confounded by the action resorted to by law enforcement officers on the scene. There appears to be no logical reasoning behind the display of force employed by state troopers and members of the mounted units who participated in dispersing the demonstrators." Even prefaced as it necessarily was with the assertion that "It is obvious that M. L. King, recipient of the Nobel Peace Prize, has declared war on the people of Alabama," it was a remarkably independent commentary.

And withal, life in the city went on after a fashion, even during the second march. A regional meeting of the Alabama Water Pollution Control Association was held as scheduled on Tuesday, hosted by Victor B. Atkins, who in addition to serving as chairman of the county Board of Registrars was also manager of the Selma Water Works, a large modern facility of which the city was very proud. Mayor Smitherman, ever the obliging chief city booster, stopped in to make a brief welcoming speech: "We invite you to take a look around while you are here," he said, "and see the progress we are making. We do have our law enforcement problems at this time, but I assure you that it has never been unsafe for anyone to walk the streets of our city."

As the march broke up, many of those who had come from a distance to join it headed back to Montgomery or piled into their cars for the long drive home. One of those doing so was the Rev. James Reeb, a Unitarian from Boston. Reeb worked on housing problems in Boston's ghetto for the American Friends Service Committee. He also lived in the ghetto with his family, and his decision to fly down and join the march was predictable. He had driven from Atlanta with several other Unitarian ministers, and now prepared to accept a ride back to Atlanta with a woman named Jean Levine. He threw his suitcase in the back of Mrs. Levine's car, but just then fell into conversation with another Unitarian minister who was planning to stay over to be available for any other needed witness. Reeb was reluctant to leave Selma after such a brief stay, and agreed with his colleague that the city's blacks were not yet out of the woods. He retrieved the suitcase and joined a group of about a dozen Unitarian ministers that was headed downtown to get some supper in a black restaurant, Walker's Cafe, on Washington Street.

Walker's is a small establishment, serving strictly Alabama soul food:

fried chicken, collard greens, big wedges of cornbread and sweet potato pie. The place was packed with marchers, and Reeb had to wait for a table along with two of his fellow ministers, Clark Olsen of Berkeley, California and Orloff Miller, also of Boston. They lingered over their rich, pungent food, which was easy to do, and just before they left, Reeb called his wife Marie to tell her he was staying in Selma one more day.

When the trio left the cafe they turned to the right, and walked down Washington Street in the direction of the Silver Moon Cafe on the corner. They had probably turned the wrong way, because Reeb had intended to go to the SCLC office on Franklin Street to talk with some black workers he had met earlier, and the office was in the other direction.

It was a fateful turn. The Silver Moon was a notorious white spa, so bad that no integrated testing team had yet tried to be served there. The Silver Moon was probably the worst place to be passing by that particular night. It was now almost dark, and as they approached the corner the three ministers didn't see four white men waiting in the shadows across the street until they started toward them, shouting "Hey you, niggers!" Olsen saw them and started to run, but got only a few steps before they were on him. He turned momentarily, saw Miller crouch on the sidewalk, hands over his head as he had been taught to do at the church, and saw Reeb being struck on the head with a club or pipe. Then Olsen was struck, dodged out into the street and was hit again. His glasses flew off and he couldn't see who was hitting him, but in a few seconds the attackers stopped and ran.

Miller and Olsen quickly recovered their senses and got up. But Reeb was unable to stand by himself; his speech was jumbled and he couldn't seem to see. They turned now back up Washington Street, up past Walker's around the corner to Franklin Street and then to the SCLC office. Reeb's talk became more coherent, and he complained that his head ached viciously. All that could be seen, however, was a slight break in the skin over his left ear.

At the office, staff members sent at once for an ambulance. By the time it arrived a few minutes later Reeb's pain was almost unbearable. The ambulance took him and his two companions to Burwell Infirmary, where Dr. William Dinkins, one of only two black physicians in a wide region around Selma, waited to examine Reeb and take an X ray. Reeb moved convulsively as the plate was exposed, however, and the X ray was spoiled. Sensing that something was seriously wrong, he clung to Olsen's hands without speaking, but soon fell into a coma.

Dr. Dinkins ordered that he be transferred at once to the university medical center in Birmingham. Only there could he get the skilled care he obviously needed from hands that could be trusted. His colleagues helped move him back to the ambulance, and headed north into the night. About ten miles out of Selma, the ambulance threw a recap and had to limp back to the city limits, stopping in a radio station parking lot where the driver telephoned for a replacement. While the men sat there waiting for it, several strange cars pulled into the parking lot and the white drivers gave them long, threatening stares.

When the second ambulance arrived, its siren did not work, and more time was spent trying vainly to fix it. A Dallas County sheriff's car pulled in and deputies hopped out, opening the ambulance door and pointing their flashlights at those within, demanding to know what was going on. Olsen told them and asked for a police escort. The deputies declined, saying they would radio ahead and that would be all they would need.

Dr. Dinkins now decided it was unsafe to go to Birmingham without an escort, and called home to ask that his personal car be brought out to him for that purpose. There was more waiting for it to appear. At length it came, Dr. Dinkins climbed into it, and with him following closely behind, the ambulance left once more for Birmingham, racing at seventy and eighty miles an hour down the dark country roads. The stretcher on which Reeb lay, breathing heavily and clearly in great pain, did not fit the restraining brackets of the second ambulance; Olsen and Miller had to hold on to it around curves to keep it from rolling back and forth. Reeb, who was lying on his back, vomited once or twice during the trip, and in that position food particles entered his windpipe, causing pneumonia in his lungs. Olsen and Miller, holding on to the stretcher in the darkened, careening ambulance and untrained in emergency procedures, did not notice what had happened. "I did nothing because I knew nothing to do," Miller said later. "I wish to God I had known."

The ambulance pulled into University Hospital after 11:00 P.M., four hours after the attack. The surgeons immediately saw that Reeb had a massive skull fracture and blood clot, complicated by pneumonia. It was clear to them soon thereafter that it was only a matter of time, and not much at that, before he would be dead.

In a room in a house in the North came a cry,
Light became dark,
Men readied to die in the dust
With a bark and a snarl
And a swing to a crash on the skull.

Two men died, not one.
Many men died, not two. . . .
The ghost, with his bat and a smile,
Sells sinks and tacks and this-and-that
And old used cars
From his house by the side of the road,
In the heat and hell
Of Selma.

—*"James Reeb," by Rev. Theodore A. Webb*

TWELVE.

The difference between the public response to the assault on Rev. Reeb, a white man, and the reaction to Jimmie Lee Jackson's murder was marked. The Reeb home in the Dorchester section of Boston was deluged with telegrams, including personal messages from both Senators Kennedy and a spray of yellow roses from the Texan in the White House. A government jet was soon dispatched to carry Mrs. Reeb to her husband's Birmingham deathbed. At the same time Jimmie Jackson's mother Viola and his grandfather Cager Lee were back on their little farm, which was not much more than a clearing with a shack on it, tending their one skinny cow and a flock of sickly chickens, forgotten in the rush of sympathy for a fallen white man.

This discrepancy was as apparent to the blacks in Selma as it was to anyone, but they took it with little outward show of bitterness. After all, Reeb had been struck down on their streets, after coming to stand with them in an hour of crisis. These facts made the disparity easier to tolerate; and besides, they had other things to worry about, the first of which was getting to Montgomery—and the second, which they didn't become aware of until Wednesday morning, was getting even as far as the Dallas County Courthouse to pay their own respects to the struggle's latest victim.

Hundreds of people streamed out of Brown Chapel about noon Wednesday and lined up arm in arm in the middle of Sylvan Street to march on the courthouse in protest of the assault. Wilson Baker and Mayor Smitherman were waiting for them at the corner of Selma Avenue, standing at one side of a line of seventeen city police blocking their path. The mayor, looking gaunt and nervous, announced that he had invoked the emergency powers of his office to ban all marches in the city until further notice. He was careful to have Baker add that he was "in full agreement" with the decision. "We are going to stop any demonstrations," Baker said flatly. His voice was tired as he tried to explain the ban without being embarrassingly specific: "It is too risky under the present circumstances—taking under consideration the facts as they now affect the city."

Some of these facts were evident behind him, in the form of several score state troopers, Sheriff Clark, and a detachment of the posse. There were several hundred troopers in Selma now, brought from Montgomery before Tuesday's confrontation in a one hundred fifty car cavalcade; but most of them, along with the bulk of the posse, were being kept carefully out of sight and action, though the posse was charitably described by the *Times-Journal* as "standing by as a second reserve force." The young mayor, after the shocks of Sunday afternoon, seemed for the moment inclined to follow the counsel of his public safety director that these agencies were not to be trusted and that the only way of salvaging any credibility for his administration's policies was to preempt them by such a device as the ban.

The marchers, led by Rev. L. L. Anderson, pastor of Tabernacle Baptist Church where the first civil rights mass meeting in the city had been held, were not exactly taken by surprise, and were ready to make the most of the situation. In fact, as they had left the church one of the senior SCLC staff members had given Rev. Anderson a list of the visiting notables who might profitably be introduced and given a chance to speak if a standoff developed. Anderson moved to do just that, and opened on a dramatic note: "Mr. Mayor, we are not here to rebel against your order, but since we have been unsuccessful in seeking to see you we feel we have no alternative but to offer our bodies as a living sacrifice." He looked down at the list, and with whispered help on the tough ethnic surnames, from a visiting clergyman at his side, began introducing people.

For the next few hours the stolid line of policemen formed a captive audience for an extraordinary outdoor civil rights meeting, one that featured the most heartfelt oratory possible from one of the most distinguished guest lists ever assembled in these years. Before the meeting was finished thirty-six people had stepped forward to pray, lead songs, and preach about the issue and event that had torn them away from the hometown routines they had been pursuing just forty-eight hours before.

Among this inter-denominational crowd perhaps none stood out more visibly than a squad of nuns from St. Louis. The Second Vatican Council, which had jimmied open so many of the locked doors in the Roman Catholic church, had just recently adjourned, so the nuns were still dressed in their traditional street-length black and brown habits. Their presence here was the logical and probably inevitable outgrowth of the council's work and spirit; but it was just the same an almost unprecedented event in American Catholicism. The Catholic missionaries of the Society of St. Edmund had been doing pioneer work in Selma for thirty years, and had built a school and the new Good Samaritan Hospital where Jimmie Jackson died and so many of Sunday's wounded had been treated. Their mission director, Father Maurice Ouellet, had worked closely and visibly with the SNCC workers in the long months before Dr. King came with the glare of national publicity. But Ouellet's work did not sit too easily with his ecclesiastical superiors in the state, and the archbishop of Mobile, Thomas J. Toolen, had given the Edmundites strict orders not to take part in any marches. They had abided by this ban, but chafed at it and wanted to make their position public. The community's superior, Father John Crowley, had done so by publishing a full-page advertisement in the *Times-Journal* on February seventh, titled "The Path to Peace in Selma." The statement made clear that the Edmundites believed the black people's struggle to be not only just and worthy of their support, but also consistent with their Christian principles.

Now the Edmundites' outpost was becoming the staging area for an assault on the entire structure of ecclesiastical opposition and resistance

to involvement of Catholic clergy in such activities. There had been
Catholic priests in the first planeload of people from Washington on
Monday, and at least two of them, Monsignor George L. Gingras and
Father Geno Baroni, came with the official approval of their bishop,
Cardinal Richard O'Boyle. By Wednesday there were scores more, and
the first of a steady trickle of nuns. Some of these came with the
approval of their superiors—though this assent was usually given in fear
and hesitation—but more did not; and none stopped to ask permission
from Bishop Toolen, which was a clear violation of hitherto sacrosanct
church custom. And by the time these Catholics had all returned
home, they had almost completely undermined the capacity of the
hierarchy to keep them out of active, public involvement in social-
change activities. Many of the people whose names later became famous in the "Catholic Left" of the later sixties and early seventies came
out of their cloisters here. It was one of the more important accomplishments of the movement, and one that was already becoming visible as
the streetcorner mass meeting went on that Wednesday afternoon.

But this was not the only demonstration underway. Not long after
the first parade had been blocked by the city police, another two
hundred fifty people walked out of First Baptist Church at the other
end of the block and headed down Jeff Davis Avenue, planning to take
another street south to the courthouse. Baker got news of this foray on
his police radio and, with the mayor, a reporter for the *Times-Journal*,
and his chief lieutenant, W. D. "Cotton" Nichols, drove quickly
around the block to head it off. He and Nichols leaped out of their car,
hurried over to the march and ordered it to halt. But the marchers,
confronted with only two officers, announced that they were prepared
to walk right past them and keep going. Baker went back to his car and
radioed for a squad of troopers to assist him. They came in a hurry, and
pushed the march roughly back into the church, using their nightsticks
freely but with comparative precision, aiming mainly at bellies and
arms.

Once that group was subdued, Baker returned to his automobile and
asked the troopers to leave a detail at that end of the block to seal off
the street to traffic. Once the scene was again quiet, Mayor Smitherman, still feeling the tension, said to the reporter, Assistant Editor
Arthur Capell, "Come on, let's get out and stretch our legs." The pair

walked slowly down to the corner, and leaned against a trooper car as they chatted. A big, burly trooper was out in the street, directing traffic with a great show of fierceness and authority; and when a break came in passing cars, he left his post and swaggered over to the two men. "Move out of here," he told them gruffly, fingering his long, black nightstick.

The mayor looked up at him in surprise, at a momentary loss for words. Capell said, "He's the mayor, officer."

The trooper wasn't listening. "Move *on*, I said," he repeated, emphasizing the order by a sharp jab to the mayor's stomach with his stick.

Smitherman stumbled backward and began fumbling for his wallet. "But I've got identification," he protested, and flashed a gold mayor's badge.

"I don't care *who* you are," shouted the trooper, raising the club again, "get out of here." The two men began walking rapidly away. The mayor was getting angry.

A second trooper car, which had observed the encounter from a short distance away, slowed up beside them, its uniformed driver not satisfied with their pace. "You heard him," he said, "get out of here." Capell showed his press pass, but the response was monosyllabic: "You too."

The two men began walking faster, but about this time a third car, driven by a trooper lieutenant who recognized the mayor, came up; when he learned what had happened he immediately spoke to the first trooper, who then put away his club, saluted the mayor smartly and returned to his post directing traffic. In a few minutes Major John Cloud had heard about the incident on his radio and had rushed over to offer a personal apology for the trooper's action. By now the mayor was philosophical: "He's a little trigger-happy," he said. "But I guess everybody is pretty tense."

As the streetcorner mass meeting was winding up its last rendition of "We Shall Overcome" for the benefit of the policemen and troopers, Rev. Anderson felt a hand on his arm. A tall, dark man with wavy, black hair, dressed in a clerical collar and a long black tunic told him he wished to speak. Anderson didn't know him, but with his dress he looked distinguished, if a little uncertain of denomination: his collar was Roman, but around his neck hung a six-pointed star of David on a steel chain. The man stepped to the front, introduced himself as

Elder William Ezra Greer, of the Zion Church of God in Christ, and a spokesman for Dr. King to this demonstration. He preached to them long and powerfully, then passed on what he said were orders from the movement's leadership to the visitors: they were not to try to leave the area of the housing project around Brown Chapel, and under no circumstances were they to patronize white-owned businesses, in violation of the boycott. Elder Greer spoke with the inflections of authority, and Rev. Anderson was much impressed by his presence and eloquence.

The group then returned to the church, for supper and more meetings. But they were back on the street by early evening, with a new plan. They told the policemen they would stay where they were until permitted to march to the courthouse, and began pulling out air mattresses and blankets to show they meant what they said. Baker strung a line of rope across the street at chest level as a marker of the point of his blockade. Within a few hours, the people on the line had christened the slender barrier "the Berlin Wall," and made up a song about it to the tune of "Joshua Fit the Battle of Jericho":

"We've got a rope that's a Berlin Wall, Berlin Wall, Berlin Wall,
"We've got a rope that's a Berlin Wall, in Selma Alabama."

New verses were added as the vigillers worked the song over among themselves:

"We're gonna stand here till it falls, till it falls, till it falls . . .
"Hate is the thing that built that wall, built that wall, built that wall . . .
"Love is the thing that'll make it fall, make it fall, make it fall. . . ."

Hundreds stayed on the street that night, and more people slept on the bare, brown benches in the church. They were not much impressed by the report that Wilson Baker had arrested three of four men who had been charged with the assault on James Reeb. Of the three, Elmer Cook, R. B. Kelley and William Hoggle, Cook and Hoggle scarcely warmed the inside of their cells before making bond and getting out; Kelley was out Thursday morning, March eleventh.

By Thursday evening, spirits on the line had begun to flag, especially since it looked like rain. But about seven o'clock Baker came to deliver personally the news that many of the people had been anticipating all day: James Reeb was dead. There had been no hope; a machine had been pumping his blood and a respirator breathing his air since Thursday morning. Early that afternoon the doctors at University Hospital decided not to add any more mechanical aids to further delay his passing. His wife Marie had been there most of the day. When she arrived, reporters at the airport had asked what she had told her husband before he left: "I said I would prefer that he didn't go," she had answered quietly. "But he said he had to go." Now she was returning home to Boston, this time on Air Force One, the president's jet.

Baker pledged to the crowd that he would rearrest the four alleged assailants on new charges of murder as soon as he could find them. He made good the commitment, but again they were permitted to make bond, under an obscure Alabama statute which permitted bail in murder cases where there were indications that the jury will not return a death penalty. Baker tried to keep City Attorney Pitts from invoking this provision on their behalf, but Pitts ignored him, and the four were once more at large within a few hours.

On Sylvan Street, the news of Reeb's death was greeted with tears and anger, then another impromptu mass meeting which went on for three hours of impassioned oratory and full-throated singing. When that had concluded, the people settled back into their makeshift bedrolls on the gravel, again vowing to stay until they could march to the courthouse for what would now be a memorial demonstration. And most stayed through the night despite the fact that the threatened drizzle soon began falling on them and their guards alike.

On Friday state representative Richard Dominick of Birmingham introduced a resolution expressing sympathy to the Reeb family in the Alabama House. But the body then voted to adjourn without acting, and the resolution was automatically killed. Representative Dominick told reporters he would not try to introduce it again.

In Washington another vigil was continuing; that was what the continuous moving picket line at the White House had become. Shortly before noon, Thursday, twelve students in a line of tourists entering the East Wing heated up the scene by flopping down in a hallway in the executive mansion and announcing they would stay there until federal troops were sent to Alabama. This was the first, and it turned out, the last time anyone had actually carried a sit-in into the White House itself; and after a flurry of consultations, while the group sang loudly "We Shall Not Be Moved," word came down from higher up to leave them alone for the moment but to keep them in one place.

The group, including both white and black young people, was in a hostile mood. At one point they spotted presidential adviser Eric F. Goldman walking to his office, and one called out "Where are you going, fink bastard,—going to get him his bullwhip?" Goldman was not amused. Nature came partially to the rescue of the White House staff, as three of the protesters had to quit their posts to go to the bathroom, and once they were up guards escorted them outside. But by six o'clock, things got tight: a reception for fifty congressmen and their wives was scheduled in the ballroom outside which the nine holdouts were sitting, and the First Family could scarcely allow them to dampen their hospitality. Guards picked the men and women up, and "walked" them to police cars. They were taken to a stationhouse in the District, charged with unlawful entry but allowed to leave without posting bond.

The reception itself was marred, however, by the news of James Reeb's death. President and Mrs. Johnson left the auditorium to return to their living quarters and place a call to Mrs. Reeb, "No matter what I could find to say to her," the president wrote of the moment, "I had no answer to the one question that kept turning over and over in my mind: How many Jim Reebs will die before our country is truly free?" Mrs. Johnson's response was more defensive. While her husband groped for something to say, "we could hear the Congressional guests and the music still playing below" she wrote in her diary; "and out in front the chanting of the Civil Rights marchers. What a house. What a life."

On another front, though, there was real movement in the capital. Attorney General Katzenbach told a press conference he was sending the president a voting bill that day. What he did not say was that the president had discarded once and for all his earlier timetable on voting rights legislation, and did so by directing Katzenbach to stop work on the constitutional amendment form of the bill. Until now, the president had shown no real signs of responding to the pressures being brought by the movement and its supporters in Congress to dump the amendment and send a bill. Liberal senators had been making critical

speeches; the *New York Times* in an editorial on February 28 urged
that a bill and not an amendment be sent; but on March 5, two days
before the attack at the bridge, Dr. King had spent two hours in the
Oval Office trying to persuade the president that a bill was what was
needed, and that it must contain provision for the appointment of
federal registrars; but Johnson had listened without making any concrete commitments. The president did little more than listen and refer
King to the attorney general.

Now all that had changed. By Thursday, March eleventh, Katzenbach was in a private meeting with Illinois Senator Everett Dirksen,
the Republican leader. This was a sure sign that serious work was now
under way, because if Dirksen went along with the bill and was allowed
to put his stamp on it, speedy passage was virtually assured, because he
could swing the crucial Republican votes needed to stop a southern
filibuster. The voluble Dirksen had earlier suggested to reporters that
he would oppose any bill that would authorize federal registrars; but
now he allowed that that was not so, and his remaining objections to
the Katzenbach draft lay in other areas, of which he would specify only
its length and complexity.

A further hopeful sign at the meeting was the presence of Louisiana
Senator Russell Long; there had been continuing rumors that the
southern bloc in the Senate would actually split over a voting bill, and
Long's willingness to join the drafting effort confirmed these indications. Without a solid southern front, a filibuster might not even be
attempted.

The drafting meetings went on until Saturday morning, focused on
formulas for determining where literacy tests should be suspended and
federal registrars authorized (all the formulas that the administration
representatives were interested in managed to leave out Texas), how
restrictive the federal supervision of registration and election procedures in affected states should be, and whether the bill should ban
outright the imposition of poll taxes. On Saturday, March thirteenth,
the Illinois senator and representatives of the Justice Department
reached agreement on these points, and reported their accomplishment
to the White House.

When he received this news the president was preparing for a face-
to-face confrontation with one of the principals in the situation, Gover-

nor George Wallace. Wallace had sent a telegram to the president on Friday, asking for a meeting on the Selma situation as soon as possible, and the president, who was looking for a chance to confront the governor with his responsibility for the protection of the rights of his state's citizens, accepted with alacrity.

This meeting, which went on for three hours Saturday morning in the privacy of the Oval Office, was one of those unique encounters which the historian wishes had been filmed or at least transcribed verbatim for all to read. The president later reported that he kept his gaze fixed directly on the governor's face the entire time; that he made a carefully calculated appeal to his pride as the chief executive of a great state, and his responsibilities as the guardian of the rights of all his people; that he urged Wallace to be true to his states rights rhetoric and guarantee that the march, which the president said should be allowed to proceed, would be adequately protected by local and state authorities, so that federal intervention would not be necessary; and he insisted that the black protesters' grievances were in great part justified, and thus the best thing that Wallace could do was to admit it and make their cause his own—that was the surest path, he said, to the national stature Wallace sought so fervently.

For his part, Wallace reeled off his standard replies, the ones he used with such adroitness in arguing rings around less articulate, smartypants Yankee reporters: he insisted that the demonstrators, led by outsiders, were the main cause of the problems in Selma, and if they would all go home the situation would return to normal; he repeated that in any case what happened in Alabama was Alabama's business, and that applied especially to maintaining law and order. But Wallace was no match for the president; he was dealing now with a man who understood from the inside the complex of history, ambition and bravado which motivated a politician like himself, and a president, moreover, who had risen in the Senate to a position of great power precisely because of his unmatched gifts for skillful, insistent persuasion. Wallace emerged smiling and impressed from the session, allowing that "Johnson's got much more on the ball than his predecessor. I have much more respect for him than I thought I'd ever have," he admitted. "I can understand now why he gets his legislation through Congress.

If I hadn't left when I did," Wallace said ruefully, "he'd have had me coming out for civil rights."

The impact of the meeting lasted almost all the way to the capitol in Montgomery. But once back in the Cradle of the Confederacy, it rapidly wore off under the abrasive action of local political needs. The next day Wallace held a press conference, at which he made it clear that the march would be allowed to proceed only when its leaders had a federal court order authorizing it, and not a moment before. He was not budging from his stance of rigid opposition, at least not in public.

On Sunday, Nicholas Katzenbach brought to the White House news that a draft incorporating the agreements of Saturday's session with Dirksen was virtually complete, and would be ready for submission to Congress by Monday, in keeping with the president's earlier pledge. Johnson met that evening with the leadership of the House and Senate to talk about how the bill could best be presented to Congress. After considerable discussion, House Speaker John McCormack of Massachusetts insisted that Mr. Johnson present it himself to a joint session Monday night, and the others agreed.

During the day Sunday the nation's cities were again alive with large and noisy demonstrations calling for action to protect the marchers and to implement their objectives of regaining the right to vote. Over fifteen thousand people rallied across the street from the White House in Lafayette Park—and the round-the-clock picketing on the sidewalk continued. Twice as many marched in New York, half of them up Fifth Avenue and the rest in Harlem; and San Francisco hosted two sizable marches, the second a long, serpentine torchlight parade. Ottawa, Canada; Norfolk, Virginia; Binghamton, New York; Bakersfield, California; even St. Augustine, Florida, had demonstrations.

The largest gathering was in Boston, where the Arlington Street Church, in which abolitionist preachers had thundered against slavery over a century before, was more than full for Jim Reeb's official memorial, and twenty-five thousand people stood in silence outside on nearby Boston Common. John A. Sullivan, for whom Reeb had worked at the American Friends Service Committee in Boston's ghetto, deliv-

ered the eulogy: "We are united today," he said, "by grief and hope.
. . . We are united by hope . . . that this death . . . will be a prelude
to victory for the voteless and that it will not be mocked by our
forgetfulness, by our readiness to be justifiably emotional. . . .

"There is now an awakening in our nation," Sullivan concluded.
"Let it be a real awakening and let there be an end to complacent
sleep."

*But nothing makes a man come to grips more
directly with his conscience than the Presidency.
Sitting in that chair involves making decisions that
draw out a man's fundamental commitments. The
burden of his responsibility literally opens up his
soul. No longer can he accept matters as given: no
longer can he write off hopes and needs as
impossible.*

*In that house of decision, the White House, a
man becomes his commitments. He understands
who he really is. He learns what he genuinely wants
to be.*

—Lyndon Baines Johnson, The Vantage Point

THIRTEEN. On Sylvan Street,
the vigil lasted through rain, and cold, and sleeplessness, and most
debilitating of all the boredom that set in once the freedom songs had
been sung for the twentieth time and all the available oratorical varia-
tions on the theme of the vigillers' presence and its significance had
been explored again and again. Wilson Baker cut the rope with a
pocketknife Friday night, complaining that he was just tired of them
singing about it all the time and making such a symbol of the damned
thing, and left them scrambling for pieces of it as souvenirs. But still
he wouldn't let them march. Behind the scenes, Baker had tried at least
once to persuade Mayor Smitherman to let the people travel in small
groups down to the courthouse for a strictly policed thirty-minute
memorial service; but the mayor flatly refused, insisting that the posse
could not be adequately controlled and he would not run the risk of
another outbreak of violence. He rebuffed a similar plea from Leroy
Collins of the Community Relations Service, after Collins thought he
had everything arranged.

Thus by Sunday, while many thousands elsewhere in the nation were
marching to memorialize James Reeb, all the black people of Selma and
their visiting supporters could do was have another mass meeting at the
barricade on Sylvan Street. "You have no permit to march," they were
told by Wilson Baker. "You may, if you wish, go individually or in

groups of two or three to the churches in town to worship, but you shall not march." Then he permitted himself a tight grin: "You men ought to know better than to parade through the streets on the Sabbath. The Good Book says, 'Go to your closet and there pray.' "

Their ranks were swelled somewhat by a contingent of a hundred Unitarian ministers, accompanied by a majority of the denomination's national board, which had been meeting in Boston the day before and recessed in a body to the rectory at the Edmundite Mission House in Selma; Father Ouellet welcomed the group to the city, and the most intensive encounter between these two very different churches was under way. Both groups chuckled over an ancedote of the process attributed to a Unitarian minister from Long Island named Farley Wheelwright, who had found himself bedded down next to a primly veiled nun on the benches of Brown Chapel at the height of the vigil. "Well sister," Wheelwright had said, "I understand we may have to stay here all night in the church. At least it's good to know that you and I are both happily married." The nun smiled demurely and replied, "But knowing the reputation of you Unitarians, I suspect that my marriage is a good deal more secure than yours is."

Monday morning the diehards sleeping in the unpaved street awakened to find the wooden barricades which had blocked their way taken down, and the troopers and policemen mysteriously withdrawn. By nine o'clock SCLC's Hosea Williams was gathering a crowd at First Baptist Church to take advantage of the opening with a march downtown. After another detailed discussion of nonviolent defense techniques and reminders of the potential seriousness of any confrontation, the group lined up and marched out arm in arm in broad ranks that extended almost the whole width of Sylvan Street, with the president of the Unitarian Universalist Church, Dr. Dana McLean Greeley, in the lead beside SCLC's C. T. Vivian.

Sheriff Clark had now arrived and saw them coming, and rushed a group of possemen into the Selma Avenue intersection to halt their advance. A squad of troopers drove up and took positions behind them. As the front rank approached, Clark got into a sound car and its loudspeaker ordered newsmen to clear the area. Then he declared that the Board of Registrars was open downtown and prospective voters could walk down to the courthouse to fill out their applications. But he wasn't going to have any marches, and the demonstrators were given thirty seconds to disperse.

Wilson Baker had been observing the confrontation from his car a little farther up Sylvan Street from the Selma Avenue intersection, and he could see it was time to intervene. But his relations with Clark were by now almost beyond repair, and he had to radio the mayor to come and act as an intermediary. The thirty seconds passed, but Clark still loomed threateningly over the line. Soon Joe Smitherman arrived, and conferred hastily with the sheriff in his car. When he had finished, Baker was ready with a line of police, who moved into the street ahead of the march and between the marchers and the possemen.

Baker approached the line of march, and asked the group to disperse, in accordance with the ban on marches in the city. Dr. Greeley stepped forward to speak for them in reply, and made an eloquent plea for permitting the march to proceed. Baker listened respectfully, but said he had to uphold the constitution of Alabama. Dr. Greeley's retort was immediate: "But what about the Constitution of the United States of America, Mr. Baker?"

As this dialogue was going on, the possemen were being moved out of their place in back of the policemen and farther back behind the troopers into their former, inconspicuous "Stand-by" position; and the obvious demotion rankled them. Why the withdrawal of forces had happened in the first place was not clear; but its result sent the sheriff into a steady, silent burn, agravating the tension between him and the public safety director.

Baker agreed to negotiate with a delegation from the march about working out a way whereby they could go to the courthouse to hold a memorial for James Reeb. With over a hundred Unitarian ministers and many of the church board members in the line backing up Dr. Greeley, the ministers had a special interest in trying to bring off this key act of symbolism while they were yet in the city. Greeley and Dr. Homer Jack of the denomination's national staff were selected for the delegation, along with Williams and Vivian of SCLC, and Elder William Ezra Greer, who though he was not very well known had been visible and active around the vigil line for most of its duration.

After a lengthy session, Baker agreed to try once more to see if some way could not be found to permit the march. With the help of staff members of the federal Community Relations Service, he began making approaches to Judge Thomas in Mobile. This was a shrewd move, because it was evident by now that the mayor would back off from his strict prohibition on demonstrations only if constrained to do so by some higher authority.

While the negotiations were going on, the rest of the marchers were asked to return to the church for a "strategy session," leaving behind a token vigil force of fifty people. The morale of this particular march had been especially high, perhaps because of the presence of so many Unitarians come to mourn the murder of one of their brethren, or perhaps because of the rousing character of the warm-up speeches they had heard, and the apparent narrowness of their escape from the tender mercies of the possemen. Whatever it was, they returned to Brown Chapel after a spirited round of singing and praying to hear otherwise sober men declaring with conviction that they had seen a trooper moved to tears by their appeals, and another visibly praying with them.

Whether these reactions were actually observed that morning, it would have been strange if all the hundreds of state law enforcement agents who had ringed the two square blocks around the Carver Homes and Brown Chapel for a week straight had been left wholly unmoved by the behavior of the hundreds of men and women who had confronted them day and night. Besides the troopers, the state had sent in Alcoholic Beverage Control Board agents and conservation officers to pull relief duty around the long perimeter. It was a cardinal tenet of Dr. King's nonviolence that a positive, loving attitude should be maintained toward the adversary; and while keeping up such a stance had not been easy during the campaign, and though it had even been momentarily abandoned by a few in a hail of bottles and bricks when the posse mounted its sweep through the project on March seventh— still, the atmosphere throughout the long days of the vigil had been one marked overwhelmingly by the spirit and expression of respect and even love, in the Christian sense of *agape* which Dr. King was so fond of talking about, toward the men across the barricades. One of the most frequently repeated songs on the Sylvan Street battlefront was "I Love Everybody in My Heart," which in the manner of most freedom songs was so simple in its lyrics that practically any name could be substituted for "everybody" to make a new verse. And so the uniformed men who had no choice but to stand for those long hours and then sit in the big blue Fords to doze as best they could were confronted with the sight of what they had been assured was a dangerous and insurrectionary assembly standing up, clapping their hands and stomping their feet in that steady, inexorable rhythm and shouting: "I love all the troopers," "I love all the posse," and even "I love Jim Clark in my *heart*," again and again, with both the melody and the philosophy combining to draw out the last word for emphasis, and sounding about as genuine as anyone could under the circumstances. "You can't make me doubt them," went the next verses, "Cuz I know too much about them, No, you can't make me doubt them in my heart. . . ." Also, faced with a veritable ecumenical council being conducted impromptu right in front of them, the troopers were obliged to listen to themselves being prayed for by one after another distinguished or at least enrobed representative of most all the great religious denominations. Given the southerner's preoccupation with religion, these earnest, often enough eloquent and unending petitions could not all have passed unnoticed.

There was little fraternization between the parties, given the rigidity of role the troopers and police were forced into and the equally genuine fear that had been instilled into the vigillers of what would happen to them if they crossed the barrier. But if the vigil had gone on much longer, it is likely that there would have been. One participant put down in verse his report of an encounter with the troopers as he tried to enter the project area, and it suggested that the witness was having some effect:

> The trooper car is, of course, waiting when you get back to your car:
> "Hey you" (flashlight beam, reflections off uniform brass, neck hairs fluorescent in headlight glare) "where you think you're goin?"

To freedom. To heaven (to hell?) To anywhere. To—

"To the church." (clear your throat quickly so your voice doesn't falter) Yes, of course: to the church.

"Lessee your identification and the registration on that car. . . ."

Pull out the wallet and start the charade, let them examine your driver's license etc., with extreme and exaggerated care, of course they have to get on the radio and check the car out through Birmingham, outside agitators are an unsavory lot and it's more than likely stolen;

But while you're standing there, looking carefully off down the nighttime street, notice the other trooper looking at you intently, *intently:*

"Where you from, William? (listen to the question: something rings in it besides antagonism, there is more than one query in the words; look up at him quick, how can you answer without exposing the concealed questions?)

"Well (you want to say give me thirty seconds to think over my answer(s) at least)—"

"What," interrupts the other trooper, "does that button mean?" and he points:

GROW—white letters on black background, Get Rid Of Wallace, what else, but you won't say that, you don't need to get beat up tonight, and besides you know that he asked it because he too heard some (not all) of the other questions in his partner's voice; so you have to answer him satisfactorily without letting it tear down the little bridge the other has extended.

"Well GROW refers to the philosophy of the whole movement . . ." etc., etc., and so on, it's hard, but the other trooper is still peering so the bridge is still there.

"MmmmmmHhmmmmmm," the questioner says; he of course knows what it really means, but your straightfaced baloney throws him temporarily off balance. Silence in heaven (and earth) for the space of about half an hour (minute). Then—

"Where'd you say you were from?" Listen again:

Reach out:

"Well, I was born" (yes I hear you) "and then we went" (can you

give me your hand?) "and after that we" (just for a moment)
"when I finished college—"
He nods a little and you know you heard; so did the other, and
his guard is up:
—"Why don't you get a good job back where you came from, and
quit messin' around down here?"
It was too good to last. . . . Just try to retreat with dignity and
without burning the bridge's remains. . . .
"Yeah, there's other ways to settle this than in the street," the
other, his guard also now up, joins in. . . .
There isn't any answer for this, so just look down at the muddy
street.
He hands you back your license and finishes up the charade:
"Tell your boss to get some identification on this car, and we're
not letting anybody into the church. Only the sheriff could
do that."

There were reports from informed whites in Selma by the weekend
that the morale of the officers on the line was getting so low that their
officers had asked the governor to replace them with National Guardsmen. No doubt part of this malaise was due to the crazy, uncomfortable
conditions the men had been subjected to for most of a week on
practically no notice. But such a decline in morale was also what was
supposed to occur, according to the theory, when an oppressor's police
force is confronted by the cumulative psychological and spiritual force
of a sustained, genuinely nonviolent movement.

A similarly impressive spirit and welcome had been shown by the
black community of Selma to the horde of outside visitors which
coursed through its mainly dirt streets in these days. Most of the local
blacks knew little of white people except what they had learned in the
context of the Black Belt's segregated, crazy-quilt class structure; and
they were thus amazed and astonished to see first scores and then
hundreds of men and women of the same shade now coming to stand
with them as they attempted to make a dent in this system. For years
afterward they would speak of these pilgrims' coming as perhaps the
most moving aspect of the most vivid period of their lives. And they
responded with a rush of hospitality, treating practically every obscure

clergyman with a bedroll as if he were a visiting church primate. Soon enough the benches and floors of Brown Chapel and First Baptist were littered each night after the mass meetings with the tired, uncomfortable bodies of people, usually the latest arrivals, trying to sleep as best they could. But this was because almost every house with a spare bed —and many without—had taken in as many of the hundreds of visitors as they could hold. At Good Samaritan Hospital a wing that had been recently closed was hastily reopened and the floor carpeted with old mattresses; under the attentions of Father Ouellet and Sister Michael Ann, Good Samaritan's administrator, it became a hostel for religious people, particularly the steady stream of Catholic nuns and priests. In their humble houses the hosts plied their guests with the best meals they could afford, and many a stranger developed a lingering taste for collard greens and sweet potato pie in the course of a short stay. At the churches, a corps of intent, perspiring women labored all day and into each night frying heaps of chicken and baking large oblong pans full of warm, crumbly corn bread, for once cooking meals for white folks with all the pride anyone could ask for.

This spirit carried over into the mass meetings, and was perhaps best expressed in them. Unitarian President Dana Greeley recalled later that his church had just issued a new hymnbook in which the amens had been deleted from the songs, the better to please the increasingly agnostic bulk of the church's clergy and congregations; and he watched with a sense of irony on Sunday evening while a hundred or more of these same ministers came into their first mass meeting and within a half hour were singing and shouting with the rest, swept up completely into the wholly evangelical and even fundamentalist rhetoric of the service, singing out those eschewed amens and unheard of hallelujahs with a gusto that would have turned them pink in their home pulpits.

The northerners were also treated to a concentrated and mind-expanding crash course on the meaning of racism, religion and the movement by a battery of eloquent civil rights preachers. If Dr. King spoke mainly in uplifting generalities, the members of his executive staff were not reluctant to be more concrete with their hearers; and none was more effective and trenchant than James Bevel. He recalled one night how he had once been enrolled briefly at a black seminary, where the level of discussion was shown by the continuing attention given to such problems as whether the Good Samaritan was black. "On the negative side of the argument," Bevel recounted, "there was the fact that the Samaritan had given the wounded man wine. If he had been a Negro he would have killed the wine before he got there. On the positive side of the argument was the fact that he left the man at the inn and said he'd pay later." It didn't take him long, Bevel said, to get himself tossed out of the place and back into the movement.

He also spoke more seriously and very bluntly about the white churches, calling them

> . . . completely ineffectual. They don't have enough preachers who believe strongly enough in what they say to live it. You white ministers are all thinking of going home to preach on Sunday. Now you just stay here. It will do your congregations much more good for you to be absent. You just let them sit there and let them think about what's happening here. You've been preaching to them all these years, and they go home, eat a great big dinner, watch TV and go to sleep. So you just stay here and listen, and leave them home alone thinking. When most preachers preach, the people go home, eat a big dinner, and then go to sleep. If we can communicate, people will stay awake and start moving. It involves more than taking a stand. Everyone is taking a stand these days, and the result is there is a lot of standing around. . . .
>
> I believe in the resurrection. I believe in it thoroughly, but I notice that in the New Testament it comes *after* the crucifixion. Will you all notice that? The only way we can get to the southern white people is by bringing out their hatred. If it requires letting them beat us, then we'll have to let them beat us, because this is the only way left open to us to communicate with them. The word on injustice must become flesh. We must be willing to die for hate-filled white children. . . . When somebody asks us "What do you want?" we should answer "What have you got?" They complain about our stealing. The average income of Negroes in Selma is eighteen hundred dollars a year. If I only made eighteen hundred dollars a year I'd steal too. When my back is hanging out

and I know that Rockefeller has six hundred suits, I know that *somebody stole my suit.*

His was a militance firmly rooted in nonviolence, however; he concluded by insisting that "If love can be constructive in Dallas County where Clark is sheriff, it will work anywhere."

Preaching like this left many of the ministers overwhelmed. "The church is too little and too late," confessed an Episcopal bishop to Bevel after one mass meeting. "But you are going to renew us. The white people are enslaved. We ought simply to be quiet."

But there was more to the meetings than just their effect on the visitors. They also moved black Selma as it had not been moved before: as the vigil went on, new faces began appearing in the line and even in the churches, albeit usually near the back door, faces of men seen normally standing silent along the curb outside the black cafes of Washington Street, men who spent their time drunk, fighting, or waiting to get out of jail. Few of them had ever been here before, even fewer had marched or taken any other part in the campaign. They lived day-to-day and hour-to-hour on Selma's block-long Skid Row, despised by respectable black people and probably by themselves as well. But now the spectacle and the force of what was happening on Sylvan Street had reached even some of them; and becoming again momentarily something they had not been in most cases for a long time, some actually came, and stood in line, and reached out bony hands from their places near the rear doors of the church to drop a creased dollar bill into the bulging collection plate as it passed.

Once the peak of the movement had passed and the glory began to fade, these men returned to their posts along the downtown streets where they were suffered to stand, or slipped back into their patterns of petty crime and self-destructive violence. They were never really noticed by the crowds, and had no visible impact on the vigil or the mass meetings; but their presence, however brief, was a sign of the magnitude of what was happening in their city in these few days.

A memorial meeting for James Reeb was held Monday afternoon, March fifteenth, in Brown Chapel, apparently in lieu of the long-

awaited gathering at the courthouse, and Dr. King was scheduled to
deliver the main eulogy. But as was typically the case, Dr. King was late,
much later than usual, almost three hours late. And the crowd which
was packed into the church, hanging over the balconies, jammed up
in all the aisles and crouched on the floor around the platform amid
the tangle of the newspeople's wiring, eventually got tired and even a
little hostile. They had sung all the songs, read all the appropriate
scriptures, and amen-ed all the long sequence of prayers and prelimi-
nary exhortations; but still Dr. King did not appear.

Finally, of course, he arrived, just in time and in good voice. He
spoke of a lesson the movement had learned from an experience he had
during the climactic days of the bus boycott in Montgomery n 1956:
the people there had organized an informal network of car pools to help
people get back and forth without having to walk or give in and ride
the segregated buses. The city officials filed suit against them for doing
this, charging they were operating a transport system without proper
authorization; and when they got Dr. King and the other leaders in
their courtroom, he could see that the judge was not on the movement's side and the city was sure to get an injunction which would stop
the car pools and, probably, kill the boycott. King described how he sat
in the courtroom filled with a gloom approaching despair, not knowing
what to do: "The clock said it was noon," was the way he put it, "but
it was midnight in my soul." The court proceedings droned on with Dr.
King about to abandon hope. Then suddenly a message was handed to
him: it said that the United States Supreme Court had just ruled that
bus segregation was unconstitutional, and that henceforth bus passengers of color in the Cradle of the Confederacy could ride public transportation seated where they wished. The high court had unexpectedly
saved the boycott and given it victory, just as the forces of resistance
seemed too strong to hold back.

The lesson was that even in the face of murder and confinement in
the close quarters of the project area, the movement was on the verge
of a great victory and must not falter or allow its momentum to flag.
The speech lifted the people's spirits again; but even more dramatic
was the announcement that came a few moments later, as if pro-
grammed to validate the prophetic character of Dr. King's sermon:
Ralph Abernathy stepped forward and said that even as they sat there

the forces of salvation had been working for them: he had just received word that federal Judge Daniel Thomas had ordered the city to permit them to conduct their memorial procession to the courthouse, and it would begin momentarily.

Grown men wept at the wonder of the moment, and soon the forces had been gathered into a mighty throng which made its way down Sylvan Street and around onto Alabama Avenue, through the heart of the city to where the green stones of the courthouse waited like the trembling walls of Jericho as the trumpets' final blast died away.

The judge had been careful to discuss the order with both the mayor and the sheriff after he had been approached about it; and Clark and Baker had announced it at separate news conferences. The order stated that the march would proceed in a column of twos; but the crowd at the church rejected this limitation, first demanding to march five abreast or not at all, then accepting Dr. Greeley's compromise suggestion of three. This was conveyed quickly to the judge, who again contacted the important white officials to get their concurrence before amending the order.

So three abreast they came, in a line that stretched ultimately all the way from the church entrance to the Alabama Avenue entrance to the courthouse. As Dr. King walked up the steps accompanied by Walter Reuther, Archbishop Iakovos of the Greek Orthodox church and several other notables, Jim Clark stepped to the glass doors from the inside and made a loud business of locking them and turning off the outside light. But he could not keep a dozen or more employees and possemen inside from peeking shamelessly through the windows in his office at the gathering that had been the focus of so much struggle and tension.

And after a week in the street, after what seemed like a crossing of their own little Red Sea, the final great memorial service for the Rev. James Reeb lasted no more than twenty minutes, and consisted—as per the federal court's prescription—of a prayer, a brief homily by Dr. King, and a single chorus of "We Shall Overcome." Most of those who took part could not see or hear what went on at the front of the line; it took most of an hour for the tail end of the march just to get within sight of the courthouse, and by that time the ceremonies had long since concluded.

But the people walked back to their still-blockaded compound feeling an immense sense of accomplishment. The barricades at the corner of Sylvan Street and Selma Avenue at last had come down to stay (although the street was still blocked farther up by trooper cars); and the line of troopers, conservation officers and liquor agents grew more porous by the hour after the march had finally gotten through. Besides, they had more to look forward to before their night would be over: at 9:00 P.M. the president of the United States would speak to Congress and the nation about them, and about the voting bill they had brought into being.

Lyndon Johnson hunched a little over the big podium in the packed House as he reached his peroration. It had been forty minutes since he had begun by telling them that "At times history and fate meet in a single time in a single place to shape a turning point in man's unending search for freedom. So it was at Lexington and Concord. So it was a century ago at Appomattox. So it was last week in Selma, Alabama." The speech had been well-received despite its length, interrupted every few lines by applause and twice with standing ovations. Now he chose to end on a personal note, with a reminiscence that stood out from the rest of an already memorable text:

> My first job after college was as a teacher in Cotulla, Texas, in a small Mexican-American school. Few of them could speak English, and I couldn't speak much Spanish. My students were poor and they often came to class without breakfast, hungry. They knew even in their youth the pain of prejudice. They never seemed to know why people disliked them. But they knew it was so, because I saw it in their eyes. I often walked home late in the afternoon, after the classes were finished, wishing there was more that I could do. But all I knew was to teach them the little that I knew, hoping that it might help them against the hardships that lay ahead.

The president had already brought old and cynical politicians in the audience to the verge of tears with his ringing declaration earlier that "We shall overcome" the legacy of bigotry and injustice that lay behind the denial of voting rights to black Americans. He had spoken, with an eloquence only intensified by his southwestern twang, about the unquestionable constitutional responsibility of the Congress to assure the black people of his region the right to vote.

Now he had them hushed again, hanging on every syllable as he reached back into his own past and forward and up into the limits of his aspirations, to speak of both with a candor, a force and an obvious integrity that he would never be able to recapture:

"Somehow you never forget what poverty and hatred can do when you see its scars on the hopeful face of a young child.

"I never thought then, in 1928, that I would be standing here in 1965. It never occurred to me in my fondest dreams that I might have the chance to help the sons and daughters of those students and to help people like them all over this country.

"But now I have that chance—I'll let you in on a little secret—I mean to use it. And I hope that you will use it with me."

Earlier he had invoked the shades of fallen American fighting men, those southerners and northerners alike "who carried Old Glory to far corners of the world and brought it back without a stain on it . . . ," particularly those now so engaged in Vietnam; but that was rhetoric. Now he was speaking what he wanted to be the truth:

> This is the richest and most powerful country which ever occupied the globe. The might of past empires is little compared to ours. But I do not want to be the President who built empires, or sought grandeur, or extended domain. I want to be the President who helped to feed the hungry and to prepare them to be taxpayers instead of taxeaters. I want to be the President who helped the poor to find their own way and who protected the right of every citizen to vote in every election. I want to be the President who helped to end hatred among his fellow men and who promoted love among the people of all races and all regions and all parties. I want to be the President who helped to end war among the brothers of this earth.

No better elegy has been written for this President and his administration; in later years he recalled it as his favorite speech, and insisted he had written it, though there were speechwriters equally ready to claim credit for its composition. There were few in the chamber or in the vast audience watching him that night who could doubt the depth of the sincerity that had just been exposed, just as within little more than a year there would be even fewer who could remember that he ever had, or ever could have spoken in such a plain and moving way.

His ending, after this peak, was almost anticlimactic:

"Above the pyramid on the great seal of the United States it says —in Latin—'God has favored our undertaking.'

"God will not favor everything that we do. It is rather our duty to divine his will. But I cannot help believing that He truly understands and that He really favors the undertaking that we begin here tonight."

*If the perverts from Washington, Boston, and other
pink punks from the North would spend their time
cleaning up the uncivil riots, murders, stabbings,
prostitution and mongrelization in their own back
yard and leave the Selma situation to the city of
Selma under the able protection of local law
enforcement, our Republic will remain free much
longer.*

> —Norman L. Hall, letter to the
> Selma Times-Journal,
> *March 18, 1965*

*I wonder what you would do President Johnson if
your daughters were insulted and possibly raped by
these dear people of yours. But you see Mr. Johnson
you don't have to worry, because you have Secret
Service men, that my taxes pay for, to guard them.
But Mr. Johnson what is going to happen to my
three little girls. The Negro has already said that
was the biggest thing they were after.*

> —Mrs. Shirley Farris, letter to the
> Selma Times-Journal,
> *March 15, 1965*

FOURTEEN. There was at least

one small segment of the president's vast audience that was not as
moved by his speech Monday night as were most others: this was a
group of several hundred college students and young people in Montgomery, who listened to the address crowded around tiny hand-held
transistor radios. They were standing in a dark street about a quarter-
mile from the floodlit, alabaster-white capitol building, over which the
stars and bars and the Alabama state flag, which was the state's Confederate battle standard, fluttered in the quiet nighttime breezes; they
were trapped there, completely surrounded by a line of city and state
police. The group had tried to march on the capitol from the campus
of Alabama State College, an all-black school, late that afternoon and
had been stopped and held in their present location by police ever
since. Leading them was SNCC's James Forman, who along with

several other SNCC people had been conducting demonstrations in the city for a week. Forman was no fan of Lyndon Johnson, and he considered the proposed voting rights bill primarily a sophisticated device for coopting and dissipating protest, and concluded that the president's use of the words "We shall overcome" was simply a "tinkling empty symbol" that had robbed the song of its integrity.

The demonstrations in Montgomery had been marked by conflict, between SNCC and SCLC staff workers and between SNCC and most local black preachers. SCLC wanted to keep control of the actions mounted in support of the Selma campaign, particularly those during these days when the voting bill was being drafted and Judge Frank Johnson was deliberating over whether to permit the march to proceed. The local black ministers in Montgomery were almost unanimously staying away from both organizations and the campaign. This attitude had had much to do with the failure of Dr. King's effort to mount a large march on the registrars' office there in February. Both SNCC and SCLC had great difficulty in finding a pastor in the city willing to allow mass meetings to be held in his church; and the march this Monday had proceeded over the vigorous opposition of the Alabama State administration.

Finally the police let the group slip away in the darkness, but Forman was determined not to submit to their intimidation. The following day he led another march, this one of a thousand people, including several hundred northern whites on their way to Selma, back toward the capitol. As they approached the capitol, Forman and a small group of other workers went ahead of the line to reconnoiter. City police closed in behind his party, cutting them off from the main contingent, and then suddenly they were attacked by the Montgomery County sheriff's posse. The possemen were mounted and led by Sheriff Mac Sim Butler, wearing a cowboy hat and swinging a cane by the tip end. Other deputies carried ropes and whips. Forman's squad first froze where they were, then scattered as the horses came thundering into them. Forman was a particular target, and he ran to a telephone pole and threw his arms around it, as if it could shelter him. A possemen rode up and smacked the pole sharply with a club just above Forman's head; the shock sent him fleeing again for cover. A little later, the city police dispersed the main body with similar tactics.

Several people were injured in the melee, and the demonstrators fled back into the black neighborhoods in a panic that soon turned to rage. Dr. King, who had spent a good deal of his time in the capital during the week trying to patch up relations between the two civil rights organizations and reopen communications with the local black clergy, hurried to Montgomery to try to contain the emotions that had been riled up by the posse's charge. By nightfall the reaction to the assault had cracked the icy disdain of the black preachers, and after King and Forman met with several of the most prominent, they had no trouble finding a church for a mass meeting that night.

At the rally, Forman was still livid with anger as he walked to the pulpit, and his was an anger that was rapidly curdling into hate. He later wrote that this was the day when he lost all remaining desire to participate in nonviolent demonstrations; and his speech to the large mass meeting reflected this sentiment. At one point he shouted that "If we can't sit at the table of democracy, we'll knock the fucking legs off!" He realized at once that profanity in church was a major breach of etiquette, especially because there were several black-veiled nuns in the congregation. He apologized for the remark and added in qualification, "But before we tear it completely down they will move to build a better one rather than see it destroyed." Still, he went on to challenge the intentions of the president: "Did President Johnson mean what he said?" He insisted that they should not settle for any more promises and argued that they should "tie up every street and bus and commit every act of civil disobedience ever seen—because I'm tired of seeing people get hit."

Dr. King, sensing that Forman's rage was shared by many others present, preached with unusual militance as well. "I'm not satisfied as long as the Negro sees life as a long and empty corridor with a 'no exit' sign at the end. The cup of endurance has run over." He insisted that "we cannot stand idly by and allow this to happen. We must get together a peaceful and orderly march on the courthouse in Montgomery." There they would confront the high-riding Sheriff Butler directly with his brutality, and given the capital city's carefully cultivated moderate image, it was fair to think they could get some solid results.

Almost two thousand people surged into the street behind Dr. King, Forman and Ralph Abernathy Wednesday afternoon, March seventeenth, despite a steady rain. Once at the Montgomery County Court-house the march leaders were taken inside for a conference with the sheriff, city officials and a delegation of influential Montgomery blacks. The conference lasted more than three hours, while the vast majority of the large crowd stood faithfully outside in the downpour; and when it was finished the leaders emerged with Sheriff Butler at their side. Butler offered the people a public apology for the violence of his possemen. The black leaders had also reached agreement with the city about procedures to regularize demonstrations and guarantee protesters freedom from bureaucratic harassment while seeking permits.

This agreement did not halt demonstrations and arrests in the city; later that same night over a hundred people were arrested trying to picket the capitol and City Hall. But the crowd outside the courthouse took the apology and agreement as victories. Moreover, they had started celebrating even before the meeting inside had concluded, because while they waited other, more important news had reached them: Judge Johnson had issued an order permitting the march from Selma to Montgomery and directing the state and federal governments to protect it.

Judge Johnson had held hearings on the march leaders' petition for almost a week, and during the proceedings had heard from all the major figures involved in the bridge confrontations on March seventh and ninth. President Johnson had the Justice Department intervene in the case on behalf of the marchers, and it was their draft of a march proposal that the judge incorporated into his decision. Attorneys for Sheriff Clark had tried to have Dr. King cited for contempt of court for marching on March ninth; but after long, probing questioning by the judge, in which Dr. King admitted that he had never expected or planned to get to Montgomery on that occasion, and intimated strongly that he had acted according to an agreement to that effect worked out by Leroy Collins, the judge declared him innocent of contempt charges.

Col. Al Lingo and other state authorities mounted Johnson's witness stand to insist they had ordered that only the bare minimum necessary force be used in breaking up the march on March seventh, and to allege that the columns of marchers had resisted them. Troopers and posse-men solemnly swore that if the march had been permitted to pass there would have been a massacre when the waiting white mob got hold of them, a bloodbath they would have been powerless to prevent.

Judge Johnson was not much impressed. In his order he declared that the evidence was overwhelming that troopers and possemen had been unnecessarily brutal, and that particularly in Sheriff Clark's case their violence was motivated by the intent to deny the blacks their right to vote and their right to peaceful protest. The right to march and protest was not unlimited in extent, he noted. "It is recognized," he wrote, "that the plan as proposed . . . reaches under the particular circumstances of this case to the outer limits of what is constitutionally allowed. However, the wrongs and injustices inflicted upon these plaintiffs . . . have clearly exceeded—and continue to exceed—the outer limits of what is constitutionally permissible." A balance had to be struck "between the interests of the public to use the highway . . . and the right of American citizens to use it for the purpose . . . of protesting their grievances. In this case the wrongs are enormous. The extent of the right to demonstrate against these wrongs should be determined accordingly." He added, "the law is clear that the right to petition one's government for redress of grievances may be exercised in large groups," and by marching "even along public highways." He directed that the size of the march be reduced to no more than three hundred persons when it reached the section of Highway 80 in Lowndes County which was only two lanes wide. This three hundred person limitation was to continue until the roadway widened again, eighteen miles further east. The primary responsibility for securing the march's passage belonged to the state of Alabama, Johnson said; but if the state defaulted, the federal government was directed to see that it was adequately protected.

When news of Judge Johnson's decision reached Selma, action was in a lull. There had been two demonstration attempts on Tuesday, March sixteenth, one stopped by Sheriff Clark and the later one by Wilson Baker. The two lawmen had come to blows the night before, at a midnight showdown in Clark's county jail. The sheriff, still smarting at the treatment of his men at that morning's Sylvan Street confrontation, swore that if Baker and his police tried to interfere with them again the sheriff would arrest the public safety director. Baker, his patience lost in a haze of exhaustion and anger of his own, shouted that if Clark so much as laid a hand on him, Baker would kill him. With that the sheriff lunged and the public safety director readied his fists; only the intervention of Mayor Smitherman between them prevented a brawl. The mayor was terrified by the violence before him; he pushed the two apart and begged them to calm down and try to deal with each other rationally. There was no fight, and no arrests of one set of lawmen by the other; but thereafter communication between the two chiefs was conducted through intermediaries.

Thus when Clark told the first group of marchers Tuesday afternoon that they would go past him to the courthouse "only over my dead body," he was probably more serious than many of those standing before him knew. And perhaps for the same reason, when Baker blocked the second attempt that afternoon, he was unusually testy with them. He told them it was unsafe to go downtown; they demanded to know why. "It is unsafe to go to the Dallas County Courthouse because of the tensions and resentment from long, drawnout demonstrations," he answered. The questioners persisted, adding that they also wanted to protest the earlier attack by the mounted possemen in Montgomery. Baker growled that he and the city had nothing to do with what went on in Montgomery, and they should go over there if they wanted to complain about it. Then he added sarcastically, "This is your show. Go ahead and make your statements and then return to the church. You claim to be men of God, and if you are you will stop this foolishness." He turned to the cameramen and photographers crowded around them. "Everybody who wants to get in on this show, get them in on it now."

Eventually that march, like so many others, turned back to the church. But instead of going in, most of the marchers sat down on the wide steps of Brown Chapel, to bask in the unseasonably warm sunshine of the afternoon. The mood was clearly one of transition and waiting; the vigil was over, and there had been no word from Montgomery about whether or when the march would be permitted to begin, so people began to relax while they waited. Sylvan Street seemed a safe haven behind its cordon of troopers; a couple of guitars appeared on the steps and what was then called a "hootenanny" soon developed, with everyone singing and clapping to the music. Baker took advantage of the break to reopen Sylvan Street through the project, clearing the remains of the vigil off the gravel and telling the people on the steps that they could not block it anymore.

The lull continued through the rest of the week, even though there were several more demonstrations. Once Judge Johnson's order was issued, the feverish, disorganized preparations for the big march, which was set to depart Sunday the twenty-first, were the main focus of activity. But initially this work engaged mostly the staffs of the two civil rights groups, and there were hundreds more people hanging around wondering what to do. Thus when four hundred people were permitted to march to the courthouse late Wednesday afternoon, the primary reason for the demonstration was not so much some new police outrage as the staff's desire to give their restless legions something to do. Similar aims were behind a more adventurous picket line of forty whites that appeared on the sidewalk outside Mayor Smitherman's home later that afternoon. Baker had not minded the large march downtown much, if only because it had received the direct approval of Judge Thomas, which was probably enough to keep Clark quiet; but this demonstration at the mayor's home, deep inside an all-white neighborhood, was crazy and dangerous. He had a schoolbus rushed to the scene to pick the people up. And once aboard, he told Harry Boyte, the white SCLC organizer who had brought them over, just what he thought of the idea. "This is stupid," he said. "You ought to call your organization the Southern Stupid Leadership Conference."

"Wilson," Boyte replied placidly, "I forgive you."

"Harry, I don't forgive you," said Baker. "Christianity has reached a new low."

As the bus drove through the city, its white passengers began singing a freedom song, in the characteristically thin and unsoulful way of white northerners. Baker's mood softened as he listened to their unmelodic voices, with their uncertain grip on the music. "What a point this movement has come to," he told Boyte. "At least before we had good singing."

On Friday there was another march to the courthouse, again with

Judge Thomas's approval—and another, much larger picket line in front of the mayor's residence. Baker once more went into a fit of pique about "misfits and mentally ill people" who wanted another martyr for purposes of publicity, and the group was piled aboard the schoolbuses and taken to the parking lot behind City Hall. There all but four of the three hundred refused to leave the building when told they could go, and lay down on the floor to emphasize their demand to share some of the privations of black prison life. Baker moved them down to the Negro Community Center a few doors away and let them stay there through the night. The group was satisfied that it was still in custody, but the center's windows were unbarred and unguarded, and there was a continuing trickle of "escapees" slipping back and forth through the alleys to the church. For a time a menacing-looking group of whites assembled across the street from the center, and those keeping watch within were sure they saw ax handles and other weapons being passed out. But they were preserved from any harm by a heavy, providential hailstorm, scattering those outside in a cold torrent of large, hard pellets.

Once this danger was past, the group turned to other activities. Several rabbis were present, and since it was Friday night they were appointed to lead religious services, which again moved even the free-thinking Unitarians in the crowd. Afterward they began a long round of folk dances, which went on until everyone was exhausted. If it was not exactly like typical oppressive black prison conditions, the evening was still a memorable one for the participants. The next morning the "prisoners" marched out of the center in a body and were given a heroes' welcome back on Sylvan Street.

But something other than demonstrations was uppermost in the minds of the crowds around Brown Chapel during these days. This was the selection of the elite group of three hundred that would be permitted to march all the way to Montgomery. Practically all the thousand or so visitors thronged around Sylvan Street hoped, once they learned of the limitation, to share the honor of "going all the way."

The job of choosing the three hundred was delegated to a white SNCC worker from California named Frank Soracco. Soracco was one of the most effective and respected workers in town, and his judgment was widely trusted; so he was the natural one for this delicate task. He took it on with considerable seriousness, too, noting with amusement how he thereupon became suddenly the most popular man in the area, besieged by smiling, importunate pilgrims each pressing on him the importance of their being part of the select three hundred. Soracco's approach, however, consistent with the general thrust of SNCC's organizing perspective, was to reserve most of the slots for local black people, those who had marched and gone to jail and faced the clubs and the horses. Except for a number reserved for Dr. King and his entourage, including spots for visiting notables he wanted to treat to a stretch on the road, only about three dozen places went to outsiders, to the church executives and congressional aides and other assorted big fish splashing around in that tiny pool. Even so, Soracco managed to include representatives from most of the major religious denominations as well as people from thirty of the states.

Soracco and his colleagues were careful to explain to the many who didn't qualify for the three hundred that this by no means meant that they need be excluded from contributing to the march. Everyone could march for three of the five days it was expected to take, and besides there was a raft of support work which needed doing as the time for departure neared and the hectic, often chaotic preparations for it assumed a more recognizable pattern.

Hosea Williams of SCLC was tapped by Dr. King to organize the logistics of the march. He issued a plea at the mass meetings on behalf of the newly formed Logistics Committee, which he said was "in dire need of personnel with formal training and experience in the following categories: portable latrines, water tanks, bath trucks, garbage trucks, medical service, camp housing, parade marshals, campsite security guards, food, office administration, finance, transportation, communications, press, public relations, electricity and the screening of marchers." Staff workers headed up many of these subcommittees, but even more were taken over by people from outside the city: David Duncan and Kenneth Murdock, for instance, two men from Chicago who worked for the interfaith Urban Training Center, between them coordinated medical services, housing, transportation, and communications. Scores of volunteers came forward to help with the thousand details of each subcommittee's task, and the march preparations quickly took on an air of nonprofessional, confused efficiency.

During these same days George Wallace maneuvered frantically to get rid of the responsibility of protecting the march without openly defying the court order. He wrote a letter to the president almost as soon as he received the decision, telling him that the state could not afford the burdensome expense which adequate protection of the marchers would entail. It would take 6,171 men, 489 vehicles and 15 buses, plus supporting units, to do the job, by the governor's calculation, and that was just too much. He suggested the White House dispatch sufficient "civilian forces" to do it.

But once again he was up against an even wilier adversary, one who understood Wallace's ploys probably better than he did himself. The president was determined to see to it that if Wallace wanted him to send federal forces, the governor would have to own up in public to his complete unwillingness to protect the march. Johnson called a press conference, read the letter to the scribbling reporters, and then pointed out loftily that the governor had the entire Alabama National Guard under his command, and that he should call them up to meet the requirements of the court order. Only then did he add solemnly that if the governor did not call up the guard, he would federalize it into action.

There was more than just buck-passing involved in his wish to force Wallace's hand. It was critical to the president's whole approach to civil rights problems in the South that the federal government should never act with even the slightest hint of haste to interpose its presence in force in place of local and state authorities. To do so would only reinforce the southern view of its region as victimized by an authoritarian and arbitrary federal power and thus, Johnson believed, intensify its resistance to other, more visibly benign aspects of his Great Society programs.

Wallace probably realized when the president's response became known that he was caught in Lyndon Johnson's net; so he prepared to do what had to be done in the proper Wallace style. He convened a special joint evening session of the legislature, which he addressed in what came across almost as a bad parody of the president's magnificent speech the Monday before. He called the marchers and their leadership "Communist-trained anarchists trained in street warfare." He said that such outrages as the proposed march were of the stuff that "ripped

Cuba apart, that destroyed Diem in Vietnam, that raped China—that has torn civilization and established institutions of this world into bloody shreds." He blasted Judge Johnson, an old favorite whipping boy, for allowing it.

But thus having made his "stand," he went on to urge all his citizens to meet this apocalyptic invasion, this challenge he had painted as almost tantamount to Armageddon itself, by simply staying home and keeping well away from it. It was a performance typical of the man when confronted with the effects of his segregationist posturing on the people whose fantasies he had fanned to light his way into office. As a U.S. attorney who worked closely on the court actions involved with the march put it, "he defies by day and cooperates by night." The bravado of his speech may even have been covering a genuine doubt that he could in fact count on his troopers to adhere to the court order once the march got into the stretches of thick, swampy undergrowth which lined Highway 80 at several spots in the grimness of Lowndes County.

The legislature, obediently playing its role, immediately passed a resolution calling on the president and the attorney general to persuade Dr. King and his cohorts to call off the march. This was followed up on Friday, March nineteenth, by another resolution endorsing the governor's declaration that the state could not afford to pay the cost of mobilizing the National Guard for the march. Wallace telegraphed the White House to that effect.

The governor's bluster may have mollified his constituents, but it also gave Lyndon Johnson what he had been waiting for: an explicit defaulting on state responsibility for preserving the rights of one segment of its population. Saturday morning he interrupted his weekend at the LBJ ranch to sign an order federalizing almost nineteen hundred men of the Alabama guard's Dixie Division and authorizing the use of two thousand more regular army troops, as well as a hundred each FBI agents and U.S. marshals, to protect the march. He called an impromptu press conference outside the ranch house, standing without a coat in a chilly wind as he read to the press the stern telegram he had just dispatched to Montgomery along with the order. "It is not a welcome duty," the message read, "for the federal government to ever assume a state government's own responsibility for assuring the protection of citizens in the exercise of their constitutional rights." But now there was no alternative, and it was a duty this president would not shirk.

By late Saturday, green army jeeps had begun rolling through Selma, dropping off soldiers carrying rifles tipped with fixed bayonets at street corners along the route to the armory. National guardsmen followed them into town, reporting sullenly to their federalized commanding officers. Among the equipment carried by the regular troops were the facilities and staff for two large field hospitals; by early Sunday morning, both were ready for use.

We lived a lifetime in four days in March.
A journey made to rid the world of hate.
Our faces charred and drawn, limping,
  striving on,
Toward those waiting at St. Jude's gate. . . .
Twas heaven on earth, a dream come true,
A memory to recall when in need or in doubt,
That's why God gave us this view.

We lived a lifetime in four days in March.
The experience was worth more than gold.
The fears, the cheers, the taunting, hating jeers,
Were a part of Christ's journey retold.
To love in return for hate, to forgive in
  your heart
Ever faithful to the cause of liberty,
To offer one's life is a small sacrifice,
Toward the dream of all men being free.

—From "God Gave Us A Glimpse of Heaven,"
  by Mrs. Juanita T. Williams

FIFTEEN.

There were several hundred whites strung out along Highway 80 just east of Selma Sunday afternoon, March twenty-first, on both sides of the road where the two earlier march attempts had been stopped. Many carried Confederate flags, and a scattering of their cars was marked with finger-painted messages: "I hate niggers," "Yankee trash go home," "Rent your priest suit here," and so forth. About 1:15 P.M. the march appeared over the rise of the Pettus Bridge, with the voices of the three thousand plus drifting down ahead of them and two big army helicopters cruising watchfully overhead.

All along the road there were uniformed sentries, standing at ease but still carrying the bayonet-tipped rifles, and the white spectators kept well back of their perimeter. They hurled shouts and occasional curses at the broad ranks as they passed, but did nothing more substantial. Only one young white man visibly lost control; he began shouting almost incoherently, then tried to make a lunge for the line. But two companions grabbed him and held on, while he screamed and screamed hysterically, his face red, his arms flailing. His words could not be made out by the marchers in the din of freedom songs and helicopter noise.

The line stopped at the spot where the march had been broken up on March seventh, and many young people lay down there briefly. Then they walked on, with Dr. King, Mrs. Constance Baker Motley, Ralph Bunche, Rabbi Abraham Heschel and many other notables crowding the front ranks. Before them a group of black marshals walked with linked arms, forcing the huge knot of photographers and reporters to keep moving and thus not overwhelm the leaders with their numbers.

The first day's march was not a long one, seven miles down the highway past the used car lots, the drive-in movie theater, and an Air Force training base, Craig Field, then south off Route 80 up a rise to a cleared field belonging to a black farmer named David Hall. Four large tents had been set up there, and an unreliable gasoline generator produced steady flickers from lights within them, as it was almost dark. The air was cold, and the temperature was rapidly dropping; this moved the leaders to call off a planned mass meeting and ship all but several hundred back to town on a line of buses, cars and a train chartered by the Justice Department to pick up the hundreds more still standing around, in order to keep them out of view of any would-be snipers.

The marchers were tired and hungry. Sack lunches had been passed out to some of them as the march began, but those provisions were skimpy and with the day's exercise and emotion they had soon wanted more. Supper, fresh and hot from the large kitchen at the Green Street Baptist Church in Selma, where a crew of black women worked sixteen hours a day for the five days of the march preparing it, arrived presently, however, carried in a yellow Hertz truck. The menu of pork and beans and spaghetti was delivered in eight large, brand-new, galvanized garbage cans by a crew of twelve whites who had not qualified for the three hundred and who instead made this their fulltime work for the march. The group was spearheaded by Dr. Elwyn Allan Smith, a Presbyterian professor of ecumenics at Pittsburgh Theological Seminary, and was staffed by others of equal erudition, who had laid aside their work in theology, hermeneutics and eschatology for the nonce to concentrate on how to carry more than a ton of food back and forth to the march three times a day, watching for attacks on their conspicuous vehicle along the way, then scrubbing the garbage cans out between each meal, and trying to sleep somewhere in between. Their tasks set a punishing pace, and after two days the group had to divide into three rotating crews of four, two to work and one to sleep, in order to maintain its strength.

The tents at the site with their flapping, open sides were poor insulation against the cold that night, and several large kerosene heaters which were hauled up to blow hot air inside didn't help much either. After dinner the exhausted archers poured into the tents and began flopping down here and there, with television crews standing around flashing their handheld spotlights and filming everything. Then someone realized that this indiscriminate bedding down, men and women together, might provide some segregationist's fevered imagination with just the fuel needed for a fantasy about sex orgies on the route, and the men were hustled up and into a separate tent. (The orgy charges were made anyway, in lurid, though rather unimaginative detail, and staff workers commented on them with irony: "Those white folks must think we are supermen, to be able to march all day in that weather, eat a little pork and beans, make whoopee all night, and then get up the next morning and march all day again.")

Outside, the soldiers camped in details all around a wide perimeter surrounding the camp, and built small fires to keep themselves warm. Many of the federalized National guardsmen, all of whom wore the stars and bars over the left pockets of their shirts, had made their displeasure at their assignment evident by their demeanor during the day. But their commander, Brigadier General Henry V. Graham of Birmingham, had been this route before; he had been in charge of the forces that compelled Governor Wallace to step out of the doorway at the University of Alabama in 1963, and here as there he had made it plain that orders were to be obeyed, and they were. James Bevel also pointed out to some worried marchers that many of the guardsmen were the kind of people who would have been strongly tempted to try a commando raid on the march if they had not been otherwise occupied, and the line was thereby doubly protected by having them in uniform and under discipline.

Frost was on the ground at sunup Monday morning; stiff, cold and still nursing many aches from sleeping on the ground, the marchers were up early in the morning grayness to eat oatmeal and sip coffee dipped out of the shiny garbage cans, then return to the road. A few among the out-of-state contingent had been demoralized by the sleep in the frigid, rough accomodations and returned to Selma; their places were eagerly taken by others. As the line pulled out of camp, a truck came bumping up the road, piled with blankets which were supposed to have arrived the night before, but had been accidentally sent to Boston instead.

Not far from the place where they re-entered Highway 80 the group passed the all-white Southside High School, and was heartened to see the students lined up along the banks of windows facing the road, waving and occasionally cheering. Not much farther down, the four lanes of the route collapsed into two, as the marchers crossed the line into Lowndes County. Here they paused to take a count and make sure only the three hundred remained. Among the whites selected to go on were such people as Sr. Mary Leoline of Kansas City, whose long habit attracted lewd remarks from watching whites like honey draws bees; the Rev. F. Goldthwaite Sherrill, a Yankee Episcopalian from Ipswich, Massachusetts; Jim Letherer from Saginaw, Michigan, who had only one leg and stumped the whole way on crutches, his armpits soon rubbed raw, while the whites he passed hooted and chanted "Left, left, left!"; and Mrs. Nannie Leah Washburn of Atlanta and her son Joe Young, two native-born poor whites from rural Georgia, heirs of the pure southern populist radical strain that hadn't succumbed to racism. Mrs. Washburn and Joe were among the most remarkable members of this unusual group: she was sixty-five and he was deaf and blind, guided down the highway by instinct, a white cane, and the proffered arms of his brethren.

To either side now the trees began to be draped with long, hanging tufts of gray Spanish moss, and they walked into the first of several stretches of thick, gloomy swamp they would have to get through before emerging almost thirty miles east into the more open terrain of Montgomery County.

The helicopters hovered lower over this area, and small army target spotter planes made buzzing passes across the line of march. Green jeeps hurried back and forth along the single open lane, as officers talked on their field radios and kept an eye cocked on the thick tree cover. These swamps were beautiful in an unnerving sort of way, their opaque waters dotted with lily pads and floating algae, dead trees standing with the bark gone and the wood weathered smooth, long strands of gray moss fluttering and their wraithlike reflections shimmering across the surface of the ponds. The whole atmosphere was different there, quieter and serene, but also alive with foreboding. The trees seemed like the stumps of burned crosses, and it was easy to imagine mutilated black bodies, the victims of Dallas County's quiet methods of social control, bloating and rising suddenly out of the mud like something in a low-budget horror movie.

But the singing kept up and in a while they were walking through dry, open country again. They passed a gravel road going off to Benton, a tiny hamlet that had just recently incorporated so that the grizzled white farmers there could begin to deal with the impact of a textile plant that was going to be built nearby by Dan River Mills Company. At Belcher's Service Station along the roadside a group of whites stood watching the line with silent, implacable hostility on their faces. Cattle had replaced cotton as the staple crop here, as it had in most of this region. But there were still many solitary, weathered pine shacks standing forlornly in the wide fields, wisps of smoke coming from their leaning brick chimneys, and people lined up on the broken porches, looking out at the passing spectacle on the highway with quiet, guarded astonishment. Later on the people they passed would feel bolder, and walk out to stand along the fences, waving and cheering; but here they stood watchfully, rags wrapped around the women's heads, the children's tattered clothes dirty, the little ones hanging on to the unpainted wood posts that propped up the roofs—all just watching. The movement had sent staff people into Lowndes County only two weeks before the attack on the first march, and most of the people in the lonesome shanties still knew of civil rights primarily as something talked about on their tiny transistor radios or shown briefly on small television sets. It would be many more months before SNCC's Stokely Carmichael, riding a borrowed horse and wearing a large floppy hat to conceal his face, had traveled enough around the cabins scattered through the county's rural wilderness to set these people irreversibly into motion.

After lunch the march passed through Trickem, which was not a town at all but just an intersection with a name. A small, dilapidated black Baptist church stood at the crossroads, and not far from it a rundown white building with a rusty tin roof that looked abandoned and thus went unnoticed by the leaders in the front line. But this building, with holes in the wall, cardboard over the missing panes of window glass and whole sections of the tin roof gone exposing the beams, was not abandoned; it was the Rolen school, one of almost a score of similar rundown structures the county maintained after its fashion for the 80 per cent black majority of its citizens. Inside it three teachers tried to teach two grades each in the three rooms, and during the winter the students had to wear their coats and boots in class because the wind came right through the walls. The latrine was out in back. A white SCLC worker jumped aboard the large, open truck at the head of the march on which the reporters and cameramen were perched, and pointed out the school to them. Most didn't believe him.

When the march left its campsite that morning, the camp was struck by a special volunteer crew, made up primarily of forty students from San Francisco Theological Seminary, but including as well entertainer Gary Merrill and TV actor Pernell Roberts. Working on a schedule much like that of the beleaguered meal crew, the seminarians spent from after breakfast till sundown taking down the huge tents, shepherding them down the highway to the next site, watching the soldiers go over each site with mine detectors, and putting them up again, grabbing a meal and then returning to Selma, exhausted, to sleep. Monday night's camp was nearer the highway, on the property of a seventy-eight-year-old black widow, Mrs. Rosie Steele. "At first I didn't think it amounted to much," Mrs. Steele explained to a reporter; "I guess I've lived too long and just didn't think things would change— until I heard the president's speech the other night. I knew he was my president too." Afterward, she no longer feared white retaliation. "When they come to me and asked me if they could use my land I felt I couldn't afford to turn them down. If the president can take a stand, I guess I can too. . . . I don't know," she finished, "I almost feel like I might live long enough to vote myself."

It was warmer Monday than it had been the night before, so a short mass meeting was conducted before the group of marchers, their new blisters treated and with neither the energy nor the inclination for the shenanigans that the Alabama legislature would charge them with in a resolution passed the next day, turned in.

Late that night a few of the marchers who were insomniac from tension and excitement gathered around a small campfire to talk and keep warm, and they heard a university chaplain begin preaching a sermon to some others using as a text the label of a vegetable soup can he was holding. When he began expounding incoherently on the theological virtue of okra, they realized that something was wrong, and another marching minister with counseling experience was summoned to escort the chaplain to a tent. His irrationality kept up, however, and by dawn he had been carried to the hospital at the City of St. Jude, a Catholic institution in Montgomery, where he began shouting out hateful curses about Episcopalians, blacks, and just about every group but his own. It was later learned that he had come only because the college organization he served raised transportation money and asked him to go represent them, unaware of how he really felt.

That night also several reporters saw a carload of young, local whites pull up outside the camp, and went to talk to them. The white youths were full of the lurid fantasies that were running wild through their communities; have you heard, they asked the newspeople, about the white woman in the vigil line who was raped so many times by her black comrades that she was taken to a white Selma hospital in a coma and had died shortly thereafter? They had not heard of it, because it never happened. Even an avowed segregationist reporter who later checked it out found conclusive proof of its falsity, but it was believed absolutely by the youths in the car and thousands of others. They were also sure that a hostile Yankee press had covered the story up.

Tuesday morning a light drizzle was falling when the camp awakened, and before they had been long on the march it began to pour heavy, large drops that splattered audibly when they hit the asphalt pavement and soon had everyone drenched. The people were at first disconcerted by the rain, and sheets of clear plastic were hastily passed out to serve as makeshift, barely useful raincoats. But then something about the rain, the very vigor of the shower and the inescapability of getting thoroughly wet, cheered them, and they began to chant "Free-

Dom! Free-Dom! Free-Dom!" with what was almost a kind of jubila-
tion, and an uplift that carried them into the Big Swamp, the longest
stretch of this terrain they had to pass through.

In the Big Swamp, Highway 80 was elevated, and as before the
regular army units sent their demolition teams well ahead of the march
to search each piling under the bridge; then groups of local guardsmen
were assigned to stand sentry duty every few yards. Before this afternoon they had stood facing the march, perhaps just to glare at this
crowd they disliked so much, or possibly offering a sign to anyone
hiding in the undergrowth that they would not be watching if someone
wanted to take a potshot or two. But now they were facing out, their
steel helmets and olive drab ponchos dripping, as their commanders
moved to tighten up their discipline.

The third night's campsite was a depressing place to have to sleep.
It was in a field owned by a black millionaire from Birmingham named
A. G. Gaston, and the dark soil had been turned by the steady rainfall
into an oozing mud that was deeper than practically everyone's shoes.
The tent crew had tried to meet this condition by covering the ground
under the tents with a liberal sprinkling of hay; but soon that had been
trampled under and the mud was as bad as before. Many people could
not stand to try to sleep in it, and two photographers got into a fight
jockeying for the best position to shoot a dozing Unitarian minister,
Richard Leonard of New York, who was sitting unevenly on a patch
of hay and was sure to fall right into the mud as he lost consciousness.
After being startled back into awareness by the noise of the scuffle,
Leonard realized what the two newsmen were after and got up to look
for another spot. Eventually the situation was eased somewhat by the
arrival and distribution of air mattresses, but that night in the mud was
still probably the low point of the trek.

A guardsman spat on a priest near a tent that night, no doubt
thinking that in the darkness he would not be identified. But the
incident was reported and the soldier found himself immediately relieved of his post and reprimanded. Someone planted a large American
flag in the mud outside the tent nearest the road, and the colors
fluttered lazily in the night breeze, giving many who passed it reason
to pause and think.

Wednesday morning dawned bright and warm; in fact, by the time the three hundred mudcaked pilgrims were on the road, it was getting hot. The coats and plastic rain ponchos that had been necessary to that point were quickly shed; but then early in the afternoon it rained again, briefly but hard, soaking almost everyone. The marchers' spirits rose steadily however, because they soon reached the far boundary of Lowndes County, and at that point the road again widened into four divided lanes. With the wider passage came the end of the three hundred limitation, and all through the afternoon cars and buses stopped along the line and discharged new marchers; by the time they passed the huge multi-colored billboard that screamed in giant italics "Help Get the U.S. out of the United Nations" there were thousands of them, exuberant and noisy, carrying banners and placards telling where they were from and why they had come.

When it arrived at the final campsite, the City of St. Jude, the march was like a tide coming in, inevitable and relentless, inundating everything. St. Jude was a large complex of unassuming, dull, red-brick buildings, housing a school, church, and medical center operated by the Catholic church, most of which fronted on Fairview Avenue, Highway 80's route into the city. Bishop Toolen, surprisingly enough, had approved the use of the complex, probably to help the city fathers avoid putting them up on municipal property.

Behind the buildings was a large playing field, on which the tents had been pitched. The shaky organization of the camping operation developed by the now-exhausted Logistics Committee collapsed completely under the pressure of the tens of thousands who poured into the field with and following the arrival of the march. Professor Smith drove in after dark with his garbage can banquet from Selma, but try as he might he couldn't find where the three hundred it was meant for were located among the continually moving and swelling mass, nor could he find any way to get the word out about supper's availability. Finally his crew decided to give their provisions out to whoever came and wanted them; and when they were gone, the men drove back to Selma for the last time in their Hertz truck.

There was to be entertainment at St. Jude's that night provided by a bevy of celebrities who had crowded into town for the last day's march. Montgomery that night had become the place to be and be seen for many important people; and when the time for the evening's show came, the large flatbed truck which was to serve as a stage was jammed with the famous personalities and a few workers who could manage to commandeer a spot for elbow-rubbing purposes. By then the crowd was immense, and pressing forward all the time to get better views, and people near the truck were squeezed until a few passed out. Harry Belafonte, Dick Gregory, Joan Baez, Peter, Paul and Mary and two score others came forward to sing, tell a joke or just say hello, and by the time they were finished it was well past midnight. The field, muddy when the people began crowding into it that afternoon, had been stirred by the forest of feet into a huge quagmire, and it was another muddy resting place for those marchers who could not find someone from the city to take them in.

Mrs. Viola Liuzzo watched the march move out Thursday morning from high in the church tower at St. Jude's. Mrs. Liuzzo was a white mother from Detroit who had spent the past week in Selma, working at the hospitality desk in the Brown Chapel parsonage getting new people settled as they came into town, and using her green Oldsmobile to ferry people back and forth to Montgomery's airport. She had driven over to St. Jude's the night before to join the last leg of the march, and declined an offer of a cot inside one of the buildings, sleeping in her car so a marcher could have the bed. Most of Wednesday evening she had devoted her apparently unfailing energies to helping in the makeshift first aid station with the marchers who were still feeling their blisters, had fainted from the heat and exertion, or were just worn out.

Thursday morning found all the dozens of march support vehicles parked on the playing field behind St. Jude's seemingly permanently set into the mud, and many people got themselves covered with the stuff helping push one car and truck after another out. Special bright-orange jackets had been sent up for distribution among the three hundred who had gone all the way, as a sign of their accomplishment. But with the haphazard record keeping and the mobs of people, an additional supply had to be obtained to satisfy all the people who swore they had marched but hadn't got their jacket. All around the area

marchers were gathering with banners and placards, so that the scene
almost more resembled a parade than a demonstration. It seemed they
had to wait for hours before the line finally began to move, but at length
it did, down Oak Street to Jeff Davis through the black sector of the
city.

Viola Liuzzo had been watching the march with Father Tim Deasy,
a priest on the staff of St. Jude's when she suddenly asked if there was
someplace nearby where she could get a better view. Father Deasy took
her to the tower, from which they could see the line stretching out,
filling the street completely for block after block, with no end yet, only
a leading edge moving ever closer to downtown and the big white
capitol.

Coming back down the winding tower steps she abruptly paused,
and told Father Deasy she had a strong premonition of evil: "Something is going to happen today," she said. "I feel it. Somebody is going
to get killed. You know, it might even be Governor Wallace himself
—he may be killed by one of his own because he has lots of enemies
down here. And they'd lay the blame on the marchers."

Father Deasy tried to reassure her; but once on the ground again she
repeated her premonition to another priest and some nuns who were
waiting. A moment later she said she was going to go pray in the
church. When she returned they went out and joined the still uncoiling
march line.

Not since the great march on Washington in August in 1963 had
so many of the important figures in the civil rights movement been
together on the same platform at a demonstration: besides Dr. King
and John Lewis of SNCC there was Roy Wilkins of the NAACP,
Whitney Young of the National Urban League, A. Philip Randolph,
Ralph Bunche, Bayard Rustin, and even Mrs. Rosa Parks, the former
seamstress whose tired feet and stubbornness had catalyzed the Montgomery Bus Boycott eight years before.

Dr. King, who gave the climactic address, did not neglect to mention
the earlier campaign. "Last Sunday more than eight thousand of us
started on a mighty walk from Selma, Alabama," he began. "We have
walked on meandering highways and rested our bodies on rocky by-

ways." But, he recalled, it was not the first time his people had had to walk a long way for freedom. "I can say as Sister Pollard said . . . who lived in this community during the boycott. One day she was asked while walking if she didn't want a ride, and when she answered 'No,' the person said, 'Well, aren't you tired?' and with ungrammatical profundity she said 'My feets is tired, but my soul is rested.' "

Behind and above him, Governor Wallace sat in his office, occasionally looking out through the drawn blinds over the window at the assembly, which stretched in a solid phalanx all the way across the cleared breadth of Dexter Avenue, back past the Dexter Avenue Baptist Church where Dr. King had held his first pastorate, all the way up to the Confederate Plaza half a dozen blocks down, and beyond it around the corner onto Montgomery Street where the big old hotels were. Despite himself the governor was impressed by the size and vigor of the crowd.

Outside, a line of state troopers stood on the sidewalk behind the speaker's platform, keeping the marchers well away from the relics of the great Rebellion that surrounded the Capitol entrance. There was a blackened old pair of cannon, a statue of Jefferson Davis, and a large bronze star marking the spot where Davis had taken the oath as president of the Confederacy in 1861. Wallace had taken his oath of office on the star, the first Alabama governor to do so, and today he had it covered with a large sheet of plywood.

The city had prepared itself for the march as if it were being led by the shade of General Sherman, flaming torch in hand. Wallace had made a televised address the night before, practically begging his white partisans once more to try to restrain themselves from responding to the march as the overwhelming, dire invasion he had consistently described it to be, and to stay as far away from the march as possible. Then he had declared Thursday a holiday for all female state employees. The *Montgomery Advertiser* published a double-page display advertisement with a long list of endorsements of the stay-away policy. And just in case, there were army troops and guardsmen stationed all over the city.

"They told us we wouldn't get here," Dr. King was saying as the "Amens" and "Preach, sir's" were coming more frequently in response. "And there were those who said that we would get here only over their dead bodies, but all the world together knows that we are here and that we are standing before the forces of power in the state of Alabama, saying, 'We ain't gon' let nobody turn us around. . . .' "

The threat of the free exercise of the ballot by the Negro and white masses alike resulted in the establishing of a segregated society. They segregated southern money from the poor whites; they segregated southern churches from Christianity; they segregated southern minds from honest thinking, and they segregated the Negro from everything. Segregation in Alabama is on its deathbed and the only thing uncertain about it is how costly the segregationists and Wallace will make the funeral. . . . Confrontation of good and evil compressed in the tiny community of Selma generated the massive power to turn the whole nation to a new course.

"The road ahead is not altogether a smooth one," he said as he prepared to close. "There are no broad highways to lead us easily and inevitably to quick solutions. . . . We are still in for a season of suffering. . . . How Long?" Here the rhythmic repetition around which his best perorations were built began:

"How long will it take? I come to say to you this afternoon however difficult the moment, however frustrating the hour, it will not be long, because truth pressed to earth will rise again.

"How Long? Not long, because no lie can live forever." The crowd knew its part, and the rising shouts followed the rise of his inflection in each new line like parts in a fugue.

"How long? Not long, because you reap what you sow.

"How long? Not long, because the arm of the moral universe is long but it tends toward justice.

"How long?" This was the climax: "Not long, because mine eyes have seen the glory of the coming of the Lord; tramping out the vintage where the grapes of wrath are stored. He has loosed the fateful lightning of his terrible swift sword. *His truth is marching on!*" The ovation went on for minutes.

A delegation of twenty people including Dr. King was selected by voice vote of the assembly to deliver a petition for full voting rights to the governor once the march had concluded. But of course the troopers kept them from going inside the capitol, and when they persisted Wallace's executive secretary came out and took it from them. The delegation agreed to try again later, and then broke up, its members joining the thousands who were moving back to the bus depot, the airport, the car pools headed for Selma, any way they could find to get out of the city before nightfall, unless they lived there. The army troops were out of sight within a few hours.

Mrs. Viola Liuzzo reclaimed her car once she got back to St. Jude's and immediately assembled a load of passengers to take back to Dallas County. She had not been following the civil rights worker's rules of the road very carefully over the past several days: she drove fast along the highway, and had stopped for gas at the white-owned stations in Lowndes County; with its Michigan plates, her green Olds had become quite conspicuous. And on the way back Thursday evening, with the troops gone, she was followed by a carload of whites, which pulled so close as to graze her back bumper several times before pulling past and racing off. Mrs. Liuzzo commented to Leroy Moton, a skinny, bespectacled black teenager who had been helping her drive, that she thought these local white folks were crazy.

As soon as their passengers were dropped off at Brown Chapel, Mrs. Liuzzo and Moton headed back toward Montgomery for a second load. On the way out of town they stopped at a traffic light, and another car pulled alongside. In it were four Ku Klux Klansmen from Bessemer, a steel town near Birmingham, among them Collie Leroy Wilkins and Gary Rowe, who were sitting in the back seat; Rowe was an FBI informer. Wilkins looked out the window and saw Mrs. Liuzzo and her black companion stopped beside them. "Look there, baby brother," Wilkins said to Rowe, "I'll be damned. Look there."

Eugene Thomas, who was driving, looked over and then said: "Let's get them." When the light changed they took up the chase, and the Oldsmobile tried to outrun them, careening through the darkened swamps of Lowndes County at almost a hundred miles an hour. Rowe later said he tried repeatedly to persuade the others to give up the pursuit, but Thomas insisted "We're not going to give up, we're going to take that car."

The Klansmen began to close in on their prey. Thomas pulled out a pistol and handed it to Wilkins, and told the others to draw their own weapons. Rowe tried once more to get them to abandon the game; but Thomas said implacably, "I done told you, baby brother, you're in the big time now." A moment later Wilkins said, "Give it some gas," and they pulled alongside the Oldsmobile.

Wilkins put his arm out the window, and as he drew even with the front windshield of the Oldsmobile, Mrs. Liuzzo turned and looked straight at him. He fired twice through the glass. The fourth Klansman, William Eaton, emptied his pistol at the car; Rowe only pretended to fire his. Then their car sped on away.

Mrs. Liuzzo fell against the wheel, dead instantly from two bullets in the head, spewing blood all over Moton, who grabbed the steering wheel and hit the brakes. The car swerved to the right anyway, crashing through a ditch and coming to rest against the embankment. Moton turned off the lights and ignition and tried to rouse Mrs. Liuzzo. Just as he realized she was dead, he saw the other car coming back and pulling up again beside the Oldsmobile. Splattered with her blood, he flopped down and played dead, convincingly. The Klansmen shined a light into the car momentarily, then drove away and headed back north toward home. Moton honked the horn at passing cars he thought were carrying other marchers; when that drew no response, he got out of the car and began running in a blind panic down the highway toward Montgomery. He ran a long distance before he finally spotted a truck he recognized coming toward him. He ran out into the road, screaming and waving, and it stopped. He climbed in, shouted a few hysterical sentences about what had happened, and passed out cold.

Within twenty-four hours President Johnson was on television, personally announcing the arrest of the four assailants, and vowing to exterminate the Ku Klux Klan. He called the Klan a "hooded society of bigots," warned members to get out "before it is too late," and pledged that "We will not be intimidated by the terrorists of the Ku Klux Klan any more than by the terrorists of the Viet Cong."

He called on the House Committee on Un-American Activities to begin an investigation of the organization immediately. He promised to propose legislation that would control these "enemies of justice who for decades have used the rope and the gun and the tar and the feathers."

SIXTEEN.

For James Bevel, the march to Montgomery was not the end of the SCLC Alabama Project, but only the beginning. The scenario in the memorandum which the local press had "exposed" in February as Dr. King's "master plan" had been aimed at producing large demonstrations in Montgomery in May of 1965 as the culmination of the campaign, demonstrations that would involve thousands of arrests. The disruption caused by the marches was expected to bring the processes of state government to a near-halt and, it was hoped, the governor to terms with the organization's demands.

This scenario had been followed only very loosely, of course, and it had included no provision at all for a fifty-mile hike from Selma. But once the march was completed Bevel returned to this original plan. In fact, in light of the momentum developed by the march, he decided its sights should be raised: the black citizens of Alabama should not settle for simply a federal voting law, he felt, but should demand the impeachment of Governor Wallace, the resignation of both houses of the state legislature, and a new, federally supervised election for all state offices.

To reinforce the impact of the mass arrests in Montgomery, Bevel wanted SCLC to institute a nationwide boycott of the state's industries and products, to add economic chaos to political disruption as the campaign heated up. He went to work lobbying for this strategy as soon as the march was finished, and quickly made some headway with Dr. King. The weekend after the rally at the capitol, Dr. King announced that he would call for a boycott of Alabama products and industries, and ask the federal government to withdraw its funds from programs in the state.

But there was also resistance to this program within SCLC, led principally by Hosea Williams. Williams believed the march to Montgomery represented an important psychological victory, in addition to having assured the passage of the voting rights act. The best way to take advantage of the opportunities the new atmosphere would open up was to implement a plan which he called SCOPE, the Summer Community Organization and Political Education Project.

Williams had been at work on SCOPE for several months, and its ambitions were large: it hoped to place a core of volunteers, mostly northern college students, in each of one hundred twenty counties throughout the Black Belt from Virginia to Louisiana (excluding Mississippi, where SNCC had conducted its Mississippi Summer Project the year before, out of which had come the Freedom Democratic Party), and through them make a concentrated regionwide push to register blacks and teach them the literacy and political skills that would give their franchise the maximum impact. Williams did not expect SCOPE volunteers to be involved in many demonstrations. With most Washington observers predicting that the Voting Rights Act would be law by Easter, or Memorial Day at the latest, SCOPE's potential appeared much greater now. Dr. King was taken with the idea, and joined Williams in announcing it at the beginning of April. SCOPE was given a budget of $480,000.

Williams urged Dr. King to give him command of all the SCLC field staff, including those in Alabama, to help implement SCOPE. That request set off an internal struggle which went on for another six weeks, because for King to agree would mean putting an end to Bevel's Alabama Project. The SCLC president always tried to stay out of staff squabbles, and here he held off making a firm decision, accepting SCOPE but also calling for the boycott and giving Bevel time to see what he could pull together in Montgomery.

That didn't turn out to be very much. Bevel had seriously misjudged the mood of the blacks in Alabama; to most of them the march had been nothing less than a kind of miracle, with wonders piled on wonders: the president's address, the coming of troops to protect them from Wallace, Lingo and Clark, the influx of whites ready to stand, suffer, and even die with them in their struggle, and soon enough a voting law which would open up the voting booths to them. They had made more history in three weeks than most of them had ever studied in their lives. Throughout the rest of the spring they were still trying to comprehend it all, savoring the memories it left, and basking in its lingering euphoria. They were also a little exhausted, especially the people in the counties around Selma who had been most actively involved.

Thus they were by no means ready to put on their marching shoes again on cue and go right back out to repeat or even surpass the march's accomplishments. And Bevel found leaders like Rev. Reese in Selma very cool to his plan to have high school students skip out to join the marches in Montgomery; most leaders shared the whites' belief in the importance of formal education, and were not willing to tolerate truancy unless there was some kind of emergency; and Alabama's emergency, they felt, had been met. Reese urged Bevel to delay the start of demonstrations until early June, when the school year would be over.

Private high-level staff meetings were held in Atlanta and Selma almost weekly through this period, trying to resolve the impasse between Bevel and Williams without success. Meanwhile Dr. King continued to give a little to both sides, promoting SCOPE at the same time that he pressed the Alabama boycott. The boycott, however, soon ran into strong opposition, not only from Alabama officials from whom complaints could have been expected, but also from President Johnson and such opinion makers as the *New York Times*, which came out against it editorially and then published an additional blast by the dean of its columnists, Arthur Krock. Union leaders didn't show much interest either, except for Harry Bridges' ILWU on the West Coast. And soon Dr. King was backing off, referring to it as mainly "symbolic" and by April 20 convening a staff meeting in Atlanta to see if there had not been "enough progress" in the state to call it off. The main problem with the boycott as Dr. King described it was that he had never mentioned in public Bevel's mass arrest–free election plan, and outside that strategic context it did not, in fact, make much sense.

By the twenty-fifth of May, when Bevel's plan had its first and last chance to go public, the handwriting was on the wall: the Alabama Project was finished. A delegation from several cities obediently assembled in the capital, and paid a call on House Speaker Albert Brewer and other officials, to present them with a petition urging "free and fair" elections. Brewer, on orders from Governor Wallace, received them quietly, listened to their pleas, and replied that theirs were local problems, and that was that.

Up until the week before, Bevel and others had been saying that this delegation would be the first of many that would descend on the capital day after day as a buildup to the demonstrations. Even Dr. King had told an audience in Wilcox County on May 11 that if the state officials didn't listen to these first visitors, "we have no alternative but to present our bodies and fill up the jails all over the state."

But it was obvious that the delegation of May 25 did not constitute the vanguard of a great upsurge of protest; Rev. Reese did not even join it, sending Rev. L. L. Anderson, who was well down on Selma's black leadership status ladder, in his stead. It was also apparent that there were not any hordes of people, young or old, waiting in the wings to clog up Montgomery's streets and jailhouse. Two days later, Dr. King's associate Fred Shuttlesworth was telling Chicago reporters that the boycott had not been "fully implemented" and probably wouldn't be, because it was meant mainly as a verbal threat in the first place. "We just threw it up in the air to show Alabama officials we could do something more than just march, sing and talk," Shuttlesworth said with a straight face. He added that the SCLC staff would meet "somewhere in Georgia" in June to decide whether to push it any further. By that time however, Dr. King had made his decision and put the Alabama field staff under Hosea Williams's direction as part of SCOPE; and James Bevel had left the state in disappointment. Bevel went to Chicago, where his restless, brilliant strategic mind found a more promising situation, and began laying the groundwork for what was to become Dr. King's massive but ill-fated open-housing campaign there in the summer of 1966.

Preoccupied with its internal politics, the SCLC national staff paid only sporadic attention to what was happening in Selma after the march. In one way this neglect confirmed the charge that SNCC partisans in the movement had made so often and were making again now—that Dr. King's organization stayed in a place only long enough to pick up a bundle of publicity for its patriarch and a bundle of cash for its budget, then moved on. But in another way, this apparent neglect completely belied the charge, because SCLC had unified the black community, had left behind it an intact organization, the Dallas County Voters League, and had brought its president, Rev. Reese, to a status within the limits of the county which was almost comparable to that of Dr. King himself at the national level. In fact, despite all the internecine sniping which went on behind the scenes during all the course of the campaign, on April 1, 1965 it could well be said that the contrasting approaches of both the organizations had been applied in the city with near-complete success: SCLC had solidified the black community behind respected local leadership; and SNCC, with its emphasis on grass-roots organizing and participation, could point to vigorous ward organizations all across the city, each with its own elected leadership and the beginnings of programs for its own neighborhoods.

Moreover, the atmosphere of intimidation in the city had been, if not completely banished, still decisively punctured. Two days after the march ended in Montgomery, big James Orange of SCLC came in to town and found several hundred out-of-town folk hanging around the street in front of Brown Chapel, disappointed that they had missed the big show and anxious for something to do. Rising to the occasion, Orange organized a march to the Dallas County Courthouse. Only two weeks before it had taken the intervention of a federal judge to make possible a march from Sylvan Street to those marble steps; but that day Orange led more than two hundred people to the courthouse in broad daylight, and then took them to City Hall as well before returning to the project, and almost no one paid the group any attention, even

though it was Saturday afternoon and all the country people were in
town.

In this atmosphere of triumph, when meetings between the mayor
and the black leadership resumed on April 7, Rev. Reese was acting like
a real leader, a man in command who was ready to press firmly the
advantages he now had in order to force important concessions out of
whites. He went in and laid on the table a long list of demands: jobs
for blacks, good visible jobs both in the city government and in the
downtown stores where the cash registers were still practically silent
because of the boycott; appointment of blacks to city boards, like the
School Board, which was self-perpetuating (and had been since Reconstruction, when the story went that Gen. Edmund Pettus got it set up
that way to keep Selma's schools out of carpetbagger hands); integration of city recreation facilities; the paving of streets in black neighborhoods; and the official adoption by the city and such institutions as the
Selma Times-Journal of titles of respect—Mr., Miss, and Mrs.—for
blacks in public and business discourse. (It was still true that in reporting the death of Dallas County's oldest citizen in 1965, a woman
named Miss Rebecca Shortridge who was one hundred and eight years
old and the daughter of a slave, the *Times-Journal* could write a long,
admiring obituary and refer to the deceased throughout only as
Rebecca.)

Reese did most of the talking at that first meeting, and he told the
whites among other things that he had reduced the number of mass
meetings to three per week, which represented a real saving to the city
in police expenses for patrolling them; so now what were they going
to do in return? He left the meeting with that question hanging over
the men on the other side of the table.

This kind of self-confident hard bargaining was bitter medicine to
have to take for Joe Smitherman and the city councilmen who joined
him at the table. Not only was it personally distasteful to the mayor
to make any concessions, but there were also forces working actively
in the white community to make it politically dangerous for him to do
so. The Dallas County Citizens Council was more alive than it had ever
been before; and under its new chairman, former mayor Heinz, it was
aiming almost all its effort in one direction: at the new mayor and his
"professional" public safety director. A recall petition was being cir-

culated, in hopes of forcing Smitherman out of office and replacing him with the old administration before the Voting Rights Act was passed and the rolls were clogged with new black voters.

The administration's response to Reese's self-assertive presentation was thus almost wholly political: it took the form of a determined stall, covered over with a patina of smiles and officeholder's cordiality. Behind the stall was the hope, based on decades, no centuries, of master-class experience, that the black community's current solidarity could not last. And when his constituency cracked, the whites figured, the bargaining power of Reese and his colleagues in the Voters League would either vanish or become manageable, and that would be enough. Besides, the proportion of blacks within the city limits was lower than it was in the county at large, and less than 60 per cent even there; and it was one thing to have a majority of potential voters according to the census statistics, among them many who were old, infirm, or unalterably dependent on whites, and another thing to have that majority both on the rolls and effective at the polls. In a place like Lowndes County, where the figures ran almost four to one black, the incumbents were in trouble; but white supremacy in Selma was far from finished. So Smitherman held out.

Soon enough the strategy began to pay off; history began to return to its familiar pattern. Moreover, the villains, if there were any, were not men and women with black skins, or even residents of Dallas County; but rather, out-of-town whites, the same people, or some of them, who had passed through the county in droves just days before and who came away with an unquenchable urge to do something for their noble black hosts and hostesses once they got home. They had been stung by the charges flung from Alabama whites that they were just on a lark, or operating out of sordid ulterior motives. Besides, the conditions of deprivation they had been shown by the civil rights workers, or walked past along Highway 80, still stood out in the memory. No, they were not going to forget Selma once the march was over.

And they didn't. Again and again people had asked the workers and the citizens around Brown Chapel what they could do once they got back home, and again and again they were told: send food, clothes, shoes and money; people are starving here, people are naked here, people are homeless here, people here have lost their jobs. And that is what the visitors did. Once they got back home, all over the nation they told their stories to rapt audiences in church halls, college auditoriums and public meetings. As they talked, they passed on the message, and soon from many points around the continent, money and supplies came trickling into Selma. As March spent itself in April, the trickle became a stream, collecting in continually growing piles in the large basement of First Baptist Church, where the image of Christ in the big stained glass window was still broken out where the posse had thrown a black youth through it on March 7. And without knowing it, against their firmest intentions, every one of the donors thus helped undermine that solidarity and spirit of the community which was what they had admired perhaps most of all while they were there.

The problem became evident almost as soon as the first relief supplies arrived: there was no one in the black community who had experience with operating a large-scale relief program; but any of the whites who knew how had now left, and the SCLC staff, tangled in its own problems, was out of town most of the time. Already there were scores of people coming around claiming to be in need, and who was to say whether their stories were true or whether they were making it up, or had not been around three days in a row telling the same story to different people. Moreover, while the piles of supplies were burgeoning, there would never be enough to feed and clothe all the poor people even in Selma, never mind Dallas County. So someone had to decide who got how much of what and why.

At once all the worst patterns of petty competition and greed were brought back into the atmosphere around Sylvan Street. And almost immediately they banished the easy trust and solidarity that had been present. Moreover, the situation was ideal for the entry of an entrepreneur, able to look beyond a few sacks of groceries to the larger possibilities that were waiting to be exploited. And almost at once someone stepped forward who seemed ready to fill this role.

That person was Elder William Ezra Greer, the man in what looked like a bishop's coat, with that not-quite identifiable metal medallion hanging on a heavy chain around his neck and that nonstop, overblown way of talking. Since Greer had appeared on the scene during the first

day of the vigil he had stayed visible ever since. In his first speech at
the barricades he had spoken as one with authority, and continued
giving orders throughout the period of the march. Among the exultant,
frightened mobs moving up and down Sylvan Street, anyone who
looked and talked like they knew what they were doing was likely to
be paid a certain amount of attention. And by the time the march was
over, Elder Greer had parlayed this fact into a position of undeniable
influence in black Selma. This was despite the fact that no one seemed
to have heard of him before, and his explanations about his background
tended to the grandiose at the same time that they were extremely
vague.

Greer wasted no time moving in on the relief scene. Barely a week
after the march he was telling a mass meeting at Brown Chapel that
a project would be activated in Selma at once to deal with what he
called fervently "the coming crisis" of white people's retaliation
against their black employees or clients who had taken part in the
movement. He declared with sweeping gestures that "a massive
drive" would be started to mobilize support from around the nation
for those who had to suffer in pursuit of their people's freedom. And
he was also describing himself to the remaining white visitors as the
"SCLC Executive Staff Person" who was assigned to the Voters
League and Rev. Reese in the absence of the rest of the staff. A few
visitors asked high SCLC people about Greer when staff people
passed through town in these days; they were invariably told that the
description was hogwash. But such debunking seemed to make little
difference; the people who asked always moved on in a few days,
while Greer stayed on. Moreover, there was still enough euphoria
remaining that no one at this point took his statements as more than
harmless exaggeration and self-promotion. Such characteristics were
not at all unknown among the black clergy or the civil rights movement, and not just in the Black Belt.

Thus it was that by the end of the first week in April, the Selma
Emergency Relief Fund, or SERF as it was to be called, was organized
and in business, with Elder William Ezra Greer in the post of "Executive Coordinator." As relief supplies began coming in in abundance,
they came to SERF, which established an office among the stacks

of boxes and piles of old clothes in the basement at First Baptist and asserted jurisdiction over the process of distribution.

Whether Elder Greer had ever been connected with a relief operation before is unknown; perhaps he had once received public assistance, and had been subject to the authoritarian bureaucracies that run southern public welfare agencies. SERF immediately began to operate like a bad imitation of such agencies. When Greer got to a mimeograph machine, the first thing that came out of it was an appeal for funds; the second was a relief application, a sheet of paper covered with a long list of questions, some of which were more than a little reminiscent of those on the despised voter registration applications downtown.

One of Greer's first targets was Dr. King himself. On April 14 a letter was sent to the SCLC leader over the signatures of Greer and several visiting whites whom he had been leading around the city, calling for "food, clothing, medical aid and cash" to be distributed in massive amounts in Selma, through SERF. The group had visited many homes, the letter said, and found horrifying conditions of poverty and need wherever they turned.

But King was only the first. By mid-April Greer had official-looking SERF stationery printed up, complete with a long, impressive-sounding list of "sponsors" and organizational representatives. Among these latter were listed the Rev. Eugene Leuning, who was described as representing the Unitarian Universalist Service Committee. Leuning was in fact the second in a series of members of a "presence" maintained in Selma by the Unitarian-Universalist Church through the rest of the spring and summer; but he had no direct connection with the denomination's service committee and was surprised and embarrassed to see his name used thus. "In some ways," Leuning wrote to Unitarian headquarters after he saw the letterhead, "Greer reminds of Adam Clayton Powell. . . . It was of course helpful to be called a service committee representative, but I could give him no such authority. But," he concluded, "emergency is emergency, and with truckloads of food waiting to come from California . . . and other things, he [Greer] takes what he can get."

And so he did. But Greer didn't do as well in distributing what he accumulated. It took no time for the disorganized little office under

First Baptist to collect a large stack of completed applications; but most of the time the doors leading downstairs were locked. People stood around all day outside for a few days once they knew there were supplies inside to be had; but not many ever got anything. The local people who were selected as Greer's assistants assimilated at once the petty bureaucratic mentality his procedures displayed, and were loath to give out anything until a "case" had been thoroughly investigated, in a most leisurely fashion, then approved and initialed by the proper responsible officials, that is, the executive coordinator. It wasn't long before the line dwindled and the rumors began to float: somethin' ain't right down there.

Moreover, it was soon enough apparent that something was *not* in order. As shipments of supplies came in—for instance the more than ten thousand pounds of food, clothing, toys, Easter baskets and medical supplies donated by the people of Michigan and delivered personally by Congressman John Conyers of Detroit—they were locked up in the bowels of First Baptist. And when the doors were opened later, it was obvious that the best supplies, the canned hams and quality vegetables, the newer stylish clothing, had already been picked out. Just who got this special service and how was a source of ever-expanding circles of rumors. Some said it was the ministers and the middle-class blacks with influence in the movement; and if it sounds incongruous for people of position to be slipping off with canned goods and used dresses, it should be remembered that in this city in that year a letter carrier for the post office was a pillar of bourgeois black society.

Others said it was the people who ·worked in the church taking advantage of their positions. There was undoubtedly some of this, because the assistants were not getting paid for their labors, and they argued openly that since they were poor too, they should be able to take their wages in supplies. There were even persistent stories about bags of groceries showing up in the country in the trunks of middle-class black people's cars, being offered for sale to the people who were supposed to be getting them free.

If it was practically impossible to verify these rumors, that only seemed to help magnify them. Rev. Reese stayed carefully aloof from the entire operation, at least at this point, no doubt at least partly because as *the* local leader, it was his role to be concerned about larger questions: there were meetings with the mayor to attend and stay prepared for, as well as a number of trips up North to make, filling speaking engagements and serving as the honored guest from historic Selma, Alabama at large liberal soirees. This was heady stuff for a schoolteacher and part-time preacher. Most of the other major figures in the local black leadership were similarly on the road a good deal during these weeks.

Toward the end of April, Greer went on tour himself, passing through upstate New York and Michigan, getting as far north as London, Ontario. Along the way he visited several Unitarian churches, and spoke at a large public meeting in Canada, on every occasion calling for help and financial contributions to SERF and the needy stalwarts of the Black Belt freedom movement. He did well, too; at the meeting in London alone he was presented with a check for seventeen hundred dollars for SCLC.

But by now the oiliness of his manner and his continuing exaggeration and free play with facts were beginning to be noticed. In Boston, the Unitarian Universalist Service Committee's executive director, Charles Vickery, got a look at the SERF letterhead and immediately burned up the telephone wires to Atlanta. He got hold of Randolph Blackwell, SCLC's program director, and asked some hard questions about this person Greer who was passing himself off as a high SCLC staff person and using the Service Committee's name without authorization. After further inquiries Blackwell told Vickery, as others had been told, that Greer was not a staff member, and that because of these complaints he had been spoken to. "Although Mr. Greer has returned to the South and has promised not to raise any more money until he sees Mr. Blackwell," Vickery wrote in a confidential memo to other Unitarian church executives, "there does remain the good possibility of a real problem with this man. . . . Mr. Blackwell made it very plain that this was not the SCLC way of raising funds and that Elder Greer was a problem to SCLC." Word of this conversation was passed along to the clergyman representing them on the scene in Selma, and the Unitarian executives began considering whether to send out Vickery's memo to all their ministers across the country.

But Greer came back to Selma talking as fast as ever, and there was still no one with clout who showed the inclination to rein him in. The day after Charles Vickery had called SCLC in Atlanta, Rev. Harold Shelley, then the Unitarian "presence," reported news of a proposed plan for moving the whole relief operation to Marion in Perry County, a proposal that supposedly came from James Bevel of SCLC. But this plan, presumably aimed at getting relief entirely out of Greer's hands, came to nothing, and if it was in fact what Bevel wanted to do, he had too many other things to worry about and would shortly be out of the picture. By May fourth Rev. Reese was telling an outside questioner that Greer had been "straightened out," adding that "he must fit in or leave." But two days later Rev. Fred Rutledge, the Unitarian minister who succeeded Harold Shelley, was taking for granted that Greer was "organizer and administrator of SERF," just as before. Rutledge was also persuaded that, whatever its problems getting started, SERF's relief operation was now finally getting the bugs out and doing some real distribution. Each of his predecessors had said virtually the same thing at the beginning of their tours. And still the rumors spread.

16. *Sylvan Street during the vigil, with the "Berlin Rope" across the road*

17. *On the line in the vigil*

18. *A march attempt during the vigil*

19. *Elder William Ezra Greer addresses the troopers during the vigil.*

20. *The rope came down . . .*

21. . . . *but the barricades remained.*

22. *Preparing for the Reeb Memorial at the Courthouse; in the center are Dr. King, Rev. Abernathy and James Bevel (in skullcap).*

23. *An uninvited march escort*

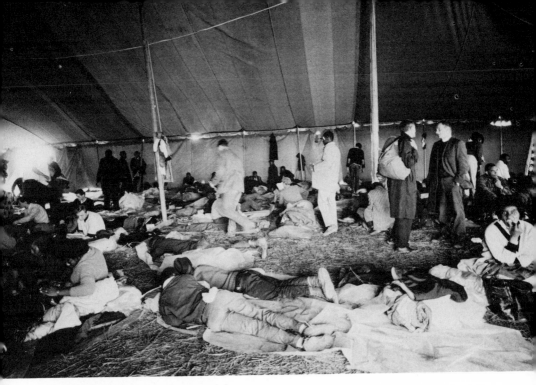

24. *Bedding down on Highway 80*

25. *Mrs. Rosa Steele's establishment, Lowndes County*

26. Gary Merrill takes a break from the tent crew with marcher Jim Letherer.

27. *Marching through Big Swamp; in the lead are James Orange, left, Bernard Lafayette and James Bevel.*

28. *At dinner in 1966 in Selma: from left, Arthur Lewis, Mrs. Wilson Baker, Wilson Baker, Muriel Lewis, Ralph and Mrs. Smeltzer*

Re-Elect

JIM

CLARK

FOR

Law and Order

Paid Political Advertising by Friends of Jim Clark.   Subject to action of Democratic Primaries May 1966

29. *The Albert Hotel during the primary campaign, Spring 1966*

30. *That year the incumbent ran on a familiar slogan.*

"We feel like Hammermill can make this community. It's just impossible to say how happy we are to have Hammermill come to Selma. They will be good for Selma and we will try anything possible to make Selma good for Hammermill."

> —Mayor Joe Smitherman, interviewed in June by a reporter from Erie, Pennsylvania, Hammermill's hometown; reprinted in the Selma Times-Journal, July 23, 1965

"The people of Dallas County are suffering from a guilt complex. Some are ashamed to admit that they are white men. These people are falling into line just as the news media wanted them to do. They are now looking for things to satisfy the Negroes with."

> —Sheriff Jim Clark, speaking to the Mobile County Citizens Council, May 12, 1965

SEVENTEEN. The white leadership must have known or at least suspected a good deal about what was happening to muddy the waters on the other side of town. But behind their own backs, they had to contend with not only the increased pressure of the Citizens Council, but also, for the first time, a public manifestation of what was referred to as "white moderation," people standing up to state in front of everyone that maybe there ought to be some changes in the way blacks were treated in Selma, that the issue was not just a matter of the city obeying evil, oppressive, and unconstitutional laws that agitators had succeeded in pushing through a gullible, vote-hungry Congress.

There had been a small group of influential white people meeting behind closed doors for some time in Selma, saying this to each other. But when a brave letter from a white Selmian, Mrs. Eleanor Hammett, appeared in the *Selma Times Journal* on March first urging those "who call ourselves 'moderates' " to "speak out loud and clear," their silence remained unbroken. None of them would repeat it in any other setting, and the meetings were devoted largely to handwringing over their felt inability to make their sentiments public in a way that would have any impact. The real problem, which they didn't have to talk about much because it was implicitly understood, was that they were *afraid* to say anything. Scared to death, despite the fact that the group included some of the wealthiest people in the city, people who presumably had the least to fear from the economic reprisals lesser souls were subject to. They apparently had little confidence in the accepted view of Selma as a peaceful city where problems could be solved by the natives without resort to or fear of violence.

It was not until after March seventh, when this violence had broken loose in their own streets, that the hold of terror began to be broken. The first white people to break out of it were an auto dealer named Arthur Lewis and his wife Muriel. Lewis was wealthy, having made money in several enterprises around Selma, wealthy enough to take up art collecting for museums, and to be able to loan paintings to the Albert Hotel for lobby decorations. He had been president of the Kiwanis chapter, and traveled widely lecturing on his home city and its history. Although he was as "liberal" about race as they came in white Selma then, Lewis had long been good friends with Jim Clark and Joe Smitherman. Lewis, who was a Jew, had kept close tabs on the Citizens Council to help keep it from becoming anti-Semitic. His religion was of course a drawback in trying to lead people out of the segregationist orthodoxy, as was the fact that he was not a native Selmian, though he had lived in the town for twenty-three years, and was a dedicated Selma booster.

Until March of 1965, Lewis had kept his opinions to himself, or worked very quietly on a private, person-to-person basis trying to soften up people like Sheriff Clark and Judge Hare. He frankly admitted to a friend during this time that he was afraid for his physical safety; he even called himself "yellow" in moments of self-disparagement. But the attack on the bridge changed all that. It jarred him out of his former role, and enabled him to put his fears behind him. By March 9 he had decided to "come out," and say whatever needed to be said, regardless of the consequences. Muriel, who had been similarly affected by the events of the previous Sunday, agreed.

After considering carefully how to proceed, the Lewises decided to write a letter to fourteen of their friends around the city, to explain what they were thinking and trying to do. The letter, dated March 19, was a remarkable document:

> This is almost the end of the ninth week of racial demonstrations in this locale, and for most of that time we have been walking on eggshells, balancing on a very thin tightrope while trying to do what we believe is right and just. But we must act differently, and think differently because Selma is our home, we love it and its people and we want to continue to live here.
>
> We have long been aware of the white racist group in Selma (and it is very large), and we have worked in a small way to change this through overthrowing the political machine that has ruled this city and county for many many years. There has been some success along these lines. . . . However, until the riot on the bridge on our terrible black Sunday we kept our views quiet. We could be called moderates but not liberals, for we believe in the rights of the Negroes, their right to free speech and their right to demonstrate in *moderation.*

They spoke of the few efforts they had made so far: talking to their friends, encouraging the moderate group to speak out and take some leadership, and spending hours entertaining some of the reporters from the major papers, networks and wire services, trying to get them to see beyond the stereotypes they had about white Selma. They had even allowed themselves to be interviewed on the record, although little of what they said had been used, apparently because of the flood of more exciting action copy: what did see print was bits and pieces, jerked out of context. The letter continued:

> Let me assure you that these actions of ours, and those that I have not mentioned here have taken courage, but we realize that we can no longer be afraid to speak out, but that does not mean that we are no longer a bit fearful, and we do not—nor should you—condemn our moderate friends for their silence. We know that this area is full of potential violence. . . .

From our friends and relatives we have heard very little, and we have needed all the love and support possible. Some few of you have been concerned and kind and to you we have tried to make our ordeal seem much less than it has been. A very few of you have seen fit to question our motives and thoughts during this time. We hope that you will continue to acknowledge us, or we shall be truly lost, and you should not feel any shame at writing SELMA on an envelope. There are decent people everywhere, and this town is no exception. I will not use our governor's method of comparison. We know we have dirt in our backyard, and just because everyone else has the same thing that is no reason why we shouldn't clean ours.

The Lewises spoke with high praise of Wilson Baker. "It is a miracle that there has only been one death in town, and for Rev. Reeb there are many here who truly grieved among the white population. . . .

"We are confused, more than ever tonight," they concluded. "We must live with ourselves, but we also want to live here. It would be so easy to be quiet, but it would not let us sleep any easier than we do now. All we ask from you is partial understanding, and compassion. We hope that you will never be faced with a crisis in your lives that even remotely resembles this, and we hope that you will understand the purpose of this letter. We ask that you do not show it to your friends or even talk about it; this information is for the people who mean something important to us." The letter was signed by both Muriel and Arthur Lewis.

Unfortunately, the Lewises' letter was not kept only within the circle of friends and relatives for very long. Tampering with the mail of civil rights workers or those considered unduly sympathetic to them was not at all unusual in Selma in those days, and a stolen copy of the letter soon ended up in the hands of the Citizens Council. There it was duplicated in quantity and circulated widely throughout the city, edited slightly in a few places to make it sound as if the Lewises were greatly exaggerating their prominence and political influence. A few days before this letter was sent out, Muriel had written to the *Selma Times-*

Journal, defending the right of local citizens to help the Community Relations Service agents in their attempts at mediation. This letter was printed, as was another one she wrote a little later to *Time* magazine, in which she asserted that "There are in Selma, as everywhere, [white] people of good faith and good intentions who were heartbroken by the acts of violence here. They will continue to try to be heard, not only by the members of the news media, but also by the people who will continue to live with this problem long after the spotlight has faded."

These few missives were enough to start the reaction coming: hate mail, threatening phone calls, and pressure on business associates downtown to shut the Lewises up. But as happened in other situations where people had taken one firm step out of a shell of fear, this opposition now served to steel their new resolve rather than weaken it. Arthur Lewis, feeling the time was ripe for even bolder action, began to move among the secret moderates, asking them to come to his house for a meeting on Friday, April ninth.

Most of the important moderates showed up: Carl Morgan, president of the City Council; Frank Wilson, a bank vice-president; Sam Hobbs, a widely respected attorney, and others, thirteen in all. Lewis had waiting for them a draft of a public statement which he wanted them to sign and publish in the *Times-Journal*. The statement was nothing radical; modeled on a declaration published two weeks earlier in the *Anniston Star* in north Alabama, the draft urged compliance with all laws, communication between the races "on a basis of mutual respect," protection of the law for each individual, and support for negotiations between differing groups as the way to reach new understandings. "By affixing our signatures below," it concluded, "we do pledge our efforts to carry out these goals."

It was probably this closing sentence which was the most shocking; but the group in the Lewis living room recoiled from the entire proposal as if the paper carried a lethal charge of electricity. Lewis got nowhere with them. In fact, just the suggestion itself was so upsetting that three days later a delegation of these same "moderates" called on Muriel, to tell her with much embarrassment and looking-at-the-floor that the Lewises' efforts were getting to be too much for them, and asking them to "withdraw" from their activities for a short, reasonable time. Later they met Arthur and repeated their plea, adding that the

Citizens Council had got wind of an effort to have a moderate public statement printed, and Chris Heinz was already maneuvering to stop it.

Thus confronted with the fear and opposition of their own, the Lewises agreed to withdraw, but only for a short time. Unfortunately, this withdrawal soon turned into isolation: Arthur was no longer welcome in the offices of his old friends, Sheriff Clark and Mayor Smitherman. The "moderates" stayed away from him as much as possible. And he had only minimal and very formal contacts with black leaders. He and Muriel began to pay the price of being first to make the kind of break they did.

But the idea of a public statement did not die; in fact, the very same day that the "moderates" were guiltily cutting themselves loose from Arthur Lewis, the Executive Board of the Selma–Dallas County Chamber of Commerce was meeting to consider whether to endorse a public statement which had been signed by seventeen of the largest Chambers in Alabama, and which was set to be published in the *Wall Street Journal* and every daily newspaper in the state a few days hence. This statement, entitled "Where We Stand," was only a little bit less innocuous than the one with which Lewis had so frightened the moderates: it supported law and order, equal enforcement of the law, the right to vote for "qualified" people, and it leaned heavily on the importance of upgraded education and an expanding economy as the real long-term solutions to the problems of the state. At the Selma–Dallas Chamber's meeting, only nineteen of twenty-six members were present, including all those who would be dead-set against any such declaration. A motion to endorse the statement was defeated by a vote of twelve to seven.

The news of this rejection spread quickly to the moderates, who had just finished talking with the Lewises. Two of them in particular, Jerome Siegel of the Committee of One Hundred, the industrial development group that had attracted Hammermill, and Frank Wilson, vice-president of the People's Bank, decided that this new statement offered them an opportunity they should seize. On Thursday, April 15, when the statement appeared as a full-page advertisement in the *Selma Times-Journal* over the names of every major Chamber of Commerce in the state except Selma–Dallas County printed in large bold type, Siegel and Wilson started to move. They called a secret organizing meeting at the Albert Hotel, attended by the presidents of the city's four banks and several other influential men in the community. The group resolved to undertake a major push to reverse the Chamber's decision, and immediately obtained the support of the *Times-Journal*'s publisher, Roswell Falkenberry.

By Friday morning, canvassers were fanning out through the downtown area, soliciting signatures from everyone they thought might be sympathetic. Some important outsiders also weighed in behind them, in the form of strategic phone calls from the top management of both Hammermill and Dan River Mills. Their companies were taking a lot of flak, the important people of Selma were told, from SCLC and other civil rights groups who were threatening a boycott of their products and getting a lot of bad publicity for them. The rejection of the statement was making their efforts to deal with these threats considerably more difficult. They hoped the Chamber's Executive Board would reconsider.

It didn't take long, with such influential expressions of interest percolating through town, for the reconsideration ball to get rolling. The Chamber president, grocer J. M. Gaston, who had said Hammermill's coming made him hear his cash registers ringing, must now have had visions of red ink flowing; he called an emergency board meeting for Saturday morning, and made sure that all the favorable members were on hand to vote. In the meantime, the county Board of Revenue and the City Council both voted to urge support for the statement. By the time Gaston gavelled the special meeting to order Saturday morning, several hundred whites, including a large roster of respectable people from old families, had signed the supporting petition.

The meeting was long and stormy, bringing out into the open the divisions within the white community for all to see. City Attorney McLean Pitts was the keynoter for those favoring adoption, and he laid it right on the line: "Hammermill and Dan River are very much concerned and feel that the Selma Chamber of Commerce is letting them down in some of the troubles they are having by being so conspicuously absent from the advertisement."

Attorney Joe Pilcher, from whom Mayor Smitherman was said to be taking much advice recently, led the opposition, and he tried to put the supporters on the defensive at once with some "startling" disclosures, which before now would have set the moderates running for cover. Pilcher revealed that a "self-appointed group of men had been meeting secretly about the race issue, and planned to "compromise" about it. This secret group, he said, included the four bank presidents, the *Times-Journal*'s Falkenberry and several others. Pilcher knew what he was talking about, of course; Selma was not a big enough town for such "secrets" to stay kept; and most of the group's members were in the meeting. But for the first time these men felt enough strength and momentum behind them that they were ready to stand and fight. William B. Craig, president of the City National Bank, admitted to being part of this group, but denied that there had been or would be any compromises of "principles of integrity under any pressure." He added, however, that both Hammermill and Dan River had phoned him to express their concern over the Chamber's rejection of the statement.

Jerome Siegel, chairman of the Committee of One Hundred and another member of the moderate group, was also attacked by opponents of adoption, who insinuated that promises had been made under the table to attract this new Yankee company. But Siegel said flatly that "Hammermill neither asked for nor received any promises on the race issue. All they want to know is whose side we are on now that we've thrown the ball right into Martin Luther King's hands by expressing this attitude of defiance toward moderation."

The mayor, who reportedly had been among the negative votes the first time around, was confronted with the fact of having held unannounced regular meetings with Negro leaders while insisting publicly that he was unalterably opposed to biracial committees. Smitherman replied that he was still indeed unalterably opposed to such committees; but the men he had been meeting with did not constitute such a committee, only a delegation from the black community. He said he would continue to hold the meetings, to see if the city's problems could be worked out.

The arguing went on, often acrimoniously, for several hours. Opponents of the statement urged the whites to unite into a solid, militant front against any yielding to integration, even the mild concessions

made by the other Chambers. William Craig responded significantly
to this proposal, however, by remarking that white solidarity might be
a good thing, but that the responsible leaders in the community
"should not lower ourselves to achieve this unity." Eventually everyone
had shouted themselves hoarse, and it was time to vote. The tally this
second time was twenty-one to eight in favor of endorsement; and
Roswell Falkenberry immediately went to work to see that everyone in
town knew about it.

Sunday's paper printed the statement twice, once in a more-than-
double-page spread, the text on one page and the hundreds of endors-
ers' names running the length of the next and several columns of a
third. A few pages later the Chamber had its own large ad reprinting
the statement over its logo. Falkenberry editorialized rather candidly
about the meaning of the board's decision: "Though some harm undoubtedly has been done, the local Chamber of Commerce . . . we
hope, reestablished the confidence of two large industries presently
planning to construct multi-million dollar plants in this area. Positively,
we believe most of the industries already located there have been
assured of the undeniable support they can expect from Selma's citizens and business community."

Publication of the statement was not much of a beachhead against
the entrenched attitudes of conservative white Selma; it soon became
clear that many endorsements had been offered out of a coldly calculated view of what was in the city's economic self-interest. But it did
bring the "moderates" out of their closets at last, and did so in a way
that enabled them to throw back the efforts to intimidate them back
into silence. If their visibility, the thing they had feared most, caused
even less damage to segregation than it did to them, at least immediately, they and the community were both better off for having them
out in the light of day.

*"The United States government has been
informed by military authorities in the Dominican
Republic that American lives are in danger. These
authorities are no longer able to guarantee their
safety and they reported that the assistance of
military personnel is now needed for that purpose.*

*"I've ordered the Secretary of Defense to put the
necessary American troops ashore in order to give
protection to hundreds of Americans who are still in
the Dominican Republic and to escort them safely
back to this country."*

—President Lyndon Johnson,
April 28, 1965

EIGHTEEN.
As the weekly bira-
cial meetings continued into May, it became evident that the mayor
was not feeling enough pressure to meet any of the black spokesmen's
demands. In fact, when they met on May fifth, the mayor tried to
divert Reese from his agenda with one of Smitherman's own. The city
was beginning the processes necessary to establish an antipoverty program, and such agencies were required to have a community-based
board whose membership reflected the target area's makeup. The
mayor offered to appoint five blacks to a fifteen-member board for the
program, and allowed Reese to argue the figure up to seven members.
But then he held firm against all his other demands. After almost six
weeks of fruitless negotiating, Reese was getting impatient, and he
threatened to mount massive street demonstrations again within a
week if the administration did not make more substantial concessions.

If Smitherman was worried by this threat he didn't show it. Three
days later, with considerable fanfare, he announced the second and
third parts of his diversionary package: he was ready to appoint a
four-member commission to investigate all charges of police brutality,
he said, and to name two blacks to it. He also offered to arrange a
meeting between black leaders and the Board of Registrars. This, he
insisted, combined with his willingness to appoint blacks to the pro-
jected antipoverty board, should be enough concessions for the blacks

to call off their boycott of downtown stores and to quit harassing Hammermill and Dan River.

The problem with these "concessions," as Reese pointed out at their next meeting, May twelfth, was that the blacks had not asked for any of them. Moreover, they were practically without any substance: the city police, under Baker, were about as well-disciplined as they ever had been, and a federal court had ordered Jim Clark to disband his posse the same weekend the Chamber of Commerce adopted the "Where we stand" statement. Smitherman would probably be forced by the federal government to have blacks on his antipoverty board anyway, if he was at all serious about getting any money for it. And the Board of Registrars would soon enough be practically out of business, once the Voting Rights Act was passed.

Reese walked out of this deadlocked meeting declaring that he wouldn't come back until Smitherman had solid proposals to offer on his set of demands; the mayor just as firmly insisted that the blacks were not showing "good faith." But he wasn't much concerned. Reese had not in fact filled the streets with demonstrators as he had promised to do, and the truth was he couldn't fill them even if he wanted to. Later in the month three groups were arrested downtown carrying signs supporting the boycott. But altogether they numbered less than two hundred people, many of those were juveniles, and most of them had come out only because James Bevel stopped by long enough to call a march together.

The meager turnout for these demonstrations was indicative of the state of morale in the black community. Attendance at mass meetings had dropped drastically; now only Dr. King could fill Brown Chapel, which had so often been packed more than an hour before a mass meeting was to begin, and the contrast between his few appearances during these weeks and the balance of the meetings was downright embarrassing. Reese was still assuring inquiring outsiders that Elder Greer was "in check"; but the flamboyant, fast-talking SERF coordinator was still very much in evidence, and the relief operation at First Baptist remained as inefficient, as shot through with favoritism, and as alienating as ever. Moreover, when Reese was out of town, as he frequently was, Greer seemed to take over his role as the major community spokesman, preaching at the near-empty mass meetings and giving orders the way he had on the vigil line out front those few short weeks ago.

By the end of May the boycott was over *de facto*, because the blacks from the country, as well as many city people, had simply abandoned it and gone back to shopping downtown. The boycott had been hard to sustain anyway, because there were no black stores or supermarkets of any size in Selma then, and the little mom-and-pop stores scattered through the black neighborhoods were gouged by their white whole-salers and in turn had to charge prices that were extremely high com-pared to downtown. Observing the boycott took enough real commit-ment to pay the higher prices at the black shops and do without what their meager inventories lacked, or to find a way to get to Montgomery or somewhere else and do one's shopping there. Thus as community solidarity decayed, the boycott was the first visible casualty. By the end of May reliable white moderates were reporting that the white mer-chants were no longer concerned about it, and had let up their pressure on the mayor to make some show of flexibility at his meetings with Reese. Sure enough, in early June the mayor began ducking the meet-ings, offering various unconvincing excuses.

Reese was soon faced with other problems besides the failure of the boycott. The mass meetings were hardly meant to be exercises in democratic processes, and the only way for people to make their feel-ings known about the people who ran them was to stay away, which they were doing in droves. But out in the wards, the neighborhood people were still gathering each week in much more open-ended ses-sions; and soon the rumors and complaints about Greer, the relief operation, and the whole disconcerting new atmosphere in their "movement" were being heard in the ward meetings. In fact, over across the river in East Selma where Ward Five had been divided in two parts, the group at Ward 5B was soon in open rebellion. A new ward captain had recently been elected there, a young, no-nonsense preacher named Fairro Brown; and when the stories of red tape, long lines and foolishness at First Baptist's basement came to him, he went over and took a look himself. Disgusted at what was going on, Brown commandeered a rickety school bus from a nearby church, drove over and demanded that he be given a load of the supplies. The SERF staff, momentarily intimidated by his aggressiveness, let him fill the seats in the bus with cartons full of food, which he took to the ward's meeting place, the Second Baptist Church.

There Brown and people from the ward set up their own relief program; and perhaps because on this smaller neighborhood level the people knew better who was really desperate as opposed to the majority who were just plain poor, it seemed to work much better there. Even Elder Greer, when he paid an inspection visit to Second Baptist, had to admit that distribution was going well. But he still admonished Brown to take a sheaf of his forms and have the people fill them out properly, a directive that Brown simply ignored.

Soon the people in Ward 5B were looking to other community problems. One of the most visible was the lack of transportation to the black high school, which was practically clear across town; the students from East Selma had to walk several miles there and back each day, and their parents did not like it. So Brown began raising money for a bus, and in a few weeks the ward treasury had collected almost a thousand dollars. But in the midst of this drive, the Dallas County Voters League sent a committee over to see Brown. The committee, led by Mr. Ernest Doyle, the first vice-president of the league, advised the ward leader that the ward group, as a part of the Voters League organization, was obliged to channel any money it collected through the parent body.

There was not a chance of that happening. The people had lost confidence in the league leadership; there had never been a financial accounting to the community for all the untold thousands of dollars that had come into the Voters League and SERF, and with all the rumors going around they were not about to let their few hundred dollars be handled that way. Brown met the challenge by holding two meetings each meeting night: first the Ward 5B group of the Voters League would transact its business, then adjourn in favor of the independent Ward 5B organization. The independent body soon had enough money to buy a bus from the city, one of the municipal buses that had stopped running when blacks stopped riding in the back earlier in the year. The bus operated between East Selma and Hudson High for the rest of the school year.

There was no comparably successful insurrection in any of the other wards, and because it was in a relatively isolated outlying section of the city, news of the fuss in Ward 5B didn't spread very rapidly. But just the same, every ward began hearing the rumors and complaints, and the voices became more insistent week by week. The response to these questions by Elder Greer and the league leaders was shrewd: they began making tours of the meetings, not to answer the rumors, but to sweep into the small gatherings like honored guests, taking seats on the platform, and disrupting the discussion by taking over the pulpit. Then they gave lengthy, very vague but highly emotional pep talks, which caught the audiences off guard and soon had them reverting to habit and "amen-ing" in between every sentence. Greer was especially good at this, leaning intently over the large, open pulpit-Bible, arms outstretched and finger jabbing in emphasis for each of his platitudinous points, then pausing when they applauded to whip out a large white handkerchief with which he mopped his streaming face and swept back his greasy, stringy hair. He carried on as if the posse was waiting outside with lynching ropes for everyone.

Before the people knew what had happened, Greer or Reese would have them singing "We Shall Overcome" and be out the door. In the meantime no one had been able to ask any of the questions that were racking their chests like smokers' coughs; and now it was late, ten o'clock, even ten-thirty, past time to go home. For most of these people getting up at five in the morning was taking it easy, and they could not afford to waste their evenings in a haze of empty rhetoric. Yet they still shrank from the implications of their questions, and deferred to their leaders, even to the self-appointed Greer, when they entered the meetings. Their grasp on this tool of self-government was not yet firm enough for them to see that these ward meetings could be a means of really making the leadership accountable. Thus as the barrage of disruptive speechmaking continued into mid-June, they responded the way they had so often before: by dropping out. Soon attendance at most ward meetings was practically nil; and when the Voters League Executive Committee followed up its incursions by announcing it would issue weekly agendas, and ordered the ward captains to confine discussion to approved topics which had been entered on the agendas in advance, there were few complaints because hardly anyone was around to raise objections.

By June, however, there was pressure on the league from another

direction which was not so easy to suppress: SCLC. When James Bevel
had moved the office for his Alabama Project to Montgomery in anticipation of its serving as field headquarters for mass arrest demonstrations, SCLC felt under the gun to bring in another full-time project
director for Selma, at least for the rest of the summer. This was
necessary in order to answer the continuing charges from SNCC of
exploitation and abandonment; besides, it would be very embarrassing
if the Voting Rights Act passed and it took a long time for Selma's
blacks to get downtown and onto the books. SCLC had to see to it that
the city's blacks stayed organized enough to be ready to move on the
courthouse quickly.

Bevel's replacement was a field worker named Harold Middlebrook.
Middlebrook was a skinny, nervous Tennesseean, who had seen action
in SCLC campaigns in Danville, Virginia; Dothan, and Tuscaloosa,
Alabama. These were local campaigns that were not widely known
outside the south, but in them he had faced up to redneck sheriffs and
Black Belt jails, and earned his stripes as an organizer. Middlebrook's
assignment was simple: canvass black Dallas County from top to bottom, get the people down to sign the appearance book and thus be in
practice to crowd the registration rolls as soon as the Voting Rights
Act became law. More was involved here than just public relations; in
less than a year there would be primary elections to fill county offices,
and that meant Jim Clark would have to face the voters. Clark had
fulfilled his role in the movement, and now it was time for him to retire,
to be replaced by a black person, it was hoped.

But Middlebrook soon had another job thrust into his hands: persuading the Voters League, and primarily Rev. Reese, to rid itself of
Elder Greer. Greer's habits became steadily more embarrassing to
SCLC, which in the minds of interested people outside the South was
solidly identified with all civil rights–connected work in Selma. An
example of the reaction toward Greer came when Unitarian church
headquarters in Boston sent out, on May 28, to all its ministers across
the country a copy of that internal memo written by Charles Vickery
of its Service Committee on May 3: " 'Elder' Greer," it read, ". . . has
approached several churches in northern New York and Canada for
funds for relief work in Dallas County, Alabama. He lists the Unitarian
Universalist Service Committee, Inc., as one of his sponsors, as well as

the Southern Christian Leadership Conference. The U.U.S.C. has not given him any permission to use their name on this appeal. . . . [I]f any money is given to him it should be by check and made out to the SCLC–Dallas County Relief. This will protect the money for legitimate purposes."

This kind of publicity SCLC didn't need and couldn't afford. Middlebrook tried several times to persuade Reese privately that Greer should be quietly dropped from SERF and the project's operation cleaned up. But he got nowhere; the league leadership refused to listen. By mid-June the SCLC project director was at the end of his patience, and was threatening to publicly disaffiliate with the Voters League if Greer stayed on. Still Reese and the others did not budge, and Middlebrook turned to Atlanta for help. The situation became so tense that a white seminarian from California named David Smith, who was spending the summer working in the white community as a conciliator, began trying to mediate between Middlebrook and Reese, though without much success. And Rev. Ben Kjelshus, who was the Unitarian representative at the time, wrote headquarters on June 20 that "it should be emphasized, as I see it, that no funds or clothing should be sent to the DCVL—at least not at this time." He suggested, however, that "developments to remedy the situation are anticipated."

Kjelshus didn't know how prophetic his statement was. On Thursday June 24, with Reese again out of town on a junket to the North, Wilson Baker walked into the basement at First Baptist with a warrant in his pocket and took Elder Greer down to the city jail. Oddly enough, the warrant said nothing about SERF or Greer's highly individual fundraising techniques. Instead, it charged him with using obscene language and the possession of obscene literature, and it had been signed by a black woman who had for a while been his close companion.

Naturally, four-letter words and filthy pictures were not what was on Wilson Baker's mind, although he did send his men down to search Greer's living quarters, and they did come up with some spicy literature that seemed to fit the bill. Rather, Baker had a long list of questions to ask Greer about certain reports he had received from people in the black community, reports having to do with money.

Before Baker had a chance to question Greer, though, two black men came to bond him out. They were Ernest Doyle and James Gilder-

sleeve, first vice president and treasurer, respectively, of the Dallas
County Voters League. The two men presented $911 in cash as a bail
bond, and slipped Greer out of Baker's grasp.

But Greer had more than one enemy, and Baker wasn't long in
getting another warrant, this one signed by a black man who lived near
Brown Chapel. It seemed that Elder Greer had made obscene remarks
and had even fondled one of this man's several comely daughters, and
this irate father wasn't going to put up with such advances.

Baker had to hustle to serve the warrant, however, because by this
time the Voters League officials had Greer at the Greyhound bus
station, waiting to leave on the next bus north. The city police got there
just at the last minute, hustling onto the idling vehicle and hauling
Greer right out of his seat. But by nightfall he was back in Baker's jail,
answering the questions and looking scared.

With the arrest of Elder Greer, the lid came off the black community's discontent. An independent meeting of ward leaders was
called while Greer sat in jail, and the people momentarily found their
voice: they wanted action and facts, they wanted to know what had
happened to all that money the Voters League and SERF had been
collecting, and why Greer had never been dealt with before now. A
committee was appointed to investigate the matter, and among its
members was Rev. Fairro Brown, representing the insurgents in Ward
5B. But this committee got no further in its meeting with Reese—who
was back in town by this time—and the other officers than had Harold
Middlebrook and SCLC. They demanded to see the books; they demanded to know who had authorized the use of Voters League money
to bond Elder Greer out of the city jail; but the only answer they got
was a refusal to admit that they had any right even to ask such imperti-
nent questions.

When the committee reported its reception, the rebellion even
spread to the next mass meeting on Sunday, June 27. Reese kept
control of the assembly only through his most emotional preaching, and
with the opportune help of James Bevel, who had come into town to
prepare for a visit by Dr. King the next day. Bevel was unhappy about
what was going on; but he told the people that their unity was their

strongest asset, and they had to maintain it even while dealing with their problems. And he pointed to Reese as the man who could best speak for a unified black community. After the meeting, however, several dissidents got together and made plans to interrupt the next evening's meeting with a demand for a new election of officers for the Voters League; the idea was to present their demand before Dr. King could speak, in the presence of the larger crowd he would draw. That same night Harold Middlebrook began trying to figure out how to unseat the officers in some less public but more permanent fashion.

By Monday evening, Reese had got wind of the plan to disrupt the meeting and had talked the dissidents out of it; and Dr. King saved himself a peck of trouble by failing to show up. But the lull was only on the surface. Wilson Baker had done much better with his questioning of Greer, who stayed in jail several days, than did the committee with the Voters League leaders; in fact, the leads that he was able to describe to the mayor were enough to make a segregationist's mouth water. Smitherman ordered his public safety director to spare no expense, to go wherever necessary and do whatever had to be done to bring this evil to light and the wrongdoers to justice. And on July first Baker, his lieutenant, "Cotton" Nichols, and a state investigator were on a plane to San Francisco, after checking out some very revealing bank records in Montgomery.

As Rev. Reese remembers it, he had ordered a complete audit of the Voters League's finances late in June, when he had realized something was awry with SERF, and had just received the results on Tuesday, July sixth, when he paid a visit to City Hall on some personal business. He never got to show the audit to anyone, though, because Wilson Baker met him at the door of his office with a warrant, and by lunchtime Reese was upstairs in the county jail.

Baker, "Cotton" Nichols and state investigator Rufus Head had returned from their California trip three days earlier, and had spent that morning testifying before the Dallas County grand jury. After lunch the jury returned indictments against Reese on three counts of embezzlement. It also subpoenaed the Voters League's financial records. All treasurer Gildersleeve could produce, however, was a check-

book. The grand jury never heard of the audit Rev. Reese later said he
had conducted.

Mrs. Amelia Boynton went to the county courthouse that same
afternoon and offered her property as a surety for the five thousand
dollar bond Judge Hare had set for Reese. But Jim Clark said her land
was not assessed at a sufficient value, and though that was patently
untrue refused to let his prisoner go. Reese spent the night in custody.

As the news of the arrest reached Atlanta, SCLC headquarters
reacted immediately. Ralph Abernathy and Program Director Randolph Blackwell caught the next plane for Montgomery, and were at
Brown Chapel in time to address the angry, confused crowd that had
gathered almost automatically after sundown for a mass meeting. Abernathy ridiculed the charges, and soon had the crowd with him: "I don't
see Wilson Baker putting any money in the plate. It's our money!" he
shouted. "If Reese needs it, we'll give it to him." He derided Baker's
comment that it was complaints by blacks that had sparked his investigation. Abernathy said it would no doubt be found that there weren't
any blacks who complained, "unless they were paid." He promised to
return the next day to get Reese out of jail, and told them not to worry
about the amount of the bail because "I can raise a thousand dollars
a minute if I want to."

"You were not in your darkest hour when you marched," he said.
"Your darkest hour is now when your faith in yourself and your leadership is being tested." But he hedged a little at the end: "Why did he
have to steal? There are Negroes right here in Selma who would have
turned their pockets inside out for Rev. Reese. . . . I'm not saying he
did or did not steal, but we must confirm our faith in him until they
come up with something else."

Wilson Baker was ready with that something else, though he waited
until the next day to present it, giving the reporters a chance to gather
and Abernathy time to make remarks that he would regret. When the
public safety director and the mayor appeared at a press conference
Wednesday, both began by speaking piously of their motives in seeking
the indictments and their concern for the black community. Baker
repeated that the probe had begun only after "the local Negroes affil-
iated with the movement came to us . . . with a complaint that some
of the leaders might be tapping the till. This investigation was at their

request." Referring to the lone Voters League checkbook, he added, "They keep very poor records. I hope they can do better than that. We can't do much investigating unless they have better financial records."

But Baker had other records to show the newspeople: he held up what he said were photographic copies of checks deposited and written on a bank account in Montgomery. A total of $7,950 had been deposited since late March, and Baker had copies of three checks which had been written on it, for $1,500, $217 and $133. These checks were the basis for the indictment: they had been issued by Reese for payments on his house and to buy furniture and clothing. The bank account was in his and his wife's name.

The mayor emphasized that Reese had been *"the* Negro spokesman for Selma. He made all the demands, most of them unreasonable." But he pointed out that Reese's name had not appeared on the most recent list of grievances his office had received from the black community, a letter sent late in June shortly before Elder Greer's arrest. Once they had started looking into the situation as requested, Smitherman added, all sorts of unsavory practices began coming to light. For instance, Smitherman alleged there was considerable evidence that food and clothing donated for relief had been taken and sold out in the rural areas. The city's intention was to "get the case wrapped up as soon as possible," Smitherman said. "We think we are in a position to prosecute."

Baker agreed. He said he had talked with members of the Voters League Steering Committee, and they had told him positively that Reese had never been authorized to use the group's funds for his personal needs, nor had they given permission for the opening of bank accounts for Voters League money outside Selma. Baker had also interviewed some of the donors on his trip, and said they had told him the money was meant for civil rights and relief work, not personal profit.

These revelations were more than the rhetorical skills of an Abernathy could paper over. The press had a field day with the news: it was on page one of the *New York Times,* and was featured on the Today Show's semi-hourly televised news reports. The Alabama press played it for all it was worth, perhaps none more snidely than the *Montgomery Advertiser.* This newspaper once won a Pulitzer Prize for its crusade against the Ku Klux Klan; but it collected no awards for its lead editorial on July 8, entitled "Civil Rights' Pigeon Drops":

> It has been known for some time that Negroes have been pressured to make donations to causes which, while they may have seemed holy at the time, turned sour, leaving them poorer but, in a bitter way, wiser.
>
> But beyond this case—and quite apart from it, since it is in the lap of the courts—it may be said that Negroes have been poorly used in many cases in recent years by their own people—who rush in, arouse the multitude and extract money in the excitement of the moment. It has been the judgement of many close to such scenes that it really amounts to nothing more than a sanctified version of the old flim-flam game known to police as the "pigeon-drop."
>
> On another level, the pigeon-drop continues to work in the civil rights movement. Disregarding the guilt or innocence of Rev. Reese, this is an abominable situation.

The worst part about such gloating was that there was enough truth in it to leave the movement momentarily unable to reply. Rev. Abernathy did not return Wednesday as he had promised, and there was no instant raising of bail money. Instead, the local civil rights staffs had to dig into their pockets and visit a white-owned Selma bonding company before they could get Reese out. And by the time they did, the mood of the community had changed drastically. Temporarily buoyed by Abernathy's oratorical extravagance, they were brought up short by Baker's photostated canceled checks. Until now, despite all the rumors, the relief mess and the leadership doubletalk, most of the plain black people in Selma had avoided concluding that Reese had any involvement in whatever was going on. It was Greer, they told themselves, or maybe some of the others on the Executive Committee, who were pulling fast ones, and Reese was just too busy and too high-minded to notice. They were willing, even anxious, to believe that the charges were just a frameup by the white folks downtown to split the movement and discredit their leader.

But once the evidence had been displayed, this rationalization evaporated. SCLC headquarters had made a strategic decision to stand behind Reese, at least until the excitement died down, and the local staff was ordered to spend all night Tuesday canvassing by telephone to turn out a big crowd to greet him on his release. But again and again the workers found themselves facing people who felt personally betrayed and completely demoralized; and most of the workers were sick at heart themselves. Two staff members, once they understood what evidence Baker had, knew the game was up and refused to join the canvass. Rev. Middlebrook, who felt much the same but was following orders, insisted they go back to work; and when they still refused, he fired them on the spot.

The canvass did not do very well; and when Reese was released, only seventy-five people were waiting for him. He led them to a mass meeting where he spoke defiantly: "The white man is not after Reese. He is after us. We must trust one another and stick together. If anybody knows about embezzlement, the southern white man knows. He embezzled my mother, he embezzled my grandmother, he embezzled my grandfather. He cannot say to anybody, 'you are accused of embezzlement,' because if we could collect all he embezzled, the white man would be in rags." To reporters he was more defensive; he did not deny Baker's evidence, but said that "any funds spent were authorized."

It was reported that after his speech at the mass meeting Tuesday night, Abernathy had gotten a fuller story from other members of the Voters League Executive Committee, and the facts had been plenty disappointing; in any case, he was now singing a different tune as well. "There may have been some practices not in line with acceptable accounting procedures," he told a reporter in Atlanta. "But I'm not suggesting that there has been any dishonesty. If there have been mistakes, they have been mistakes of the head and not of the heart."

"What can they do for an encore?"
"This is the question uppermost in the minds of
the followers of Alabama Crimson Tide football as
they begin to look at the day by day reports on fall
practice at the home of the 1964 national
champions of football."

—Selma Times-Journal, *"Football*
Edition," September 5, 1965

NINETEEN. SCLC's SCOPE

Project did not turn out nearly as well as its sponsors had hoped. The
most important reason was that despite the continual predictions of
imminent passage, the Voting Rights Act was not actually sent to the
White House for the president's signature until the second week in
August. In the Senate the southerners held what was for them an
innocuous "non-filibuster," but that lasted five weeks. Then several of
the ambitious House liberals, including John Lindsay who was running
hard for mayor of New York City and had a lot of black and liberal
Jewish voters to please, tied up the bill some more with a long and
ultimately pointless fight for the insertion of a complete ban on poll
taxes into it.

As the weeks passed, rumors circulated among the summer volunteers that President Johnson had made a deal with the southerners to
the effect that in return for only a token show of opposition, he would
let the bill be delayed until SCOPE was almost over, so they would not
be inundated by a flood of black voters in their home districts right
away. This was probably not true, because comparatively speaking the
bill was whisked through the congressional labyrinth in very short
order. But even so there were hundreds of SCOPE workers walking
dusty streets in hot little Black Belt towns all summer with not much
to do. Everybody was waiting for the bill to be passed, so few people

felt much urgency about standing in long lines at registration offices.

Moreover, with almost a half million dollars to play with, SCLC's legendary disorganization became an industry in SCOPE. The top staff members, as well as any underlings who could get hold of a credit card, spent an inordinate amount of time traveling around the country supervising, organizing, and maintaining liaison, and doing so on the first-class sections of jetliners, behind the wheels of air-conditioned rent-a-cars and from rooms at the best integrated motels along the way. The money went fast, without a great deal to show for the expenditures.

Selma was an exception to this rule. Rev. Middlebrook had worked diligently with the group of volunteers assigned him to keep people trickling down to the courthouse to take advantage of the speeded-up registration procedures already in effect there because of Judge Thomas's injunction. And through all the weeks of May and June, as the morale and spirit of the community had steadily declined, this effort was kept up alongside his attempts to grapple with the other problems that were developing.

After Reese was arrested and the Voters League constituency had disappeared, Middlebrook and his volunteers still spent much of their time doing the slow, time-consuming canvassing that was their main job. Within a few days after Reese's release, that was about all the movement activity there was in the city; that and the infighting which the whites had been waiting for and which quickly became the dominant fact of life in the black community.

Wilson Baker had left for another trip north as soon as he had finished his press conference on July seventh. This time he was gone a week and visited New York, New Jersey, Pennsylvania, and Ohio, talking with more people who had sent checks to the Voters League or the now-defunct SERF. When he returned on July thirteenth, he said he had plenty of statements that the money had never been intended for the personal bank accounts of local leaders, and that he was expecting more indictments to be issued against more people in the near future.

The same day, Elder William Ezra Greer made his last appearance in Selma, before the recorder's court in City Hall. He pleaded guilty to one charge of swearing in the presence of a young girl. Judge Edgar Russell fined him twenty-five dollars, sentenced him to six months' hard labor, and filed three other warrants which were outstanding against him. The six months was suspended pending "good behavior" when Greer's attorney allowed that his client did not intend to stay in the city.

What happened to Baker's new evidence is not clear; no further indictments were ever issued, and Rev. Reese and his colleagues in the Voters League leadership acted as if nothing had happened. They continued centralizing their control over the wards, calling a meeting of ward captains in late July at which Reese asserted, as one attender wrote, "that the Voters League is the responsible organization in the county and that all programs should be cleared through the President. No committee meeting can be called without approval and knowledge of the President." Reese also announced at the meeting that he was making an "administrative decision" to combine Wards 5A and 5B into one unit—clearly an attempt to unseat the maverick Fairro Brown in 5B. These pronouncements did not mean very much; there were hardly any ward organizations left to control by now, and in East Selma the insurgents were not paying much attention anyway.

At another meeting at the end of July, Reese's associate Ernest Doyle showed other local leaders a copy of the Voters League constitution, which few of them had ever seen before. It contained a clause providing that the first vice president would automatically succeed to the presidency when the incumbent's term expired. This meant that Doyle would take Reese's place on January 1, 1966. This was a prospect that the other leaders were not prepared to accept. There was nothing they wanted less than the perpetuation in office of the people whom many believed had first led Reese astray. And several of them began meeting privately soon afterward to figure out a way to prevent it.

Out of these rump meetings came a double thrust: first, a county-wide organizing effort, begun in late September, to pull together a representative group that could petition the Office of Economic Opportunity in Washington for approval as the official antipoverty agency in the county, which was then possible under the law. If they were successful, control of a large block of federal money would be taken away not only from Reese and the Voters League, but just as importantly away from Smitherman and the county officials, and placed in the hands of the poor blacks who were supposed to be the main beneficiaries.

At the same time, a direct competitor to the Voters League appeared, with the name the Dallas County Independent Free Voters Organization. Once the Voting Rights Act had finally passed and a federal examiner was dispatched to Selma, as expected the rolls began to balloon with the names and marks of black people, and the total came steadily closer to reflecting the slender black majority. With these numbers came dreams of black officeholders—even, in place of Jim Clark, a black sheriff. The Independent Free Voters Organization was determined to make these visions into daytime realities.

Through the fall of 1965 and into the winter of 1966 these two new groups struggled against the Voters League and the whites for the allegiance of the black community and the proceeds of their newly won franchise.

On August 11, 1965, the Watts riot began, the first of the really big urban conflagrations of those years. Watts was top front-page news in Selma throughout the rest of the week, as Los Angeles burned and the National Guard hunted snipers. All through the South whites began locking their doors more carefully and laying in extra supplies of ammunition for their hunting rifles. Watts might be more than two thousand miles away, but some of the Black Belt whites' most terrifying nightmares were being played out in color on their own living room television screens. The blacks also had TV sets, and the whites knew they were watching too. Watching and thinking—what?

Despite the paranoia, there was little energy left over in black Selma after the infighting and the continuing efforts to get people down to sign up with the federal voting examiner, and the city lay somnolent in the punishing August heat. When Wilson Baker slipped a disc early that same week and went into the hospital for ten days, he was scarcely missed, at first.

Then on August twentieth, the next Friday, thirty people who had

been arrested during the first (and last) public demonstration in
Lowndes County, a picket line in front of the stores in the town of Fort
Deposit, were suddenly released from the county jail in Hayneville.
Among them were two whites, Jonathan Daniels, an Episcopal
seminarian from New Hampshire who had been working in Selma and
the surrounding region all summer, and Father Richard Morrisroe, a
priest on vacation from his predominantly black Chicago parish. The
group had been released without explanation after spending almost a
week in the jail, crammed into small cells and denied bail; now they
were ordered off the jail grounds and were left standing on a corner of
the town square, across from the old, rundown Lowndes County Courthouse with no way to get out of the town and out of the view of the
hostile local whites. An SNCC worker among them volunteered to go
over by Varner's Cash Store, a ramshackle red building mainly patron-
ized by blacks, and to call Selma and get someone out to pick them up.

On his way back from making the call, the SNCC worker noticed
a white man sitting inside the door of the store holding a rifle and a
pistol. At that moment Jon Daniels and Father Morrisroe, walking with
two black girls, Ruby Sales and Joyce Bailey, came toward the store.
They wanted to go in and get cokes, hoping to wash the taste of a
week's jail provisions out of their mouths.

Ruby Sales was halfway up the store's steps when the armed man
came running out the door, his rifle raised, yelling: "If you don't get
off this god-damned property I'm going to blow your damned brains
out! And I mean get off!"

Jonathan Daniels was walking right behind Ruby, and had only a
second to react; he grabbed her and pushed her to the ground as the
other man pulled the trigger of his shotgun. The blast caught Daniels
full in the stomach at point blank range. He was thrown back twelve
feet into the street and was dead almost instantly.

Father Morrisroe, a few paces back, grabbed Joyce Bailey's hand,
ducked around a car and began to run with her. The man on the steps
fired again, and the charge struck the priest in the back. He skidded
to the ground, alive but grievously wounded.

The killer, a Lowndes County deputy sheriff named Tom Coleman,
walked calmly past his victims and across the wide grass park to the
courthouse. There he picked up a telephone and called Col. Al Lingo

in Montgomery. "I just shot two preachers," he reported laconically. "You better get on down here."

Lingo came in a hurry, while the Lowndes County Solicitor charged Coleman with murder but assured everyone who inquired that he and the deputy sheriff, who was from an old, well-known family, were good friends and there was really nothing to worry about. Coleman was in custody only a few hours.

Back by Varner's store, Father Morrisroe lay moaning in the street for more than an hour, his slain companion's blood coagulating in the dirt, before someone came to pick them up and carry him to Baptist Hospital in Montgomery. There he was in surgery for almost twelve hours, but survived.

Jim Clark heard about the shooting and he arrived in Hayneville about the same time Lingo did; they were probably among the first to be told that Coleman's defense would be that the dead seminarian had attacked him with a knife, and he fired in self-defense.

The Dallas County sheriff knew that Daniels had been in Selma for months, and was known in the black community there. With the smoke of Watts still hanging in the air, the smell of a little gunpowder and blood was enough to send his mind racing. He drove back to Selma convinced that a riot was imminent there, as the blacks learned of the death of another one of their agitators and moved to avenge it as their California cousins had tried to do. He had soon received a report of riot plans being made in the black section, which was all the proof he needed.

Within hours the sheriff, like Major Benjamin Grumbles a hundred and twenty years before, had reactivated his posse and taken it to a mass meeting of whites near the edge of town. There he told them that they had to be ready to liquidate the niggers who tried to riot, and assured them he was ready to lead the defense of the city. He briefed several downtown merchants about the advisability of covering their display windows with plywood, to protect them against bricks and looters, though not bullets. And he was preparing to mount machine guns atop the buildings along Broad and Washington Streets, to keep the thoroughfares open in whatever way was necessary.

Across town, the report of Jon Daniel's murder and the shooting of Father Morrisroe was met with quiet, bitter sadness. Sudden, violent, unjust killings were not new to these people, and their response was to mourn rather than seek revenge. No one suggested that the example of Watts was worth repeating in Dallas County.

Harold Middlebrook was out of town for the weekend, and an assistant named Jimmy Webb was in charge of the SCLC staff during his absence. Webb was young and excitable, but when he learned of the shootings, his response was entirely conventional: he began making plans for a march and vigil downtown Saturday afternoon. The demonstration would probably not be anything spectacular; Daniels was not that well known in the black community, and with the local movement at a standstill since the arrest of Reese, the turnout was not likely to be very large even for such an occasion as this.

Wilson Baker had just come out of the hospital and was resting at home; it was his absence that had permitted the sheriff to bring his fevered fantasies back into the city streets. But Friday night when he learned of Clark's fortifications and Webb's proposed vigil, he moved at once to set up a meeting in his office the following morning with the civil rights workers who were still in town. Webb would be leading his people into a death trap; his vigil had to be stopped, for the blacks' safety and to expose Clark's deadly foolishness for what it was.

By morning, with the black community still calm, Baker had succeeded in tracing Clark's rumor of a riot back to one of the sheriff's own deputies, where it apparently had started. But it took two hours of convincing to get stubborn Jimmy Webb to believe that Baker was not just trying to sidetrack a memorial to Jon Daniels with his talk about Clark and a panicky armed posse waiting at the courthouse. Finally, however, Webb agreed to call it off, and a friend drove him back to Sylvan Street. There he came upon a small group of young people standing on the sidewalk singing freedom songs and talking about marching downtown on their own. He had just persuaded them to abandon the idea when a sheriff's car cruising by saw him speaking to the group and pulled over. The grim-faced deputies grabbed Webb, hustled him downtown and charged him with inciting to riot. It took Wilson Baker's intervention with Justice Department officials to get Webb out on bond.

That Sunday night a memorial meeting was held in the safer confines of Brown Chapel, after the white Episcopal church in Selma had declined to permit any services to be held there for a dead seminarian of its own communion. After the meeting Harold Middlebrook, Jimmy Webb and several other workers gathered in the back of the church to hear reports from projects in several other communities. While they talked, the door opened and Wilson Baker entered. The public safety director was restless and he had something to say to them. It was about Jim Clark: the man was not fit to hold office, and someone had to be found to run against him in next year's election, someone with sense who could have a chance of winning. But it wasn't easy to find willing candidates, and if no one else would stand, he would run himself. He wasn't really politically ambitious, Baker insisted; he would just as soon go back to quietly teaching police science at the university in Tuscaloosa. But he had had enough of Clark, and would try once more to retire him before giving up. If he had to run, he said he hoped he could get some of the black votes that were now going to have to be counted.

While he talked, the door opened again and Rev. Reese came in. Reese was not invited to meetings like this anymore, and his entry was as unexpected as Baker's. The two men greeted each other politely, and Baker soon left.

Wilson Baker did run for sheriff against Jim Clark, and Rev. Reese supported him to the hilt. Baker had originally agreed not to make another race for the job when Smitherman had hired him eighteen months earlier, because of the mayor's friendship with the sheriff and his desire to minimize competition between the two men. But after all the publicity he had received during the voting rights campaign, Clark was convinced that he was a national figure of sorts and the time was ripe for a run for statewide office. In fact, he was determined to go straight for the top, and announced his intention to run for governor. When he did that, Baker felt released from his commitment, because now Clark would not be in the sheriff's contest. Late in January 1966 Baker had the mayor tell Clark of his intentions, but Baker added that he would run only if Clark agreed that to do so would not violate his pledge not to oppose him. Clark told the mayor he was agreeable.

But then George Wallace, who had fought unsuccessfully to repeal the constitutional provision that prohibited Alabama governors from succeeding themselves, announced that his wife Lurleen would run as a stand-in. That squashed the ambitions of several aspirants, including Jim Clark, who knew that no one could run as a symbol of segregation and get anywhere against a Wallace. So the sheriff retrenched and started campaigning for re-election, denying for good measure that Baker had ever asked to be let out of his pledge not to run against him.

The campaign was a long and bitter one, and it seems that the disposition of the embezzlement charges against Rev. Reese was one small piece of interplay within it. Reese's trial had been postponed twice, from the original date in early October until December, then again when the trial—and acquittal—of James Reeb's alleged assailants was placed ahead of it on the December docket. Then one morning in March, 1966, Solicitor Blanchard McLeod abruptly called the case to trial, and told Judge Hare he was in no position to prosecute because members of the Voters League Steering Committee were now saying that they *had* given Reese permission to use the money found in his Montgomery account. Hare quickly agreed and dropped the charges.

Many people in the black community assumed and said that Reese must have made a deal with Baker to get off, trading support against Clark for his freedom. But Baker swore that this was not the case, that Solicitor McLeod and Judge Hare were supporters of the sheriff and would not have gone along with anything that would have helped his challenger. Rather, Baker believed that the dropping of charges was a ploy by the sheriff aimed at painting Baker as a vindictive persecutor of blacks who was trying to frame an innocent man. The truth here, as in most such situations, is hard to ferret out; but it is a fact that Jim Clark, after all was said and done, did try to get black votes in the primary, throwing at least one big barbecue for blacks. (Nor was he the only big segregationist who was learning to sing a different tune in that election: Al Lingo, who had left the state troopers to run for sheriff of Jefferson County, which included Birmingham, visited a black mass meeting there, ostentatiously dropped a five-dollar bill in the collection plate, and asked for black support. He didn't get it, and lost overwhelmingly. This was also the year that George Wallace learned how to

pronounce Negro "Knee-grow" rather than "Nigra.") Already the new
black vote was something to reckon with. But Clark's solicitations
didn't do him much good either.

It was not long after the dropping of charges that Reese and the
Voters League announced their support for Baker and began working
hard for him among the black community's more than seven thousand
new voters. The Dallas County Independent Free Voters Organization
believed on the other hand that a black could win, even though white
votes were still in the majority, if a three-way race developed between
Clark, Baker and a black candidate. They had a candidate, too, a man
named Samson Crum. But Reese and a number of other prominent
blacks who did not see eye to eye on many other issues felt that the
entry of a black candidate would only assure Clark's re-election, and
they put pressure on Crum to withdraw. Crum was nearing retirement
as a postal worker, and they got to him through his job; he pulled out,
and the contest was fought between the two white candidates.

On primary night, May 3, 1966, Baker pulled slowly ahead as the
boxes from mostly black areas came in. But the next day, as had
occurred before, strange things began happening. The sheriff appeared
before the county Democratic Executive Committee to challenge six
of the predominantly black boxes, which contained enough votes to
give Baker a clear majority and the nomination. Without them he
would have had only a plurality and would have had to face Clark again
in a runoff. The committee chairman was Alston Keith, one of the most
fervent old-line segregationists in the county; and the vice-chairman
was former Mayor Chris Heinz of the White Citizens Council; and it
did not take the body long to accept Clark's objections and throw out
the boxes.

But Wilson Baker was ready for such shenanigans this time around,
and the Justice Department, which had taken a special interest in the
race, was standing by as well. Clark was expecting a fight in the local
court, where he had a friend in Judge Hare. But the challenger's
attorneys went to Judge Thomas's court in Mobile as soon as the
committee's decision was made, to file a federal suit against the proceeding. They found that Judge Thomas was conveniently out of town
for several weeks on what was described as a "business-vacation trip."
But the lawyers were not to be easily foiled; they swung back north to

Montgomery and found a ready listener in Judge Frank Johnson. Johnson issued an order directing that all the boxes be impounded in the custody of federal agents until Judge Thomas could return and hold a hearing.

After the hearing was held in mid-May, Judge Thomas ordered the Democratic Executive Committee to count the six boxes and award the nomination to Baker. Baker's victory was saved by the first Justice Department action in history involving a local primary. The suit—and Baker's election—were made under the provisions of the Voting Rights Act which Baker had worked so doggedly, and so much more intelligently than his opponent, to prevent.

Clark ran on a write-in in the general election that fall and came close to winning, but not close enough. His political career had been ended, and its ending was the first tangible outgrowth of the blacks' successful struggle to regain the franchise. It would be seven more years before the effects of the deep divisions in the black electorate were healed enough to finally put blacks into office in Selma. When at length blacks were elected in Selma it was Rev. Frederick Reese, emerging from a long period of eclipse, who led a group of five black men into City Council seats in the municipal elections of 1972.

EPILOGUE.

There are other stories that could be told of Selma 1965. One of them is how the southern civil rights movement of that decade came to an end there, with only the splendor of the march to Montgomery's success preventing the fact of its finality becoming immediately apparent to all. This other story has been intentionally avoided here, first of all because in it the Selma campaign is but the closing chapter in a drama much larger in scale and span of time. But even more important, it has been avoided because to focus on it, as have many other writers, is to become bogged down in a mass of ambiguous, often tawdry and largely irrelevant detail which only obscures the greater significance of the campaign. The black community's misfortunes following the march which have been described earlier are suggestive enough of what was happening elsewhere. More important than these local disappointments is the fact that the voting rights campaign seems to have accomplished its long-term objectives. These ends, which Dr. King based on his commitments as a Christian minister and an heir to Gandhi's *Satyagraha*, always went beyond gaining the ballot to making possible some real reconciliation among the black and white citizens of Dallas County—and the South. And as this book was being written, in the spring of 1973, a remarkable degree of reconciliation had taken place there as a result of the campaign. For instance, the schools had been fully and peacefully desegregated, an achievement that—even under court order —still eludes much of the urban North; Wilson Baker had been re-elected sheriff almost unanimously, and not least because he provided black and white a superior quality of professional, fair law enforcement; and on a more mundane level, ordinary black citizens like Mr. Lonzy West, a housepainter who signed the first warrant against Elder Greer, were again able to find steady work, after being punished with years of unemployment for participation in the voter registration campaigns.

None of these items is meant to imply that the people of Dallas County have transcended the dark side of human nature, or even solved all the problems of 1965, but rather to mark the extent of change there —and because of the struggle there, elsewhere—with such a comparatively small human cost. In the ghettos of Washington, Brooklyn, and other northern cities, shells of riot-burned buildings still stand, underlining the continued despair that destroyed them, but also serving as monuments to the futility of its hopeless, outraged explosions. In Selma, and indeed throughout the South, the character of the region has persisted, but the climate of the culture has become markedly more humane. There are even reliable reports of the beginning of a reverse migration, a trickle of proud, educated black men and women away from the ersatz emancipation of the North back toward their parents' homes, and this after four generations and more of a stream in the opposite direction. Some others, those whose parents marched in the select three hundred along Highway 80, or maybe made the last day's trek themselves, are staying.

These are developments that the Selma campaign helped bring to pass, and they are uniformly promising. Beside them the deaths of Jimmie Lee Jackson, James Reeb, Viola Liuzzo, and Jonathan Daniels stand out as genuinely redemptive sacrifices in a time when the meaningless massacre of scores of thousands was becoming a national policy; the beatings and the arrests, even the disappointments of SERF and the paralysis of the summer, seem paltry prices to have paid for the value received.

That it was so has made the history worth retelling. There have been too few Selmas in our time; we must not let them slip from our memory.

Among the other stories in Selma 1965, one deserves brief attention: In late October 1963, a minister of the Church of the Brethren named Ralph Smeltzer paid a call on the national SNCC headquarters in Atlanta. There Smeltzer, a fair-haired, deceptively quiet, conservatively dressed man, was told how Mrs. Annie Lee Cooper and three dozen of her co-workers at the Dunn Rest Home in Selma had been summarily fired by Mr. Dunn not long before, after he saw them lined up at the courthouse trying to register. We met Mrs. Cooper ealier, when she decked Sheriff Clark at the courthouse in January 1965. Reverend Smeltzer was told that none of those fired had since been able to find work with white employers, and he was asked if his church could offer them any assistance.

Smeltzer was serving as a race relations specialist for his denomination at the time, and decided to visit Selma to look into the situation. His inquiries confirmed the story he had been told, and he went to work setting up a relief project. The Church of the Brethren operates a large international relief and assistance program, and his plan was to get help from its staff in establishing a small sewing factory in Selma, where the Dunn victims could find permanent work.

As he pursued the details involved in the project, however, Smeltzer's attention was increasingly drawn to the tense and oppressive racial situation in the city at large. SNCC workers were agitating among the city's black youth; Jim Clark was harassing them and others, with no one to stop or restrain him; the situation looked and obviously was explosive. In the spring of 1964 Smeltzer obtained permission from his superiors to work as a conciliator and mediator in the city.

Through a long and irrelevant series of complications, the sewing factory never got started. But over the next eighteen months Reverend Smeltzer worked quietly and steadily away at his new task of opening up communications between black and white in Selma and trying to bring about some modicum of reconciliation and justice in their relationship.

His first job was to come to know Selma intimately, both the black and white communities. "I have to get to know this city better than most people who live here," he wrote in one of numerous memos to himself on the subject. And he did: he studied the history, the economy, the politics and the religion of the region intensively and thoroughly. During later visits he interviewed practically all the people who either carried weight in the black and white sections or knew who did. Where officials like Mayor Heinz met his inquiries with a barely disguised invitation to get the hell out of town, he fell back and developed contacts with people who had important access to these officials. Based on this material he drew up detailed analyses of the black and white power structures, and the political groupings within each.

As he moved about the city, Smeltzer kept bumping into white people who would say to him privately, once he had gained their trust, that they knew segregation was evil and must go; but each was convinced he or she was alone in this sentiment and was afraid to express it publicly. Smeltzer began quietly putting these people in touch with each other, in what was the beginning of the "moderate presence" in the city which finally emerged with Art and Muriel Lewis's courageous stand and the struggle over the Chamber of Commerce declaration after the march. In the black community he found leadership fragmented into competing cliques; here he worked with the various erstwhile community spokespeople, trying to get them to sit down and come to some understanding that would enable them to join forces. He was an early advocate of the elevation of Reverend Reese to the presidency of DCVL as a way of achieving this unity.

It was slow work, and Smeltzer's memos to himself are dotted with reminders that he must above all be patient in his efforts. His style was carefully low-key and nondirective: he stayed strictly neutral between the two communities and among the factions within each; he kept confidences, listened more than he spoke, asked questions more than he made statements, and rarely attended any of the meetings he catalyzed. Even so, he was often afraid for his physical safety in the city, especially after an incident in late spring 1964, in which two Presbyterian officials visiting church schools for blacks in Wilcox County were set upon and beaten savagely by a white motel owner, who decided they must be outside agitators. Wilcox Sheriff P. C. "Lummie" Jenkins declined to take the incident seriously, and the county grand jury returned no indictment when it got around to considering the matter. With Jim Clark and his possemen roaming the Selma streets without restraint, Smeltzer was right to be cautious and concerned.

Once his community analysis was complete, Smeltzer began to move strategically. His plan, as he described it, was first to make himself indispensable to leaders in both communities as a source of information and a communications link between them; then to use this position to prod the white leadership toward dilution and abandonment of their diehard segregationist posture, and the blacks toward building a disciplined, representative leadership that would press resolutely but peacefully for basic but moderate advances. By the end of 1964 he had come near achieving indispensability; but while he was encouraged with the privately expressed willingness of many white businessmen and officials to comply with the Civil Rights Act, the terrorism of Clark and the violence boiling just below the surface in much of the white community had still kept them from making any break with the public united front against compliance.

Smeltzer looked forward to the impending SCLC direct action campaign with foreboding. He knew how completely such a movement could disrupt a community's life. In fact, he felt so strongly about what was coming that he stepped briefly out of his usual unobtrusive role in an attempt to make the white leadership aware of what they were facing. On January 6, 1965, Smeltzer called together several of his key contacts in the board room of the Peoples Bank and Trust Company building. At the meeting he laid out in detail for them what he knew of SCLC's plans, and tried to show how serious the potential for disruption, violence, and federal intervention were. He also suggested a number of concessions which, if made by the city and county government in time, might be able to make the city less of a sitting duck and enable it to avoid being the main target of Dr. King's drive. The key to these concessions was easing the stringency with which the Board of Registrars was applying the state's restrictive voting regulations.

Smeltzer's forecast was, of course, prescient. His proposals were both moderate and sophisticated, reflecting an understanding of both the community and the movement. But he got nowhere. The whites simply did not believe that the situation portended anything like he had described, and felt themselves under no pressure to work for the changes he outlined with any more vigor than they already were. When the lengthy session concluded, Smeltzer had failed to pierce their complacency.

As the campaign unfolded and outstripped even his direst predictions, Smeltzer kept in almost daily contact by telephone with key people on both sides: among them were, in the black community, Reverend Reese and Reverend Claude Brown; and among the whites, Arthur Capell of the *Selma Times-Journal*, who was Mayor Smitherman's confidant, along with Art Lewis, who was in close touch with Sheriff Clark and Judge Hare until his public break with segregation in March. It appears to have been Smeltzer's mediation that set up the negotiations in early February, from which emerged the Board of Registrars' decision to open an appearance book before it was ordered to do so by the federal court. This minuscule concession almost opened the way to continued negotiations, which might ultimately have produced a local compromise that would have forced Dr. King to shift the focus of the campaign elsewhere; but as we have seen, the situation and the SCLC staff did not permit it to happen. Smeltzer also assisted the agents of the Community Relations Service who arrived after the March 7 attack, orienting them to the situation and feeding them the contacts they needed to carry on their own mission of preventing further violence.

After the march, Smeltzer returned to Selma for a visit and was gratified by what he found. Despite the ordeal that the city had undergone, prospects for progress seemed good: in his memos he describes Reverend Reese as being in a strong bargaining position and carrying himself like a real leader; the white progressives were winning the struggle over the Chamber of Commerce statement and would not be silenced again. Smeltzer concluded that the time was right for him to phase out of his role in the city, which he did over the next few months. He found a successor in David Smith, a Methodist seminarian from California who took leave from his studies to spend the summer in the city. Smith found quarters in the white community and went to work as a conciliator in the same manner as Smeltzer had. As the situation deteriorated, he found himself with plenty of work to do and played a similarly important role.

Ralph Smeltzer is an unusually methodical man, and this characteristic clearly had much to do with his effectiveness in Selma. He took notes during every telephone conversation he held about Selma, and wrote summaries of each interview he conducted. His community analyses were worked out in painstaking and comprehensive detail, and updated as they were affected by new information. All this was entered in longhand in the pages of a small black looseleaf notebook he carried with him.

Predictably, Smeltzer threw nothing away, and after concluding his Selma work he assembled all his notes, plus dozens of file folders full of relevant news clippings, pamphlets, magazine articles, correspondence, and other materials, for the Church of the Brethren archives in Elgin, Illinois.

These files were made available to the author during the latter stages of the research for this book. That they became the most valuable single resource for interpreting what happened in the white community during and after the voting rights campaign should be evident from the footnotes as well as the preceding paragraphs; but even more than that, they unveiled a ministry about which the author previously knew virtually nothing but which was unquestionably one of the most phenomenal performances in a situation that produced many startling phenomena.

Only the barest sketch of Reverend Smeltzer's work in Selma has been given here, intentionally so, because any adequate treatment would deserve a book of its own. It is the author's hope to stimulate some other student of the period or of the Christian ministry to undertake the fuller study of Smeltzer's work which would result in such a volume. To study and learn from such a distinguished example is to begin to pay it proper tribute.

There are many others whose assistance was necessary for this work, and who likewise gave it freely. The first on the list chronologically, although unwitting helpers, still deserve note. They are Frederick Wiseman, distinguished maker of documentary films, and Dean Peerman, veteran managing editor of *The Christian Century*. It was Dean Peerman's decision to publish the author's review of Frederick Wiseman's great film *High School* which led to the publisher's inquiry which in turn produced the agreement for this project.

Krister Stendahl, dean of Harvard Divinity School, and William Hutchison, Charles Warren Professor of the History of Religion in America there, later extended help far beyond what was warranted by the inconclusive character of my tenure at the school. Mr. Nathaniel Bunker of the Resources and Acquisitions Division of the Harvard College Library encouraged and assisted the research and was generous in judging its potential value to scholars as an addition to the library's collections.

Carl Seaburg of the Unitarian Universalist Association staff was very cooperative in making available the denomination's archives at its headquarters in Boston. He also helped track down the ministers who had maintained the Unitarian presence after the march. Many of the ministers themselves were similarly responsive.

In Selma, Mayor Joe Smitherman, Sheriff Wilson Baker, and Councilman Frederick Reese all endured extended questioning with patience and provided candid replies. Reverend Claude C. Brown(see footnote to page 17) who brought food and messages to the author and his fellow prisoners at Camp Selma in February 1965, was equally unstinting in his hospitality thereafter. The career of Reverend Brown, spanning forty years in Dallas and Wilcox counties, is still another Selma story worthy of some perceptive historian's careful attention. Mr. and Mrs. Lonzy West, Mrs. Amelia Platts Boynton Billups, the fathers of the Society of Saint Edmund Mission House in Selma, Gordon and Judy Gibson, Conrad and Ora Brown, and Dan and Pat Bing likewise cooperated in the work, as did numerous others whose interviews became part of the Harvard Library Selma Collection.

In Washington, Dr. George Docherty, pastor of the New York Avenue Presbyterian Church, his late wife Gerry, and his associates Jack McClendon and Thelma Odum assisted the project in ways too numerous to mention. It is one of the author's greatest regrets that Mrs. Docherty did not live to read this account of a movement which meant so much to her and in which she took part so creatively.

Several score people from around the nation responded to queries for information and recollections of their participation in the march, and provided many important fragments of information. They are too many to list here, and must accept this belated general expression of gratitude. One among them, however, requires special attention, and that is Mr. Richard Leonard of New York, who generously provided a copy of the 160-page manuscript account he wrote of his recollections of the vigil and march, a vivid and eloquent work that deserves publication on its own.

In the course of a marathon effort to type and re-type this manuscript, the help of the author's wife, Letitia Hastings Fager, and brother, Michael Allen Fager, was of incalculable aid, notwithstanding the confusion that resulted from having three typewriters going at it simultaneously. And last but not least, the tenacity, courage, and new life contributed by Ms. Carol Browne of Atlanta cannot be underestimated.

Bibliography

At the height of the campaign, of course, newspapers and magazines around the globe were full of reporting about Selma and the march. But the best newspaper source for studying the Selma campaign is the one closest to home. The *Selma Times-Journal*, under heavy pressure from several directions at once, still managed to do a superior, professional job of honest and balanced reporting. Other Alabama newspapers, such as the *Birmingham Times-Herald* and *News* were occasionally helpful, as were the *New York Times* and *Washington Post*. Except for the "Frederick Douglass Free Press," several issues of which were published in mimeographed form by the Selma SNCC staff in late 1964–early 1965, there was no newspaper in the black community at the time of the campaign. The Smeltzer papers include an extensive collection of clippings about Selma, most of them pre-1965, and covering other subjects as well as civil rights issues. The complete collection is in the archives of the Church of the Brethren in Elgin, Illinois; a microfilm copy of most of this material, excluding most of the clippings, is in the Harvard College Library. The Civil Rights Documentation Project, now located in Howard University, Washington, D.C., has extensive taped interviews, most of which have been transcribed, with many of the leading participants in the campaign, and the author regrets that they were unavailable to him during his research. Similarly, the large collection of papers from the records of SCLC in the library

of the Martin Luther King, Jr. Center for Non-violent Social Change
in Atlanta were still unavailable to researchers when this book was
written, but they should become a major resource when they are
opened up. Extensive information about the participation of nuns at
Selma is contained in the archives of the National Catholic Conference
for Interracial Justice at Marquette University, Milwaukee.

BOOKS AND ARTICLES

Adler, Renata. "Letter from Selma." *The New Yorker*, 10 April
1965, p. 121ff. Also reprinted as Chapter One in her book *Toward a
Radical Middle*. New York: 1969.

Cash, W. J. *The Mind of the South*. New York: 1941.

Docherty, Dr. George. Sermons preached at New York Avenue
Presbyterian Church March 7 and 14 1965, privately printed by the
church.

Fager, Charles E. "Jail in the Black Belt," *The Register-Leader*.
Unitarian Universalist Association, Vol. 148, No. 5, May 1966.

Fleming, Walter. *Civil War and Reconstruction in Alabama*.
Tuscaloosa: University of Alabama Press, 1905.

Forman, James. *Sammy Younge, Jr.* New York: 1968.

Gitlin, Todd, ed. *Campfires of the Resistance*. New York: 1971.

Going, Allen J. *Bourbon Democracy in Alabama*. University, Alabama, 1951.

Goldman, Eric F. *The Tragedy of Lyndon Johnson*. New York:
1969.

Good, Paul. "Beyond the Bridge." *The Reporter*, 8 April 1965,
p.24ff.

Hackney, Sheldon. *Populism to Progressivism in Alabama*. Princeton: Princeton University Press, 1969.

Hardy, John. *History of Selma*. Selma, 1879.

Jackson, Walter M. *The Story of Selma*. Decatur, Alabama: 1954.

Heinz, W. C. and Lindeman, Bard. "Great Day at Trickem
Fork." *Saturday Evening Post*, 22 May 1965, p. 30ff.

Ianniello, Lynne. *Milestones Along the March*. New York: 1966.

Johnson, Lady Bird. *A White House Diary.* New York: 1970.

Johnson, Lyndon Baines. *The Vantage Point.* New York: 1971.

King, Coretta Scott. *My Life with Martin Luther King, Jr.* New York: 1969.

King, Dr. Martin Luther, Jr. "Behind the Selma March." *The Saturday Review*, 3 April 1965.

Leonard, Richard. Untitled manuscript describing march experiences, 1965. Cambridge, Massachusetts: Harvard College Library.

Lewis, David. *King: A Critical Biography.* New York: 1970.

Louis, Debbie. *And We Are Not Saved.* New York: 1970.

Mendelsohn, Jack. *The Martyrs.* New York: 1966.

Mikell, Robert. *Selma.* Charlotte, North Carolina: 1965.

Miller, William Robert. *Martin Luther King, Jr.* New York: 1968.

Rapier, A. F., *The Tragedy of Lynching.* Chapel Hill: 1933.

San Francisco Theological Seminary. *The Chimes*, vol. 11, No. 4, San Anselmo, California: September 1965.

Schneider, William, ed. *The Jon Daniels Story.* New York: 1968.

Southern Christian Leadership Conference. *Newsletter,* March 1964.

Southern Commission on the Study of Lynching. *Lynchings and what They Mean*: Atlanta: 1931.

Unitarian Universalist Association. *To Bear Witness.* Boston: 1965.

United States Congress. *Testimony before the Joint Select Committee on Ku Klux Klan,* vols. 8–10(Alabama), 1871.

Williams, John A. *The King God Didn't Save.* New York: 1970.

Williams, Juanita T. "The Impact of Education, Socio-Economic Status, and Self-Concept on Out-of-State Participants in Selma, Alabama Movement Dissent March 1965." Master's thesis, Atlanta University, n.d.

Zinn, Howard. *SNCC: The New Abolitionists.* Boston: 1964.

Notes and References

ABBREVIATIONS: STJ—Selma Times-Journal
DCVL—Dallas County Voters League
UUA—Unitarian Universalist Association

Page 5 "The judge claimed . . ." Lewis to Smeltzer, 24 July 1964. The judge's views were also recorded by Yankee reporters, including Paul Good, in "Beyond the Bridge," *The Reporter*, 8 April 1965, p. 24.

Page 6 "So Clark stayed away . . ." Capell to Smeltzer, 28 August 1964, 3 October 1964; Capell and Baker to Smeltzer, 30 December 1964; Capell to Smeltzer, 31 December 1964, and 6 January 1965.

Page 6 "Dr. King and his . . ." Cf., for example, the SCLC *Newsletter*, March 1964, in which a five-part plan was announced which included "massive" nonviolent direct action, to regain the vote for blacks in Alabama. Dr. King told reporters that the demonstrations "might" begin in thirty days. They didn't. Later SCLC joined SNCC in designating Selma as the target of a "major push" for the summer of 1964; cf. Smeltzer, Speech Notes, 5 May 1964. See also page 41.

Page 7 "Baker understood . . ." Cf. a speech he later gave to the Crestwood Civic Club, noted in the *Birmingham News*, 18 April 1965; cf. also the *Selma Times-Journal* (hereafter referred to as *STJ*), 18 February 1965, in which a front page editorial "Sanity and Realism Must Come to Selma," reprinted statements made by Smitherman and Baker before the campaign began that were along similar lines.

Page 7 "Baker moved first to head . . ." This incident is described from Baker's account of it.

Page 9 "The Voters League in turn . . ." Cf. Reese to Smeltzer, throughout December, 1964.

Page 12 "Once during the 1830s . . ." This tale is recorded in John Hardy, *History of Selma*, pp.15–16.

Page 13 "Many of the early settlers . . ." The early chapters of W. J. Cash, *The Mind of the South*, were very helpful in putting Selma's early history in context.

Page 14 "While he supported slavery . . ." Cf. Hardy and Walter M. Jackson, *The Story of Selma*. Dallas County voted Whig regularly until the mid-1850s; and when delegates were elected to the secession convention in 1861, a slate of "cooperationists" or mild secessionists opposed the dominant immediate secessionist candidates. The cooperationists lost, of course, but garnered over 20 per cent of the vote; this was in sharp contrast to what happened in surrounding counties, where if there were any cooperationists, they were unwilling or unable to even enter the contest and the vote for immediate secession was unanimous.

Page 14 "In March 1865 . . ." This account is from Hardy.

Page 14 "In 1869 and 1870 the Ku Klux Klan . . ." Cf. *Testimony before the Joint Select Committee on Ku Klux Klan in Alabama*, 1871, vols. 8–10. There are lengthy lists in the index to these hearings of "outrages" in other counties not far from Dallas, but none in either Selma or Dallas County. General Pettus testified (p. 399) that numerous resolutions were passed by meetings of white men opposing mob violence, but without mentioning the Klan.

Page 15 "But it never showed . . ." General Pettus's statement to the Joint Committee, *ibid.*, p. 385ff, is full of disdain for the mass of Klansmen, even as he solemnly insists that no such organization ever existed. The only two "outrages" he ascribes to his home county (p. 375) involved assaults on *white* men by groups of *blacks*.

Page 15 "And when the state . . ." General Pettus, sagely insisting on his political innocence and naiveté before the Joint Committee, *ibid.*, *supported* Negro suffrage, service on juries, etc., in 1871, no doubt because he was talking to a panel of radical Yankees, but also probably because he was not terribly afraid of the effects of these measures, especially if former Confederates like himself could obtain pardons and re-enter active political life. Sheldon Hackney, in *Populism to Progressivism in Alabama*, traces the political developments that culminated in disfranchisement at the end of the century; his analysis suggests that Pettus was not putting the congressmen on very much, if at all.

Page 16 "Nor was it unknown . . ." In the *STJ*, 9 December 1965, a large obituary was headlined "Well-known Negro Dies Wednesday," and it began: "Senior Citizen Suzie Morris Brown, wife of Payton Brown, died Wednesday morning. . . ." But "Senior Citizen" Brown was not Negro at all.

She was a white woman, a Selma native, who had married a black man. Their son, Reverend Claude Brown, still lived and worked in Selma as this was written, and he had had a long and distinguished career as a Negro leader and minister. He was pastor of the Reformed Presbyterian Church on Jeff Davis Avenue, on the border between the black slums and the genteel white neighborhoods; it was in his church that the Concerned White Citizens of Alabama were to gather in March 1965(see Chapter Nine).

Page 16 "In this situation . . ." Cf. Rapier, *The Tragedy of Lynching.*

Page 17 "It was a hard-fought campaign . . ." The *STJ* followed a strict policy of non-involvement in local campaigns at that time, reporting only the entry of candidates into the various races and the final results. Additional information comes only in the campaign advertisements published during the primary race, supplemented by personal interviews. This was also the year of George Wallace's first try at the governorship, when his campaign ads even in the Black Belt listed segregation very low on his platform.

Page 18 "Because of the civil rights laws . . ." See note to page 7 above, "Baker understood . . ."

Page 19 "Baker hoped to duplicate . . ." Cf. David Lewis, *King: A Critical Biography*, p.265.

Page 19 "That the Alabama Councils . . ." Lewis to Smeltzer, 4–5 June 1964.

Page 22 "One ancient, wrinkled woman . . ." These anecdotes are taken from the two January issues of the "Frederick Douglass Free Press," a mimeographed newspaper published by the Selma SNCC staff in late 1964 and early 1965, except for the account of the Ward Three meeting on pp.26–27, which the author attended.

Page 24 "But before he left . . ." Baker (Smitherman) to Smeltzer, 4 January 1965.

Page 28 "At the Selma Del . . ." *STJ*, 18 January 1965.

Page 31 "Wilson Baker had a spy . . ." or so he said, and the author believes him. But the identity of the unwilling double-agent will not be disclosed here.

Page 36 "They had planned to be . . ." This account of the preparations for the march is based on Reverend Reese's recollections.

Page 41 "(To be filled out . . .)" These excerpts are from a sample application printed in the Congressional Record, 9 February 1965, pp. 2422–2423.

Page 41 "Judge Thomas was a native . . ." Jansen-Smeltzer, 16 July 1964.

Page 45 "Mrs. Cooper was no stranger . . ." It was her firing by Dunn in October 1963 that brought Ralph Smeltzer to Selma; see Epilogue.

Page 45 "He pointed to an antenna-like device . . ." The "doohickey" speech is as the author, who was present, remembers it. It was not mentioned in the press accounts, although it was the high point of the meeting.

Page 47 "Baker didn't like having . . ." Capell to Smeltzer, 29 January 1965.

Page 47 "At a special executive . . ." Smeltzer to Boyte, 26 January 1965.

Page 51 "When the King . . ." Dr. King's letter appeared in an advertisement in *The New York Times*, 5 February 1965.

Page 51 "Before he was ever jailed . . ." *Congressional Record*, 10 February 1965, p. 2510.

Page 52 "The men were in a bay . . ." The description of the imprisonment is from the author's recollections as one of those arrested and later moved into King's cell.

Page 54 "Attorney Peter Hall . . ." This anecdote is again from the author's own memory as one of those arrested.

Page 54 "One group was taken . . ." The camp here was Camp Selma, and the conditions are as the author observed them during five days confinement there.

Page 57 "Just then it seemed . . ." Cf. Coretta Scott King, *My Life with Martin Luther King, Jr.*, p. 259.

Page 60 " 'I've had enough of this' . . ." Eric F. Goldman, *The Tragedy of Lyndon Johnson*, p. 404.

Page 61 "In fact Johnson had no intention . . ." This is in contradiction to his statements on this matter in *The Vantage Point* (p.161) but was reported to me by Professor Doris Kearns, and is borne out by later events.

Page 66 "Inside the courthouse he ran into . . ." Pitts recalled his advice to Clark while testifying at the sheriff's contempt hearing, cf. *STJ*, 18 May 1965.

Page 66 "You asked me . . ." *Campfires of the Resistance*, Todd Gitlin, ed., pp. 36–37.

Page 74 "Among them were Jimmie Lee Jackson . . ." In addition to press accounts, the author has here relied on Jack Mendelsohn's *The Martyrs*, which devotes a chapter to Jackson, pp. 133–152.

Page 74 "Then a trooper picked him up . . ." Trooper Fowler was never more specifically identified.

Page 75 "Selma's Confederate general, Edmund Pettus, gave . . ." See the notes for page 14.

Page 77 " 'This is dirty pool' . . ." So Baker remembered the remark, which is in character.

Page 81   "On Thursday night, James Bevel . . ." This is how Bevel described the episode to the author at the time.

Page 82   "The people were treated to . . ." The author is very fortunate here to have access to two sermons by Dr. George Docherty, pastor of the New York Avenue Presbyterian Church in Washington, D.C. Dr. Docherty was present at this service, and recalled the texts and quotes from Bevel's sermon in his own preaching on March 7 and March 14 1965; it is from these that this description is taken, as well as several details of Dr. King's travels on 1 March 1965.

Page 85   "The rain had not let up . . ." The author's recollections of this funeral, which he attended, have been aided by Mendelsohn, *The Martyrs*.

Page 91   "The troopers were also limbering up . . ." John Carter Lewis told his story in federal court in Montgomery later; see *STJ*, 14 March 1965.

Page 92   "But this time, as on the . . ." Interpretations differ about the reason for King's absence, and this writer has had no success in reconciling them, but is obviously more friendly to him than others, such as James Forman in *Sammy Younge, Jr.* and John A. Williams in *The King God Didn't Save*. Williams' trashy, undocumented put-down would be beneath comment except that it states baldly a view that many others hold privately, and with about as much basis.

Page 93   "As they reached the high point . . ." This anecdote was relayed to the author by Wilson Baker, and it, like the one noted on page 77, is in character. The balance of this account of the confrontation is based on conversations with him, Mayor Smitherman, Mr. Clarence Williams of Selma(Cf. Harvard Selma Tapes, Reel 4, Tape 5, Side 2), a study of newspaper accounts, personal recollections, and the Smeltzer papers.

Page 95   "As one group of marchers . . ." Clarence Williams, *ibid.*

Page 96   "Other blacks were coming in . . ." *Ibid.*

Page 99   "HE DIDN'T COME . . ." Gitling, *op. cit.*

Page 101   "During the day Monday . . ." This account is as the mayor recalls it.

Page 101   "He had had many run-ins . . ." The "carpetbagging . . . liar" comment was apparently first uttered in 1957 when Wallace was a circuit judge in Barbour County, his home area. He attracted considerable attention in the state by refusing to turn over county voter registration records to Johnson's court, in the face of a threatened contempt citation. Judge Johnson said later that Wallace had in fact arranged to have the records in question made available in order to avoid the contempt citation, and the comment was part of Wallace's continuing façade of defiance. We will see this pattern at work again as the Selma events unfold.

Page 102   "There is uncertainty as to . . ." Dr. King steadfastly denied that any agreement was made, cf. his article in *The Saturday Review*, 3 April 1965, p. 57. David Lewis, however, in his *King: A Critical Biography*, p. 281, makes a convincing case that there was.

Page 105 "Most of the others . . ." This summary of Dr. King's rationale is taken from a long unpublished and untitled narrative of the march by Mr. Richard Leonard, a participant, based on his notes at the time (*see* Bibliography); the manuscript was very helpful to the author in drafting the account of these weeks.

Page 107 "One of those doing so . . ." The accounts used here are those of Reeb's two companions at the trial of his alleged assailants, cf. *STJ*, 8 and 9 December, 1965; and *The New York Times*, same dates; a good deal has also been borrowed from the chapter on Reeb in Mendelsohn, *The Martyrs.*

Page 111 " 'In a room in a house . . .' " This poem is in Reverend Webb's correspondence with the author.

Page 114 "Once the scene was again quiet . . ." This anecdote comes from Capell's account of it in *STJ*, 10 March 1965.

Page 115 "As the streetcorner mass meeting . . ." Greer's appearance is as Reverend Anderson recalled it on the Harvard Selma Tapes, Tape 8, Side 1, 670ff.

Page 116 "Within a few hours . . ." Richard Leonard helped compose this song, and recorded the lyrics in his manuscript.

Page 118 "At one point they spotted . . ." Goldman, *The Tragedy of Lyndon Johnson*, p.312.

Page 118 "President and Mrs. Johnson . . ." The quote is from *The Vantage Point*, p. 161.

Page 118 "While her husband groped . . ." Cf. Lady Bird Johnson, *A White House Diary*, p.251.

Page 120 "This meeting, which went on . . ." There are summaries of the meeting in Goldman, *The Tragedy of Lyndon Johnson*, pp. 313–14; LBJ's *The Vantage Point*, pp. 162–63; and press accounts of the President's impromptu press conference the same day.

Page 121 "John A. Sullivan, for whom . . ." The quote is from Mendelsohn's *The Martyrs*, p. 174ff.

Page 124 "Both groups chuckled over . . ." The anecdote is recalled in a sermon in the Unitarian Universalist Association Archives in Boston (hereafter referred to as UUA) entitled "The Tragedy and the Triumph: Selma, Alabama, U.S.A.," p.5.

Page 125 "Dr. Greeley stepped forward . . ." This exchange with Baker is as Dr. Greeley remembered it in an interview with the author.

Page 126 "The morale of this . . ." A detailed account of the tent crew's experiences can be found in *The Chimes* of San Francisco Theological Seminary, Vol. 11, No. 4, September 1965. This entire issue is a detailed and comprehensive account of how one religiously-based community was moved to respond to the Selma campaign.

Page 127 "One participant put down in verse . . ." This verse is the author's, an excerpt from a longer poem entitled "Contact," composed at the time.

Page 129 "There were reports from informed whites . . ." Jantsen to Smeltzer, 13 March 1965.

Page 130 "If Dr. King spoke mainly . . ." The account of Bevel's speech is from the Leonard manuscript, spliced together with quotes from *The Chimes*, San Francisco Theological Seminary, Vol. II, No. 4, p. 12. The author is very grateful to Rev. James Arnot of Minneapolis, who was among the tent crew and who made this account available.

Page 132 "A memorial meeting for James Reeb . . ." Reverend Robert Senghas of Wellesley, Massachusetts was good enough to recall this meeting for the author.

Page 135 "It had been forty minutes . . ." The text of this address is in Lynne Ianiello, *Milestones Along the March* p. 111ff.

Page 138 "There was at least . . ." Much of this account comes from James Forman's *Sammy Younge, Jr.*, pp. 98–101, as well as newspaper reports.

Page 144 "And once aboard he told Harry Boyte . . ." Cf. William Robert Miller, *Martin Luther King, Jr.*, p. 216.

Page 144 "On Friday there was another march . . ." Details of the second picket line at Smitherman's home have come from the newspaper accounts; Richard Leonard's manuscript; and an interview with Reverend Harcourt Klinefelter, one of the participants and "prisoners"; cf. Harvard Selma Tapes, 17 and 18.

Page 145 "The job of choosing the three hundred . . ." This is from Mr. Soracco's own account of his work given on tape to the author.

Page 146 "Hosea Williams of SCLC . . ." The source for this information about the march logistics is the Master's thesis by Williams' wife, Mrs. Juanita T. Williams, which for brevity's sake will be listed here as "Impact of Education" (*See* Bibliography). This unique piece of scholarship is available (at least) in the libraries of Atlanta University and Harvard College.

Page 150 " 'We lived a lifetime . . .' " These lines are from a poem, "God Gave Us a Glimpse of Heaven," by Mrs. Williams, one of several original verses and numerous original aphorisms in "Impact of Education," p.141.

Page 151 "Supper, fresh and hot from . . ." The yeoman labor of the food brigade was described in detail by Professor Elwyn Allan Smith on Harvard Selma Tape 1, Side 1.

Page 152 "The orgy charges were made anyway . . ." In extensive, purple detail, but without any documentation, by Robert Mikell in *Selma*, and by Congressman William Dickinson of Montgomery in the House of Representatives beginning 30 March 1965. Cf. *The New York Times*, 31 March 1965, and the *Congressional Record*, 89th Congress, Vol. III, Part 5, pp. 633f; Part 6, pp. 8592–8600; for rebuttals see pp. 8600–8607. Congressman Dickinson presented a series of unconvincing affidavits and photographs, but was careful to confine his statements to the House floor, where he was immune from libel and slander suits, until it became evident that no one was going to take action against him. Later that year a publication entitled "Sex and Civil Rights" took up the cudgels, not much more persuasively.

Page 152 "James Bevel also pointed out . . ." This comment was recorded by Richard Leonard, and it gave him some comfort along the more isolated stretches of the route.

Page 153 "Not far from the place . . ." The response of the students at Southside High was personally observed by Richard Leonard, or the author would not have believed it.

Page 155 "But this building, with holes in the wall . . ." The only reporters who paid much attention to the facts of the Rolen School were W. C. Heinz and Bard Lindeman, writing in *The Saturday Evening Post*, 22 May 1965, p. 20, where they included a picture of it on page 93.

Page 155 " 'At first I didn't think . . .' " *Ibid.*

Page 156 "Late that night a few . . ." *Ibid.;* and Richard Leonard's manuscript.

Page 156 "That night also several reporters saw . . ." This is from Renata Adler's "Letter from Selma," in *The New Yorker*, 10 April 1965, p.121ff. The avowed segregationist was Mikell in *Selma*.

Page 159 "Mrs. Viola Liuzzo watched . . ." This account is summarized from Mendelsohn's chapter on Mrs. Liuzzo in *The Martyrs*, pp. 176–95.

Page 166 "For James Bevel, the march . . ." Bevel's postmarch plans were referred to frequently in papers from these weeks in the UUA Selma Presence Files in the denomination archives.

Page 166 "The scenario in the memorandum . . ." This memorandum, referred to earlier (*see* page 52), was excerpted in the *Birmingham Post-Herald*, 2 February 1965, p. 2; Mikell reproduces it in full in *Selma*, p. 28ff.

Page 169 "Two days later, Dr. King's associate . . ." Cf. the *Chicago Sun-Times*, 28 May 1965.

Page 171 "The Dallas County Citizens Council . . ." This summary of the Citizens Council's campaign is based on Smeltzer's reports from his white sources.

Page 175 " 'In some ways' Luening wrote . . ." This letter, dated 14 April 1965, is in the UUA Presence Files in the denominationa archives, as are most of the materials mentioned in this connection.

Page 177 "Toward the end of April . . ." An article in the London,

Ontario *Free Press* dated 24 April 1965 recounts Greer's success as a fund-raiser there. Other indirect references are made in the UUA Presence Files, cf. the letter from Ms. Elaine Rodriguez to John C. Fuller, 29 April 1965.

Page 178 "By May fourth Rev. Reese . . ." Reese to Smeltzer, 4 May 1965.

Page 180 "The first white people . . ." This account of the Lewis's development is based largely on the Smeltzer records.

Page 181 "The letter, dated March 19 . . ." The text, as bowdlerized and reproduced by the Citizens Council, is in the Smeltzer materials.

Page 183 "This letter was printed . . ." The *Time* letter was published in the issue of 2 April 1965, p. 11; the *STJ* letter on 16 March 1965, p.4.

Page 183 "Lewis had waiting for them . . ." The text of this draft is in the Smeltzer materials.

Page 190 "In fact, over across the river . . ." The details about Ward Five-B come from the author's own recollections and the narratives of two residents recorded on the Harvard Selma tapes: Clarence Williams, Reel 4, Tape 5, Side 2, 715ff; and Reverend Fairro Brown, Reel 6, Tape 7, Side 1, 350ff.

Page 194 "This kind of public relations . . ." The developing conflict between local SCLC and DCVL leaders over Greer's role is extensively described in the letters from this period of the UUA Presence ministers, and also in the letters to Ralph Smeltzer from David Smith.

Page 195 "An independent meeting of Ward leaders . . ." Cf. Fairro Brown, Harvard Selma Tapes, Reel 6, Tape 7, Side 1, 670ff.

Page 200 "Two staff members, once they understood . . ." The workers were the author and his wife, who were subsequently re-hired and made responsible directly to Atlanta.

Page 200 "It was reported . . ." By David Smith, to Ralph Smeltzer, 7 July 1965. The Abernathy quote in Atlanta is from *Time*, 16 July 1965, as also is Reese's comment after his release.

Page 203 "They continued centralizing their control . . ." Notes taken at this meeting by Reverend Leon Hopper are in the UUA Presence Files, without a date, but it refers to the meeting as being held on a Wednesday, most likely 21 July 1965.

Page 203 "At another meeting at the end of July . . ." Recounted by David Smith to Smeltzer, 1 August 1965.

Page 204 "At the same time a direct competitor . . ." The DCIFVO is described by Clarence Williams, Harvard Selma Tapes, Reel 4, Tape 5, Side 2, 300ff.

Page 204 "Then on August twentieth . . ." Here again the main source is Mendelsohn's chapter on Daniels in *The Martyrs*, supplemented by the accounts in William Schneider, ed., *The Jon Daniels Story*.

Page 206 "He drove back to Selma convinced . . ." David Smith to

Smeltzer, 24 August 1965, describes Clark's actions; it was Smith who notified Baker, and his quick response may have prevented an ugly confrontation. Reverend John Ruskin Clark, the UUA Presence minister at the time, described Baker's meeting with Jimmy Webb, *et al.*, in his letter of 28 August 1965 in the UUA archives.

Page 208 "While they talked, the door opened . . ." Smith to Smeltzer, 24 August 1965.

Page 208 "Late in January 1966 Baker . . ." This account is from both Baker and Smitherman independently; the author was unable to obtain Clark's version.

Epilogue, Page 212 "But even more important . . ." The approach referred to here is exemplified in James Forman's *Sammy Younge, Jr.*, pp.73–116; John A. Williams, *The King God Didn't Save*, pp. 78–85, 200–202; and Debbie Louis, *And We Are Not Saved*, pp. 273–277. Williams' comments in particular are so offensive and inaccurate as not to merit comment except that again he articulates sentiments held by not a few veterans and supporters of the movement who should know better.

Index

93, 102, 130–31, 152, 166ff, 178, 189, 195–96; conceives of march to Montgomery, 80–81; in Chicago, 169–70; talks about nationwide boycott of Alabama, 167

Billups, Mrs. Amelia Platts Boynton. *See* Boynton, Mrs. Amelia Platts

Binghamton, New York, support for protection of march, 121

Birmingham, Alabama, 6, 18, 47, 69

Birmingham News, 221

Birmingham Times-Herald, 221

Black Belt, 7, 13, 26, 31, 53, 69, 85, 105, 129, 167

Black Muslims, 27

Blackwell, Randolph, 97, 177, 197

Blalock, Ira, 65

Boston, support march, 106; support for protection of march, 121

Boycott of white-owned businesses in Selma, 70, 80

Boyd, Malcolm, 100

Boynton, Amelia Platts, 10, 197, 219; announces boycott, 80; arrested, 33; tear-gassed, 94

Boyte, Harry, 144

Brown Chapel, African Methodist Episcopal Church, 8ff, 25, 27, 33, 39–40, 49, 56, 58, 67, 76ff, 85, 102, 112, 116, 124, 130, 132, 143, 145, 159, 163, 170, 172, 197, 207

Brown, Rev. Fairro, 190–91, 195, 232

Brown, Mrs. Suzie Morris, 225

Brown, Rev. Claude C., 217, 219, 226

Browne, Carol, 220

Bruce, Celeste, 22

Bunche, Ralph, 151

Bunker, Nathaniel, 219

Burwell Infirmary, Selma, 96, 168

Butler, Sheriff Mac Sim, 139ff

Camden, Alabama, 31, 69

Camp Selma, 53ff, 219, 227

Capell, Arthur, 25, 43, 114–15, 217, 224, 227–28

Carmichael, Stokely, 154

Carter, Harmon, 28

Cash, W.J., 222, 225

Cavanaugh, Mayor Jerome, 106

Chamber of Commerce, Selma-Dallas County. *See* Selma-Dallas County Chamber of Commerce

Cheek, Rev. George W., Sr., V

Chicago, support march, 106

Chimes The, of San Francisco Theological Seminary, 229

Christian Century, The, 218

Church of the Brethren, 218, 221

Citizen, The, 20

City National Bank, Selma, 186

City of St. Jude, Montgomery, Alabama, 156, 158–59

Civil Rights Act of 1964, 6ff, 26, 42, 61, 216

Civil Rights Documentation Project, The, 221

Clark, Sheriff Jim, 4ff, 16ff, 24ff, 31, 33ff, 38–39, 41, 44ff, 54, 59; attacks first march to Montgomery, 93–94; goes to Hayneville, 216; in Vaughan Memorial Hospital, 68–69; in Washington, D.C., 87; loses election, 211; ordered to disband posse, 189; speaks to Mobile County Citizens Council, 179

Clark, Rev. John Ruskin, 232

Cleveland, support march, 106

Cloud, Major John, 91, 93, 104, 115

Coffee County, Alabama, 16

Coleman, Tom, 205–06

Collins, Leroy, 102, 123

"Committee of Fifteen, The" 9, 80

"Committee of One Hundred, The" 184, 186

Community Relations Service, 102, 123, 217

Concerned White Citizens of Alabama, 87, 226

Congress of Racial Equality, 102

Conyers, Representative John, 176

Cook, Elmer, 116

Cooper, Mrs. Annie Lee, 44–45

Craig Field, 151

Craig, William B., 186–87

"Crimson Tide," University of Alabama football team, 3–4, 201

Crocker, L.C., 82, 87, 91

about march in face of restraining order, 101–02; dissuaded from going on first march, 92; hit by Jimmy George Robinson in Albert Hotel, 29; in Montgomery, 63; march in Montgomery, 140–41; meeting with northern Congressmen, 59; Nobel Peace Prize banquet, 47; plot to murder, 78; speaks at end of march in Montgomery, 161–62; speaks at Reeb's memorial service, 132–33; talks about march in New York, 92; talks to Lyndon Johnson, 119; threatened in California, 78; visits Lyndon Johnson, 77; visits Perry, Lowndes, Dallas, and Wilcox Counties, 83–84

King, William Rufus, founder of Selma, 13

Kjelshus, Rev. Ben, 194

Klinefelter, Rev. Harcourt, 230

Krock, Arthur, 168

Ku Klux Klan, 14, 17–18, 20, 26, 72, 76, 80, 163ff, 199, 225; founded, 75

Lee, Cager, 74, 111

Legal Defense Fund, National Association for the Advancement of Colored People, 54

Lehman's Pontiac Showroom, 93

Leoline, Sister Mary, 153

Leonard, Richard, 157, 219, 223, 228ff

Letherer, Jim, 153

"Letter from a Selma Jail," 47, 51

Leuning, Rev. Eugene, 175

Levine, Jean, 107

Lewis, Arthur, 215, 217, 224, 226, 180ff

Lewis, David, 223, 226, 228

Lewis, John, SNCC Chairman, 35, 79, 93–94, 96, 161, 228

Lewis, John Carter, 91

Lewis, Muriel, 215, 180ff

Lewis, P.H., 79

Lindeman, Bard, 222, 231

Lindsay, John, 201

Lingo, Colonel Al, 46, 72, 76, 86, 91, 141, 168, 205–06, 209

Liuzzo, Viola, 159–60, 163, 213

Lloyd, Robert Alison, 29

Logistics Committee, for march, 46, 158

Long, Senator Russell, 119

Longhorns of Texas, University of Texas football team, 4

Lord, Bishop John Wesley, 100, 104

Louis, Debbie, 223, 233

Lowndes County, Alabama, 80, 81, 83–84, 87, 142, 153–54, 158, 163, 172, 205

Mack's Cafe, Marion, Alabama, 74

Malcolm X, 56ff

March to Montgomery, arrival in Montgomery, 158; confirmed by King, 86; first attempt, 92ff; idea for, 81; Johnson calls up troops, 148–49; march begins, 150ff; order permitting march issued, 141ff; rallies at capital, 160ff; second march attempt, 103ff; second march attempt enjoined, 101

Marengo County, Alabama, 15, 80

Marion, Alabama, 31, 54, 69, 72, 78, 80–81, 85, 178; night march, 73–74

Marshall, Burke, 7

Martin, James, 51

Martin Luther King, Jr. Center for Nonviolent Social Change, Atlanta, 222

McLendon, Jack, 219

McCormack, House Speaker John, 121

McLeod, Blanchard, 39, 41, 209

McRae, Willie, 44

McShane, Chief Marshall James, 100

Meany, George, 62

Medical Committee for Human Rights, 92–93

Mendelsohn, Jack, 223, 227ff

Merrill, Gary, 155

Miami, Florida, 4

Middlebrook, Rev. Harold, 193ff, 202ff, 207ff

Mikell, Robert, 223, 230

Miller, Orloff, 108–09

Miller, William Robert, 223, 230

Miller's Ferry, 31

Mississippi Freedom Democratic Party, 29, 167

Moldavan, Alfred, M.P., 92

Montgomery, Alabama, 10, 58

Montgomery Advertiser, The, 161, 198

Montgomery bus boycott, 133, 160

Montgomery County, 153

DATE DUE